BEYOND THE LEARNING ORGANISATION

In memory of my Grandfather, Rudolf, and for Greta

Beyond the Learning Organisation

Paths of organisational learning
in the East German context

MIKE GEPPERT

Gower

Published by
Gower Publishing Limited
Gower House
Croft Road
Aldershot
Hampshire GU11 3HR
England

Gower Publishing Company
131 Mainstreet
Burlington, VT 05401-5600 USA

British Library Cataloguing in Publication Data
Geppert, Mike
    Beyond the learning organisation : paths of organisational
    learning in the East German context
    1.Organizational learning - Germany (East)
    I.Title
    658.3'124'09431

Library of Congress Control Number: 00-135333

ISBN 0 7546 1450 6

Printed in Great Britain by
Antony Rowe Ltd, Chippenham, Wiltshire.

Contents

List of Figures and Tables

List of Abbreviations

BTF	Behavioural Theory of Firm
CEO	Chief Executive Officer
CIP	Continuous Improvement Process
CMEA	Council for Mutual Economic Assistance
GDR	German Democratic Republic
OD	Organisational Development
SDA	System Dynamics Approach
THA	*Treuhandanstalt* (East German privatisation agency)
TINA	There Is No Alternative
TOA	Theory Of Actions
TOP	Team Orientated Production
TQM	Total Quality Management

List of Interview Partners

Interview code   **Position**

Case study A:
1a[1]   Former Managing Director
2a   Managing Director
3a   Manager
4a   Personnel Manager
5a   Works Council
6a   Manager
7a   Manager
8a   Manager
9a   Engineering Manager
10a   Team Leader

Case study B:
1b   Managing Director
2b   Manager
3b   Manager
4b   Manager
5b   Works Council

Case study C:
1c   Managing Director
2c   Manager
3c   Manager
4c   Labourer

Note

1   The figure after the interview-code counts which interview is being referred to with respective interview partner. Interview code 1a/2 (chapter 4, p. 69), for example, refers to the second interview with the former Managing Director of case study A.

Acknowledgements

When you read this study you will understand that its preparation, quite similar to the theme of our project, was an open and compound learning process. There are two points I would like to make.

On the one hand, I wanted to research a topic which has not given much consideration in conventional organisational learning discussions. Thus, it required a lot of encouragement from colleagues and friends. I first and foremost wish to thank Arndt Sorge (University of Groningen) who has supported me in my work through many discussions and his expert advice. Despite having moved to the Netherlands in the middle of my research project, he continued to be a source of great support. So, I thank him especially for his patience shown throughout the entire, sometimes rather difficult research process. Moreover, I am particularly grateful to colleagues and friends who read numerous drafts of this study and provided me with valuable feedback, such as Maja Apelt (Universität der Bundeswehr Hamburg), Günter Bechtle (Humboldt-University Berlin), Johan DeDeken (Humboldt-University Berlin) and Stefan Kühl (University of Munich). I am specially thankful to my colleague Karin Lohr (Humboldt-University Berlin) who, beyond reading my work and discussing it with me, was of great assistance to me during some of the more challenging phases of my research. In addition, I want to thank John Child (University of Cambridge) for the support he gave during a visit to the UK in arranging very stimulating discussions with other academics researching similar issues at the Judge Institute of Management Studies in Cambridge in the summer of 1996.

On the other hand, my decision as a native German to write this study in the English language required not only a lot of self-discipline but a great deal of learning and, moreover, active support. Here I am most grateful to Kay Adamson (University of Sunderland), Beverley John (University of Wales Swansea), Lora Renz-Moritz (Humboldt-University Berlin) and again to Johan DeDeken, and Arndt Sorge for their assistance in revising the English manuscript and hopefully improving my 'German English'.

For research interviews, access to companies and documents, I thank managers, employees and works councils in my sample companies. Thanks also to the students who worked together with me in the intensive research phase of the project, such as Marek Krause (now University of Jena), Andrè Metzner (now in a research group of Daimler/Chrysler).

Moreover, I wish to acknowledge the Hans-Böckler Foundation, and mention especially Werner Fiedler, for their support of my research.

Last but not least I want to thank my family and my friend Peggy. I am profoundly grateful to Peggy for loving me and not disowning me during the process.

Finally, in spite of all the help that I received, I take the responsibility for any errors that remain in this study. Thus, when you find some, then I want to thank you in advance for bringing them to my attention.

Mike Geppert
Swansea

1 Introduction

In contemporary management literature, the idea that managers and even organisations should not just learn, but create widespread capabilities for learning to learn is gaining in popularity. The concept of learning to learn which Bateson (1992, pp. 219–40) called 'deutero-learning' is seen as the most important life skill at the edge of the new millennium (Honey, 1999, p. 9). The reason for the increasing interest in the creation of learning skills can be understood as a consequence of modernity. Well-known arguments in certain sociological discourses look upon reflexive thinking and learning as being the proper responses to the transformation of industrial society into a 'risk society' (Beck et al., 1986). Similarly, management research interprets advancing competition in global markets, the loss of lifelong job prospects, and the rising obligation of individuals to assume more responsibility for their life and work etc. as threats requiring an improvement of the familiar methods by which people learn (Honey, 1999). Consequently, this author and eight other 'so-called learning gurus' recently published 'A declaration on learning' to inspire and promote thought and debate about the benefits of learning for management, for organisations and for society as a whole (Honey, 1999).

This study does not, however, wish to negate in its entirety this thesis, which impressively underlines the recent surge in interest in the topic of learning in modern capitalist societies. Our problem with such arguments is that the conclusions reached by such experts are often ostentatious and have little relevance for and differ from what actually happens when actors learn among each other. However, it is not our intention to debate the outstanding importance of organisational learning for the purpose of comprehending the problems arising within the transformation of well-established management and organisational practices. And yet in contrast to customary organisational learning approaches which focus on organising and planning in order to develop promising learning recipes, our study is concerned with the social practice of organisational learning.

This project is a departure from common organisational learning approaches used to develop a particular sociological understanding of organisational learning processes. Both conceptually as well as empirically we introduce a particular perspective of analysis, the enactment concept, to study organisational learning as an interactive process. We want to accent the social embeddedness of organisational learning and thus consider how actors and groups of actors actually learn. Through the application of a comparative research perspective, we will show that differences in social context do in fact matter. Consequently, we will confront some of the fairly tentative arguments in the traditional organisational learning debate such as the influence of organisational slack resources, participation, experiences of others or planning, with the concrete learning practices.

This study is an attempt to combine the arguments of two seemingly different academic research approaches. On the one hand, there is the widespread discussion inspired by intervention researchers such as Argyris and Schön, (1978, 1996) or Senge (1990) in which not only the importance of organisational learning is emphasised, but also the necessity to create learning organisations which are seen as a kind of tool with which to meet the challenges of the global economy. Higher-level learning in particular is interpreted as a more or less context-free course which can be voluntarily created with the help of skilful intervention research. On the other hand we have neo-institutionalism, one of the most popular approaches in current organisational sociology, which views the idea of managerial voluntarism with scepticism. Whereas the first approach stresses higher-level organisational learning as a chance to create more human, participative and emancipatory work forms in modern organisations, neo-institutionalism emphasises that the chances for such forms of organisational learning are limited in typical organisations because institutional structures and frames within capitalist societies are constraining. In this sense it is believed that institutional pressure allows managers little room to develop strategic choices. In conclusion, the conception of this study not only critically addresses the neglect of social institutions in common organisational learning approaches, but also reconsiders some neo-institutionalist arguments which overestimate the role of institutions at the expense of the role played by creativity and the emergence of strategic choices within the processes of organisational learning (e.g. DiMaggio and Powell, Meyer and Rowan).

We started our research project by concentrating on the analysis of organisational learning processes in the social and economic transformation of East Germany. Thus, when we look back over the course of our research process, we have to confess that the focus of our research project shifted over time from being a study of managerial and organisational processes in East

German firms, to one of theory building. But it should be also clear that, if there ever was an ideal ground for practising organisational learning very widely, then it was in East Germany in the transformation of socialist combines into capitalist enterprises. Accordingly, it is an ideal testing ground in order to examine if and how learning concepts are applied in practice, and what we can learn from this, in turn. It was also to be assumed that organisational learning endeavours, in this context, were not institutionally neutral, to say at least. On the basis of our comparative research design, a certain understanding of the dialectic relationship between organisational and institution building was developed. In retrospect, we can insofar conclude that the quite remarkable conditions of societal change appeared to be beneficial in helping us better to study the consequences of micro-level learning processes on the macro-level of society and vice versa.

This study consists of six chapters, including this introduction. In chapter 2 we start with a brief discussion about the origins of common organisational learning approaches. After that we focus our attention on the arguments of one of the most prominent schools in the organisational learning discourse, the intervention research approach. Our illustration of how organisational learning is understood by these scholars reveals that those within the mainstream of this research tradition have concluded that the creation of learning organisations is the ideal response to dealing with the challenges of a global market economy. The first part of chapter 2 finishes with a summary of some key arguments of common organisational learning approaches. The second part of this chapter begins with a critical reflection on the basic ideas of intervention research and confronts them with the main arguments of neo-institutionalist approaches which emphasise the role of institutional environments in understanding the transformation of modern organisations. However, we will see that both concepts would appear to have a one-sided view about the role of institutions within the process of organisational learning. Whereas intervention research underestimates the role of institutions in the organisational learning process, neo-institutionalism overestimates the manner in which institutions influence organisational behaviour. At the end of this chapter we therefore recommend trying to understand and analyse organisational learning from an enactment perspective. Here, the concern of inquiry turns from analysing individuals who learn in order to overcome learning blockades and the question of how institutions force organisational actors to complete adaptive learning modes, to an examination of how actors and groups of actors socially construct the constraints and chances with which they are confronted in the ongoing process of organisational learning.

In chapter 3, the methodological part, we explain the development of our research design. It will be accentuated that our study must be seen as an experience-based project where every chapter has a specific function in the research process as a whole. As such, the study is in and of itself a learning process. Therefore, the company studies in chapter 4 have a more descriptive function, while the discussion in chapters 5 and 6 is more concerned with conceptual questions relating to the comparison of organisational learning in different social contexts and a reflection on the role of institutions within the learning process. Besides the illustration of the different phases in the research process, we also give information about the content and the number of the interviews, and explain the selection of our three case studies and interviewees.

Chapter 4 contains trajectories of learning in three East German companies and begins with an abstract about the origins of the firms we have analysed. What follows is an illustration of the process of organisational learning from a process perspective where we describe how internal and external interrelations were transformed after the 'wall came down'. The influence of these processes on participation and human resource management is also examined. Each case study report finishes with a brief synopsis recapitulating the starting conditions and the enacted conditions, closing with remarks about the further learning prospects of the firms.

The observations in the company studies served as the bedrock for the comparative discussion of our empirical findings in chapter 5. According to our suggestion put forth in chapters 2 and 3, we will apply seven leading arguments within the conventional organisational learning debate as a guideline to explain and compare the differences in how actors and groups of actors in each firm actually learn and thus create chances and limitations for future organisational learning. As a result of this critical deliberation, we will see that the meaning of key patterns which were accorded a great deal of categorical significance in conventional organisational learning approaches such as manner of participation, planning or learning from the experiences of others can mean something quite different within the context of the learning practices of these three firms. The argumentation of this chapter ought to be read as a detailed illustration of our thesis that the micro-dynamics of organisational learning cannot be discussed with disregard for the institutions which constitute and are constituted by the manner in which actors actually learn with and from each other.

The final discussion in chapter 6 refers back to the main objective of this study to develop a closer understanding about the dialectic between organisational learning and institutions. Correspondingly, we reflect on the results of our comparative research project from a more theoretical angle by pointing to three institutional tensions which actors and group of actors face when they learn interactively with each other. However, next to the relational dimension, in this chapter we also stress the significance of local cultural systems for the emerging dissimilarities in the processes as well as in the outcomes of interactive learning patterns in each of the companies analysed. In conclusion, we stress the benefits of the enactment perspective developed here and suggest analysing paths of organisational learning. Such an analytical concept circumvents both the undersocialised nature of conventional organisational learning approaches which simply neglect the role of institutions in the creation of deutero-learning, as well as the oversocialised view of neo-institutionalist scholars who simply see no place for deutero-learning because of the compelling nature of institutional isomorphism.

2 Theories of Organisational Learning, Institutional Settings and Enactment

2.1 Introduction

The discussion about organisational learning and learning organisations is quite popular in current organisation theory. Miner and Mezias (1996) have succinctly pointed out that organisational learning is an 'ugly ducking no more'. The discussion has gone from the periphery to the centre of interest of contemporary organisation studies. Scientific journals, readers and conferences about this topic have become fashionable. There is a growing interest in organisational learning and its consequences for organisational development both in theory and in practice. Easterby-Smith et al. (1998, pp. 261–3) have identified two central questions in the discussion: 1) how *does* an organisation learn?; and 2) how *should* an organisation learn? These two questions are at the centre of two distinct epistemological communities. The first is largely made up of academics, while the second consists more of practitioners such as consultants and human resource managers.

However, beyond this specific research tradition the intention of this study is to approach the problem of organisational learning from a sociological perspective. Such a perspective places the social character of learning within organisations at the centre of its analysis. Organisational learning processes are conceived of as socially embedded into a more less institutionalised social context. In this sense it is assumed that routines and social practices are not so much the outcome of unconstrained learning processes within the learning organisation, but rather emanate from certain institutional conditions.

We will develop the conceptual question of how organisational learning and social institutions are intertwined in three steps. At first, we will return to the main arguments that emanate from the debate about organisational learning. We will demonstrate that the role of institutions in the process of learning has been neglected or underestimated (section 2.3). After that we will discuss how one of the most popular approaches in current organisation theory, the neo-institutionalist approach, discusses the relation of institutions and learning within organisations. We will see that contrary to the rather radical and promising assumptions of organisational learning approaches, the chances to advance the learning capabilities within and of the whole organisation as a system are questioned (section 2.4). At least we will suggest another approach which avoids both the undersocialised assumptions of conventional organisational learning theory, and the oversocialised view of neo-institutionalism (section 2.5).

Adopting Weicks enactment theory (1995a) we will seek to develop an understanding of organisational learning that considers both its institutional embeddedness, as neo-institutionalism stresses, as well as the processes of competence development and group learning, that is central to the concerns of theorists and practitioners of organisational learning.

Contrary to the tendency in organisation science of using rather abstract metaphors to foster an understanding of organisational learning,[1] the main purpose of the present study is to come closer to the actors' learning experience. Because the existing discussion about organisational learning tends to focus more on cognition and individual learning, one can find only a few attempts that try to establish a link between on the one hand the conceptualisation of organisational learning and on the other hand the social experiences of the actors involved. (Weick and Westley, 1996, p. 441). Such an integrated perspective opens the way for empirical research of processes of organisational learning that is not biased by idealised and normative presumptions about how organisations and their members are supposed to learn.

2.2 The Roots of Organisational Learning in Organisation Theory

Looking back to the history of organisation theory there seems to be a dualistic bias that, if only indirectly, still prevails in the current discussion on organisational learning and learning organisations. One perspective focuses on the formal aspects of organisations. At the centre of this type of analysis are the division of labour, focal and functional processes, organisational structures and spans of control. The alternative perspective conceives of organisations as natural systems. This type of analysis focuses less on the formal structure of an organisation, but instead more on its informal aspects. It thereby seeks to gain a clearer understanding of the human relations within formal organisations. The members of organisations are not treated as impersonal parts of a mechanical system that have to be guided and controlled. Instead scholars working in this tradition have sought to improve work conditions. In this sense the discussion about informal aspects of organisational life can be seen as being in critical opposition to classical management theories that tend to neglect such aspects as human needs, motivation and self-actualisation of man.

In line with the latter, the human relations approach, dualistic concepts of organisation became established. Especially in the modern management literature where a growing number of polar types such as rational *vs* natural, formal *vs* informal, mechanistic *vs* organic, participative *vs* hierarchical appear. In all these models, the problematic relation between two ideal typical poles of organisational life is being assessed. However, in contrast to the discussion about organisations as rational and natural systems, succeeding theoretical perspectives searched for optimal combinations of both organisational aspects and relate them to the specificity of the organisation's task environment. These models of organisation are now interpreted as open systems. In this sense it is assumed that organisations are in reality combinations of formal and informal modes of coordination. Such combinations can be seen as the result of differences in tasks, staff, markets and technologies with which every organisation has to deal with its specific environment.[2]

In the next section we will examine in more detail how the current debate about organisational learning refers to established theories about modern organisations bearing in mind the before mentioned arguments. There seems to be two research traditions to which the organisational learning approaches directly or indirectly relate:

- the *socio-technical systems* approach, in which learning in and between teams is seen as an appropriate method to satisfy the technical and social needs of organisational systems;
- the *information-processing* view, in which organisations are also seen as open systems which have to learn to reduce the amount of information that is processed in accordance with the degree of task uncertainty.

Both approaches deal more or less with the same question: How are organisations as open systems able to deal with the environmental challenges caused by economic and technological change? Both argue that with increasing turbulence or changes in the task environment traditional mechanistic forms of organisational design have to be replaced by more organic design principles. Moreover the socio-technical approach suggests that economic and social goals of a business firm can be combined in such a way that the improvement of human relations and social success will also lead to economic success. As we will see, in the current debate about organisational learning the leading ideas from both approaches can be applied and developed further. However, this discussion went so far that some researchers and consultants celebrated the learning organisation as a new 'one best way' for (post-)modern organisations to deal with the challenges of global markets and new technologies.

2.2.1 Organisations as Socio-technical Systems

The term socio-technical system was introduced by Trist and Bamforth, two researchers from the legendary Tavistock Institute of Human Relations. They first used the term 1951 in their classical studies about the introduction of new technologies and work systems in British coal mining. Their notion of open socio-technical system was further developed as a framework for the study of organisations as a whole or at certain levels such as departments and work groups (Brown, 1992, pp. 39–88).

The research of the Tavistock Institute can be considered to be part of the tradition of human relations movements that stressed the social aspects of work and organisation, this in sharp contrast to the 'scientific management' approach that focused more on production engineering. The idea of socio-technical systems can be seen as an attempt to overcome the distinct fixation on formal aspects by classical organisation studies in the tradition of Weber and Taylor, and on informal aspects by the human relations approach. By adopting an open systems approach the researchers from the Tavistock Institute sought to avoid both studying 'organisations without people' (typical for the scientific management approach) as well as studying 'people without organisations' (the main weakness of the human relations approach) (Staehle, 1973, pp. 9–61). Their aim was to replace the design principles of the 'old' bureaucratic paradigm by the 'new' socio-technical one. But contrary to the one-sided social imperatives of the human relations approach, scholars in this tradition argued that the requirements of technical efficiency have to be combined with human needs. Table 2.1 shows the differences between the 'new' socio-technical paradigm and the 'old' paradigm based on technological imperatives.

Regarding our problem of how the socio-technical systems approach influences the current organisational learning debate it can be said that at the centre of interest stands the question: how learning conditions of individuals and work groups in organisations could be improved. In this context, Trist has pointed out that:

Table 2.1   Key features of the old and the new organisational paradigm

Old paradigm	New paradigm
The technological imperative	Joint optimisation
Man as an extension of the machine	Man as complementary to the machine
Man as an expendable spare part	Man as resource to be developed
Maximum task breakdown, simple narrow skills	Optimum task grouping
External controls (supervisors, specialist staffs, procedures)	Internal controls (self-regulating subsystems)
Tall organisation chart, autocratic style	Flat organisation chart, participative style
Competition, gamesmanship	Collaboration, collegiality
Organisation's purposes only	Members' and society's purposes also
Alienation	Commitment
Low risk-taking	Innovation

Source: adapted from Trist, 1981, p. 42.

> ... it was not true that the only way of designing work organizations must conform to Tayloristic and bureaucratic principles. There were other ways, which represented a discontinuity with the prevailing mode. The technological imperative could be disobeyed with positive economic as well as human results (Trist, 1981, p. 9).

The basic idea was that any productive system includes both a technical organisation which refers to layout of equipment and specification of process, and a social organisation that specifies individual tasks and the relationships between individuals who perform them. At the centre of the research and counselling process stands a 'goodness of fit' between these two designing principles. The development of more human work principles within organisations was discussed at two main levels: job design and the design of entire organisation. The first level was directed to the redesign of single places of work and to the development of autonomous work groups. The latter stressed the importance of adaptability and flexibility by shifting the design principles of the organisational system.

1   The question of improving the job design is seen as a problem of motivation and increase in job satisfaction. It is assumed that workers not only want the creation of 'enriched' jobs, but that employees with some desire for 'higher order' need satisfaction, perform better and feel more positive when their jobs rates high on the 'core dimensions' of motivation. According to psychological writers the improvement of intrinsic motivation on the job ought to be interpreted as important for individual and group learning. Complementary to rather extrinsic dimensions of job design, such as fair and adequate pay, job security, benefits, safety and health, it was claimed that the creation of more intrinsic job properties can give space for individuals and groups to learn on the job and go on learning on the job. Contrary to traditional work organisation with rather formal conditions of employment, in socio-technical systems the job itself should become of the foremost significance. Intrinsic job properties such as variation and challenge, continuous learning, autonomy, recognition and support etc. are of prime importance for the joint optimisation of technical and social systems. The improvement of the intrinsic quality of jobs can be accomplished by creating autonomous work groups. They indeed found that team work will lead to a higher degree of task autonomy and to more self-regulated works' activities (ibid., pp. 29–37).

2   If the early studies of socio-technical systems mainly focused on the job and group levels, later on research became more holistically oriented. In the late sixties and in the seventies the researchers became increasingly interested in how the design principles of an organisation as a whole can be changed. The problem of self-regulation within autonomous work-groups was linked to the problem of designing organisations. In line with the aforementioned discussion about job design that saw intrinsic motivation as fostering a 'joint optimisation', the later studies considered the positive effects 'redundancy of functions' (ibid., pp. 38ff.) had on the development of improved redesigning strategies. This was seen as an essential answer of organisations to become more adaptive and flexible:

> There are two basic principles, both of which display 'redundancy' in the systems theoretic sense. In the first, the redundancy is of parts and mechanistic. The

parts are broken down so that ultimate elements are as simple and inexpensive as possible, as with the unskilled worker in a narrow job who is cheap to replace and who takes little time to train. The technocratic bureaucracy is founded on this type of design. In the second design principle the redundancy is of functions and is organic. Any more component system has a repertoire which can be put to many uses, so that increased adaptive flexibility is acquired. While this is true at the biological level, as for example in the human body, it becomes far greater at the organizational level where the components – individual humans and groups of humans – are themselves purposeful systems. Humans have the capacity for self-regulation so that control may become internal rather than external (ibid., p. 38)

According to the first question – how can the conditions for learning in and of human work groups be improved? – another question that is broadly discussed in the present discussion about organisational learning appeared. This central question concerns the way in which the learning capacity of the organisation as a whole can be improved. Management is presented with a choice between two design principles, and following the recommendations of the Tavistock researchers, managers are expected to abandon traditional bureaucratic modes of learning in favour of organisational design strategies that are based on redundancy of functions. Looking back on the history of industrialisation the authors come to the conclusion that bureaucratic and technocratic forms of organisation, in which the ideas of Weber and Taylor are matched and operationalised, fit best with environmental conditions of mass markets which they called 'disturbed-reactive" (ibid., p. 39). They assume that with increasing environmental turbulence the stable state of traditional markets and technologies gets lost. In this analysis, an environment appears that exhibits both a high level of complexity and a high degree of uncertainty. The author characterises this environment as 'turbulent fields' (ibid.) and see it as a new challenge of modern capitalist firms.

Tavistock researchers also treated socio-technical systems as things or entities with their own goals, needs or 'primary tasks', that are distinct from the members and groups which compose them. They assume that the system has to be continuously designed to accommodate the functional needs of an organisation to survive, or, in economic terms, to make profits. This means that all activities and relationships in the organisation must be appropriately structured to fulfil the firms' functional needs (Brown, pp. 81–8).

We demonstrated that design principles, such as intrinsic job design, self-regulating work groups and redundancy of functions, are all positively valued because of their human potential. This is seen as a functional requirement through which organisational systems are able to meet the challenges of more complex and competitive markets. That is the reason why this type of approach has become increasingly attractive for managers as well as work counsellors who are interested in integration and in preventing conflict by fostering participation and consensus. These interests were among the factors that led to the broader application of the socio-technical systems approach in the practice of consulting business. The central ideas of the approach had an immense, if predominantly indirect, influence upon debates about organisational learning. Especially the arguments about redundancy of functions, continuous learning in work groups, and about role participation were taken and developed further in so called action research, which has had a significant influence on the current organisational learning debate (Argyris and Schön, 1996; Morgan, 1986, pp. 77–109; Senge, 1990, et al.).[3]

2.2.2 *Organisations as Information Processing Systems*

We saw how the socio-technical systems approach was, just like the tradition of the human relations movement, mainly concerned with the problem of reconciling technical and social requirements within organisations. The model of information-processing is interested in the question of how organisational decision-makers are able to reduce the complexity that emerges in the course of executing tasks. Initially research was centred around attempts to develop more human working condition. Later on, the focus shifted to legitimise the original goal of humanisation by referring to the requirements of an environment, typical for late capitalism, that is characterised by customer-dominated markets whose have replaced mass markets.

The focus of the information-processing view, on the other hand, was on the knowledge and the effectiveness of management decisions. This view argues that the main problem that managers are faced with when environmental uncertainty increases, consists in anticipating and planning decisions.

Researchers such as Simon and his colleagues at the Carnegie Institute of Technology in the United States developed their theory about cognition within organisations by criticising the idea of instrumental rationality. They assume that decision-makers do not have the knowledge to know all the alternatives for making rational decisions, nor do they have an overview or are they capable of controlling all the consequences of implementing those alternatives. Simon (1955) highlighted the problem that all attempts in organisations at being rational are essentially limited. He introduced the concept of 'bounded rationality' to capture the idea that the basic function of organisational design structures such as programmes, rules hierarchies and goal setting ought to be interpreted as both a method and the outcome of processes of human problem-solving and rational decision-making by individuals. Organisations, Simon claimed, have a design or have specific structures, precisely because of the fact that rationality in organisations is inherently limited (Hatch, 1997; Walter-Busch et al., 1996). This in spite of the fact that precisely at this point in time organisational sociology became more aware of the problem of organisational learning, and further research on the problem was stimulated.

The main programmatic statement was originally developed in the classical book *Organizations* from March and Simon (1958) and again underlined by Simon (1996). March and Simon argued that members of organisations, because of their limited human rationality divide, routinise and confine their decision-making processes in order to make them manageable. As Simon puts it:

> For purposes of discussing organizational learning, organizations are best viewed as systems of interrelated roles ... Roles tell organization members how to reason about the problems and decisions that face them: where to look for appropriate and legitimate informational premises and goal (evaluative) premises, and what techniques to use in processing these premises (1996, p. 177).

Simon and his followers claim that organisations, using specific role systems such as programmes, plans, rules, standard operation procedures etc., become capable of reducing the complexity of organisational reality.[4] In this sense organisational routine is seen as a necessary tool that allows then to adjust to the uncertainties inherent to processing information.

Moreover, it is taken for granted that the decision-maker is confronted with programmed and non-programmed situations of decision-making. Programmed decision-making is based on and leads to the institutionalisation of organisational routines and to an established role system. In relation to the problem of organisational learning, the assumption is that programmes sustain adaptive learning through their continuous routinisation. Even non-programmed decisions are seen as possibilities for learning, because the choice of alternatives which decision-makers are faced with, are not given in advance, but must be sought out by a rational process of searching. The chances for learning and understanding non-routine events appear, because established organisational routines release the attention of decision-makers.

The original aim, understanding organisations as information-systems, used up a lot of the attention of many researchers. Galbraith (1974) provides us with an important example of an attempt that sought to use the information-processing approach in order to generate a better understanding of the process whereby organisations try to adjust to a situation in which task uncertainty increases. We already pointed out in our discussion of the ideas of Simon et al. that the appearance of non-programmed decision-making situations cannot be handled with the established forms of internal coordination because the ability for planning decreases and the necessity for non-routinised communication increases. The problem of information-processing under greater task environment can be summarised as follows:

> The basic effect of uncertainty is to limit the ability of the organization to preplan or to make decisions about activities in advance of their execution. Therefore it is hypothesized that the observed variations in organizational forms are variations in the strategies of organizations to 1) increase their ability to preplan, 2) increase their flexibility to adapt to their inability to preplan, or, 3) to decrease the level of performance required for continued viability. Which strategy is chosen depends on the relative costs of the strategies (ibid., p. 432).

Galbraith, though, failed to offer a workable model to calculate the costs of information-processing, even if he made some suggestions on how to improve the capability of an organisation to deal with this problem. But apart from the suggestion that with increasing uncertainties, decreasing possibilities to control behaviour by rules and programmes have to be replaced through controlling outputs by setting targets and goals, his main recommendations are limited to the problem of design strategies. Those strategies are presented as methods that complement conventional routines whenever uncertainties that arise with the emergence of non-routinised tasks are identified. As in the socio-technical systems model, this approach too, makes a distinction between mechanical and organic organizational forms. The first are related to familiar decision-making situations that can effortlessly be planned and programmed. The latter are related to rather inexperienced tasks that require more flexible and ad hoc processes of decision-making. In this sense, Galbraith has identified two complementary design strategies through which routinised information-processes can be complemented. A first strategy seeks to 'reduce the need for information processing', whereas the second wants to 'increase the capacity to process information' (see Figure 2.1).

The first strategy recommends the creation of organisational slack resources and self-contained tasks. Slack resources such as the increase of planning or budget targets or inventory buffers are seen as the right method to reduce the overload of the established role system, at least if the number of non-programmed events increases. This strategy also intends to provoke a shift from input to output control (ibid., pp. 433–5).

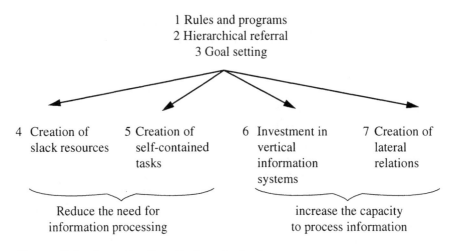

1 Rules and programs
2 Hierarchical referral
3 Goal setting

4 Creation of   5 Creation of   6 Investment in   7 Creation of
   slack resources   self-contained   vertical   lateral
                         tasks   information   relations
                                               systems

Reduce the need for   increase the capacity
information processing   to process information

Figure 2.1   Organisation-design strategies

Source: adapted from Galbraith, 1974, p. 433.

The second strategy considers the investment in vertical information systems to be very important, because a quantification of data increases the effectiveness of information-processing. This strategy seeks to compose lateral relationships, such as direct contact, liaison roles, task forces, teams integrating and managerial linking roles, whenever traditional organisational routines fail to cope with the increased task uncertainty (ibid., pp. 435–6).

The main message of the information processing model can be summarised as follows: When the complexity of the task environment increases, the organisation has to shift its focus from structural design towards some kind of process design which has a more organic quality. Thus the tasks of managers are compared with strategic designers that are not able to maximise, but are in a position to satisfy their intended goals of learning. In this sense, the outcome managers hope to accomplish may not be considered to be the best possible way, but it can be seen as good enough considering the level of existing uncertainty. Thus, organisational learning is understood as routine-driven process. Only when the original intentions and developed learning programmes fail to meet in a satisfactory way the conditions imposed by the situation, can managers start to search actively for processes that allow for the generation of new alternatives.

In the current organisational learning debate, the ideas of the information-processing perspective are being developed further in two directions. The first stream leads immediately to the quite popular discussion about how to create the learning organisation. Scholars working in this tradition argue that by making rational choices actors achieve satisfying decisions, which again improves the information-processing capacity of the whole organisational system. The organisation becomes capable of learning to learn. This is an important turning point in the debate about organisational learning. As we will see, the argumentation of the information-processing model were combined with cybernetic premises to develop recipes for the creation of learning organisations. In the first part of section 2.3 we will reconsider the development and main arguments of this approach.

The second stream refers to the critics of theories about cognition within organisations and is rather pessimistic about the possibility of developing more reflective and radical organisational learning approaches. As we will see in the first part of section 2.3, there are scholars who are convinced that in organisations only incremental learning approaches are possibly (for example the so-called behavioural theory of firm). In the second part of that section we demonstrate that the ignorance of neo-institutionalist approaches of the key arguments of the mainstream discussion about organisational learning has its roots in organisation theories about cognition decision-making.

2.2.3 Implications of Prior Models for the Mainstream Debate about Organisational Learning

The conditions that lead to the creation of learning organisations are mainly to be found in abstract technical terms, such as technological change, the advance of globalisation and growing competition (Easterby-Smith et al., 1998, pp. 259–72). From such a vantage point, the role of social context and institutions tends to be neglected. One should bear in mind though that the term 'learning' is not a neutral one. This directly follows from our view on the essence of an organisation. As we have seen both, the socio-technical systems and the information-processing perspective, conceptualise organisations as systems. Even if the definition of organisations as systems is well established in the current discussion about organisational learning and learning organisations, the question remains which aspects of learning in and by systems one should take into consideration. The choice of emphasising one particular aspect, such as the structures of information processes, the process of human development, the issue of participation, the correction of errors often depends upon the disciplinary and methodological background of the researchers.[5] In this sense we can conclude that in spite of the confusion in the research field as observed by Easterby-Smith et al., the systems view does seem to be an approach that is broadly shared by researchers and practitioners interested in organisational learning.

Besides the theoretical evidence which conceptualises organisational learning in terms of the perspective suggested by the systems model, there is another consequential implication: both research traditions are closely linked to organisational development (OD). This is not so much an academic discipline, but an umbrella for various practical intervention methods. The basic idea of OD is that organisational learning processes can be initiated, directed and controlled by skilled practitioners and managers. We saw that the socio-technical research tradition can be more related to a trend in OD which is focused on human development. The technical goals of the firm are then presumed to be perfectly compatible with human needs. Individual behaviour is expected to change organisational structures and individual behaviour by means of continuous learning processes that are mainly understood as team learning. Consultancy programmes that were developed in relation to socio-technical ideas focused on the improvement of working conditions and democracy at the work place. There was a boom of such consultancy programmes, in particular in countries ruled by Social Democrats such as Norway or Germany during the 1970s.

The joint optimisation of social and technical systems needs remains important in the present discussion about organisational learning. The development of human resources is seen as a requirement that has to meet the demands of management to develop more flexible and more innovative organisations. When the socio-technical approach was used to convince both managers and organised labour, the information-processing perspective was mainly applied to the interests of management. From an information processing view, the main interest was to design an innovating organisation and to create a learning organisation. In this sense the information-processing concept had an impact on both the scientific discussion, as well as on practical management processes.

However, we can conclude that complementary to these early approaches, in the current debate about organisational learning and learning organisations, the focus of analysis has moved from designing structures to designing processes. Moreover, such aspects which where stressed by socio-technical systems and information-processing approaches such as humanisation, the role of learning routines or the search for more flexible designing principles are still relevant in the current organisational learning discourse. In the next section we will discuss how both the theoretical link of organisational learning models to the systems perspective as well as its typically close links to consultancy has had an impact on the present discourse about these issues.

2.3 The Idea of Organisational Learning

2.3.1 *Organisations as Brains: Incremental and Radical Forms of Organisational Learning*

If in the early discussions in organisational theory the term organisational learning had rather a secondary meaning, one can observe that recently there is an increasing interest in the subject. This has led to the establishing of organisational learning as a distinct research field, that now faces problems of confusion (Easterby-Smith et al., 1998, pp. 259–72). As in organisation theory itself, the researchers who entered the field have very different disciplinary and methodological backgrounds. Even if the mainstream arguments continue to be related to the original decision-making and systems theory, the study of organisational learning has become a 'broader church'. Students, consultants and practitioners who are interested in the question of organisational learning often have a professional background in management science, business administration or even in cultural anthropology and sociology. With the establishment of organisational learning as a fashionable field of research there have been a growing number of publications which try to put order into this conceptual diversity. Especially in the 1990s a lot of articles, books, readers or special issues of scientific journals have sought to present synthesising typologies about the subject.[6] However, each of these efforts to structure the debate about organisational learning and the learning organisation has its own focus about the purpose of organisational learning, what learning means, where it takes place, how to implement it, as well as about the research methods that need to be adopted (Easterby-Smith et al., 1998).

It is obvious that the most influential arguments can be traced back to the idea of self-organisation. In this view the design of organisations is compared with learning processes in human brains which are not only information-processing systems with more or less organic design principles, but also able to learning to learn or to self-organise (Morgan, 1986, pp. 77–109). It is assumed that the process of reorganisation cannot be merely understood in terms of adaptive learning by improving established programmes and certain routines, but should also be seen as a chance to increase the capacity of organisations to see thing in new ways, to gain new understandings, and to produce new patterns of behaviour. Thus, similar to earlier approaches, the socio-technical systems perspective and the information-processing view, have proposed to conceive of organisational learning as a process that seeks to improve the learning capacity of the members of an organisation or of the organisation as a whole. Such improving of the learning capacity continues to be a central question in the literature on organisational learning. Students still stress the importance of linking the learning advances of individuals with the level of organisational learning (for example, Kim, 1993, pp. 37–50).

Moreover, we have to be aware of the fact that the use of the 'brain metaphor' has had important consequences for the continued discussion about organisational learning (Morgan, op. cit.). According to this idea the most prominent scholars in the field have argued that research in organisational learning must include both, how learning processes inhibit and promote organisational development towards self-organisation (Argyris and Schön, 1978 and 1996; Morgan, op. cit.; Senge et al., 1990). They have sought to combine the idea of brains as information-processing systems with the cybernetic notion of self-regulation.

The cybernetic turn from adaptive learning systems to learning systems that are capable of 'learning how to learn' can be seen as pivotal in the current organisational learning debate (Argyris, 1996; Argyris and Schön, 1996; Miner and Mezias, 1996). It led to a separation between students in the tradition of theory of action (TOA) such as Argyris and Schön (1978) and Moingeon and Edmondson (1996) and scholars that follow the tradition of the behavioural theory of firm (BTF) such as Cyert and March (1963), March and Olsen (1976). The main question separating both approaches concerns the extent to which organisations are just capable of incremental learning, or whether they can also develop the capability of learning to learn in order to be able to change more radically. Thus, on the one hand there is the sceptical fraction such as BTF which questions if at all it is possible to improve the effectiveness of the process and the outcome of organisational learning. On the other hand, there are the intervention-oriented researchers who believe in the transformation of learning and thinking styles. Compared with the basic assumptions of intervention research[7] which are at the centre of this section, the concept of organisational learning as advocated by the BTF is not only indefinite about the possibilities of higher-level organisational learning; it is also more academic and less practice-oriented, more descriptive than prescriptive and normative. In brief, researchers in the tradition of the BTF propose to adopt what could be termed a 'neutral' approach to the relationship between learning and effective action or desirable outcomes (Argyris and Schön, 1996; Easterby-Smith et al., 1998; Edmondson and Moingeon, 1996).

However, in spite of strong methodological and conceptual differences between the two leading perspectives in the current debate about organisational learning, some scholars working in the TOA perspective have sought to draw attention to commonalities. Argyris, for instance, has conceded to the BTF approach, that not only higher-level organisational learning would lead to more freedom, changing the status quo, but also routine-driven (lower-level) forms of learning (1996). Moreover, he sees similarities between his understanding of lower level learning and the BTF views on the issue: both, he claims, tend to stress the limiting effects of organisational routines within lower-level learning processes.[8]

We not only want to argue that academic attempts on both sides have sought to foster a convergence of both lines of thinking, but also that the most visible discussion moved the focus from organisational learning as such to the creation of the learning organisation. Both approaches continue to maintain the distinction between incremental and radical modes. The radical mode of organisational learning is valued more positively and interpreted as a kind of new 'one best way'.

In the next two sections we will start by discussing how the brain metaphor studies of organisational learning gradually adopted the idea of the learning organisations, which came to be understood as a new field of research as well as a new model of management practice. At the centre of our argument will be the basic ideas of 'two of the most visible researchers in this field' (Edmondson and Moingeon, 1996, p. 5), Chris Argyris and Peter Senge. They may well have started from quite different directions: Argyris focused on the individual learning level, while Senge focused on the level of the learning systems. But in spite of these differences, they both ended up with the same conclusion, arguing that creating learning organisation would require intervention strategies that improve both the adaptability as well as the effectiveness of the learning processes.

Next, we will demonstrate that, on the one hand, the turn from organisational learning towards the learning organisation supported the growing circulation of this idea both within the academic community and within the practice of management. On the other hand, we will show how following the growing publicity, accompanying the underlying trend towards oversimplification, it led to an overestimation of rational choices and to an optimism about the possibilities managers dispose of, to design learning organisations more effectively.

Finally, we will confront the radical ideas about organisational learning and learning organisations with one of the most prominent trends within current organisation sociology.

These researchers adopted doubts about possibilities of higher-level learning from BTF and developed an even more sceptical view about the chances of systematic organisational development. That brought them close to the intention of our own study, to analyse organisational learning from the perspective of organisational sociology. Organisations are not understood as self-enforcing learning systems, but as being institutionally embedded in society.

2.3.2 The Intervention Research Perspective of organisational learning

Contrary to other organisational learning approaches in the tradition of BTF that limit the focus of their research to the analysis and description of learning paradoxes and learning traps, intervention research does not stop at the level of diagnosis, but formulates therapies how to overcome the problems of defensive routines and learning disabilities (Argyris and Schön, 1996; Senge, 1990). Distinguishing two learning levels of learning, is one of the main issues that makes intervention research different from other organisational learning theories. However, depending upon the specific interests of researchers or consultant, additional levels of higher learning levels are sometimes identified.[9] In answering the following three questions we will reiterate the main questions of intervention theory:

1) how is organisational learning understood;

2) how is the appearance of defensive (that means non-effective) learning loops explained;

3) how can the members of organisations eliminate defensiveness and develop alternative models of learning?

Subsequently, we will draw attention to the question of how intervention research went from analysing organisational learning processes to claiming to create a learning organisation.

1) What does organisational learning mean? The idea of learning is borrowed from cybernetics and research about human brains (Argyris, 1992a, p. 8; Argyris and Schön, 1996, p. 21). An often cited example which distinguishes between lower level and higher level learning is the house thermostat. The thermostat is programmed to detect and correct errors of a heating system and prevents a room becoming too cold or too hot. In reference to this rather technical example, learning occurs when actors detect and correct mismatches or errors. Error detecting and correcting is called single-loop learning. This type of learning is compared with individual problem-solving in an organisational context. It is assumed that individuals learn as long as they have a satisfying solution for a certain problem. However, taking the house thermostat example it is further assumed that single-loop learning is not enough – in particular in the case of complex and non-programmable situations.[10] In such a context, double-loop learning is considered to be necessary. The programme of the thermostat or the established methods of individual problem-solving are challenged. The distinct new quality of double-loop learning is that it goes beyond the search for and elimination of mismatch. In the process of double-loop learning the underlying programmes of the learning process are themselves subject to questioning and change. Figure 2.2 shows the difference between the two learning forms.

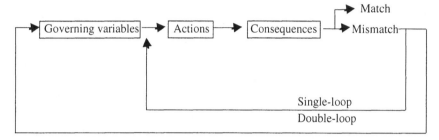

Figure 2.2   Single-loop and double-loop learning

Source: adapted from Argyris, 1992a, p. 8.

We already saw that the distinction between different learning levels is a central issue in intervention research. Subsequent generations of scholars have adopted this idea from Argyris and Schön, and have developed their own typologies of lower and higher levels of learning. Senge developed a theory about the learning organisations that has a lot of affinities with the TOA. He argues that lower level learning is not a sufficient condition for increasing an organisation's adaptability. Senge sees adaptive learning as a matter of 'coping', while the development by organisations of generative learning has more to do with 'creating' (1990, p. 14). Some authors even distinguish between three levels of learning.[11]

The underlying idea of this model is not that learning occurs when people discover a new problem or invent a solution to a problem. Instead it assumes that learning is a reflexive and output-oriented process. Argyris describes this process as follows (1992a, p. 9):

Learning occurs when the invented solution is actually produced. This distinction is important because it implies that discovering problems and inventing solutions are necessary, but not sufficient conditions, for organizational learning. Organizations exist in order to act and to accomplish their intended consequences.

Organisations are interpreted as tools to meet specific goals and human action is a consequence of organisational design. Like the socio-technical systems approach and the information-processing both view the structure of organisational design as a precondition that either enables or inhibits the chances of individuals for double-loop learning. It has to be noticed though, that researchers such as Argyris who work in the tradition of intervention research, do concede that the emergence of double-loop-learning in organisations rarely occurs. That is why they conclude that in order to study double loop learning one actually has to create it (Argyris, 1996, p. 81).

This conclusion has two consequences which will be discussed next. On the one hand, intervention research seeks to understand learning blockades explained in terms of self-reinforcing defensive patterns and routines that inhibit the appearance of double-loop learning. On the other hand, it seeks to identify and describe the conditions under which these sources become more explicitly ineffective and as a consequence, ripe for change. Thus, starting with a definition of organisational learning which looks at how individuals (Argyris, 1992a) and teams (Senge, 1990) improve their learning capabilities, the research process became focused upon a diagnosis of counterproductive learning effects and on a therapy for developing intervention strategies.

2) How the emergence of defensiveness in organisational learning is explained
Intervention researchers think that actions in organisations are value- or belief-driven. They assume that actions in organisations seek to give meaning to those actions or are based on the intention to achieve specific outcomes. However, researchers often found that the actual behaviour in organisations has little to do with the justifications people give to those actions. This has led to the distinction between two kinds of TOA: the 'espoused theories' according to which individuals claim to follow and the 'theories in use' (Argyris, 1992a; Argyris and Schön, 1996) or 'mental models' (Senge, 1990) which members of an organisation actually, but without awareness, practice. The discrepancy between saying and doing causes problems for organisations and requires them to develop productive modes of learning that include an effective processing of information.

The actors' unawareness of their routinised and skilled actions is seen as a source of failure. Moreover, organisational success in the market place induces managers to improve their established single-loop learning programmes (Argyris, 1992b, p. 85). Such programmes, as well as the routines and skills that actors really use, in the end become purely defensive. In this sense the leading question is how a defensive strategy leads at the individual level to a low freedom of choice and a reduced production of valid information, while at the level of organisations as whole systems it results in self-enforced inhibiting learning loops. Such defensiveness is manifested by 'conditions of undiscussability, self-fulfilling prophecies, self-sealing processes, and escalating errors' (Argyris, 1992d, p. 219). This situation is understood as an obstacle preventing productive learning to occur, as actors remain unaware of their own responsibility for spreading defensiveness. Senge (1996) describes the problem of defensiveness as a form of 'learning disabilities' which lead actors in organisations to blame others for their own failures, to concentrate on short-term events rather than on a long-term vision, and to have a linear explanation of systemic phenomena.

Another important point is that the appearance of defensive routines and of learning disabilities is not only interpreted as blockade of higher level learning in particular capitalist or Western organisations, but as a trend that can also be observed in different national cultures. Both the taken-for-grantedness of organisational defensive routines as well as their specific effects on human decision-making are claimed to be universal qualities of organisations.

> We have found that human beings have master programs in their heads about how to deal with embarrassment or threat. Although the specifics vary with age, education, position in the company or functional discipline, the underlying master programs are the same. Indeed, they do not differ across cultures such as North America, South America, Western Europe, Africa, India, China and Japan (Argyris, 1992c, p. 134).

This statement is a good example of the underlying universal philosophy of intervention research. First they see theories-in-use as a kind of basic cultural property of modern organisations which cannot easily be changed or 'un-learned', because it has been learned by socialisation, be it education in early life or success during the performance of a job. They contemplate that under such conditions actors have less or close to no possibilities to learn from their failures. This make it hard for individuals to detect and correct their errors in difficult situations. Even in case they fail to understand the meaning of information given by others, they continue to act as if they try to avoid embarrassment and threat (Argyris, 1992b pp. 84ff.; Senge, 1996, p. 301).

Secondly, beyond the actors ignorance about their own defensiveness, intervention researchers assume that socialisation is the product of a 'universal human tendency' to act rationally on the basis of four basic values: 1) a need to control; 2) a desire to maximise winning; 3) a will to suppress emotions; and 4) an inclination to be as rational as possible. They conclude that in case actors try to act in accordance with all these values, their actions would become contra-productive for deeper learning and would fail to comply with the underlying premises of their behaviour (Argyris, 1992b, p. 90).

Thirdly, the observed defensive behaviour of actors such as face-saving, negative feeling, hostile communication, risk avoidance, rigid routines, are also to be understood as the consequence of established organisational structures[12] that only enable single-loop learning and prevent the emergence double-loop learning. The underlying definition is that organisations are tools purposefully created to achieve specific goals. This requires organisations to develop more or less mechanistic designing strategies which again influence the choices of actors to act and learn alternatively.

This leads us to the question about therapies recommended by intervention researchers following their diagnosis of counterproductive effects of inhibiting learning loops, defensive behaviour and structural conservatism.

3) How members in organisations can learn how to learn   The problem discussed above, defensiveness, is the starting point for considerations on the development of alternative forms of organisational learning. In the same way as the appearance of defensiveness is understood as an universal problem in modern organisations, intervention research approaches suggest that the liberation from these self-enforcing learning blockades is the general task of intervention research. Or, to put it in medical terms, besides the problem of diagnosis, it is also intended to check the chances of therapy by developing learning recipes and their implementation.

Argyris describes his understanding of intervention research as follows:

> The action scientist is an interventionist, seeking to help members of client systems to reflect on the world they create and to learn to change it in ways more congruent with the values and theories they espouse (1992d, p. 220).

One can draw two lessons from this quotation. First, intervention research is a normative model that refers to the idea that actors can be helped to learn more effectively and according to more human ways of behaviour. Second, the quotation is based on the idea that more congruence between the two forms of theories of action, between espoused theories and theories-in-use, will lead to more productive learning results. Actors are thought in principal to 'espouse' the recipes that can lead to 'deeper' learning, but tacitly developed learning disabilities prevent them from doing what they wish to do (ibid., pp. 213–46).

The initial idea of intervention research is to interrupt the defensive single-learning loops by the confrontation with a learning model that not only espouses new values, but also transform them. The main interest of intervention research is to make tacit knowledge explicit as to change deeply anchored defensive learning modes into more productive ones. The key feature of the alternative 'productive learning model' is open communication. It is assumed that previously undiscussable issues must be uncovered. The interruption of self-enforcing and dysfunctional defensive learning loops is seen as an adequate solution that enables actors to test and correct the underlying values of their actions. The differences between the defensive single-loop learning model and the productive double-loop learning model is characterised as follows.

Table 2.2   Defensive and productive organisational learning modes

Defensive	**Productive**
Characteristics	
• soft data	• hard data
• tacit, private inferences	• explicit inferences
• conclusions not publicly testable	• premises explicit, conclusions publicly testable
Supported by	
• tacit theory of dealing with threat	• (explicit or tacit) theory of strategy formulation
• set of tacitly interrelated concepts	• set of directly interrelated concepts
• set of tacit rules for using concepts to make permissable inferences, reach private conclusions, and private criteriato judge the validity of the test	• set of rules for using concepts to make permissable inferences, reach testable conclusions, and criteria to judge the validity of the test

Source: adapted from Argyris, 1992d, p. 221.

The intention of intervention research is to help actors to achieve an organisational development process from stage X to stage Y, i.e. from the defensive to the productive learning model. The same idea can be found in Senges best-seller *The Fifth Discipline – the art and the practice of the learning organization* (1990), in which he criticises the learning disabilities of traditional organisations and recommends five 'new "component technologies"' to move from stage X to stage Y.

The basic idea of intervention research is to educate the decision makers and to examine and develop mental models or theories-in-use, that prevent learning in so far that negative behavioural patterns are being replaced by productive ones. Actors should learn to acquire instrumental learning skills such as 'organizational inquiry' (Argyris and Schön, 1996, p. 20) in order to change defensive into productive modes of organisational learning. This includes a change of risk-avoidance into risk-taking, of relations of distrust into relations of trust, of hostile into friendly communication, of rigid into flexible rules etc. (ibid., p. 29). These processes are documented in literature by various examples, experienced in practising intervention research.

However, in spite of the fact that the initiation of higher-level organisational learning without the help of an external interventionist is seen as nearly impossible, intervention research approaches expect organisations to develop capabilities to learn how to learn or what Argyris and Schön (1978), in reference to Bateson (1992, pp. 219–40), have called 'deutero-learning'. This type of learning is to enable the actors to develop broader capabilities self-organisation that are explained as a reinforcement and a restructuring of mental models without external impulses from intervention research. In other words, organisations are seen as continuous and reflexive learning systems.

All in all we can summarise that the researchers such as Senge (1990) or Argyris and Schön (1996), much in line with earlier approaches such as the socio-technical systems view, repeatedly stress that the creation of higher-level learning processes will not only gain economic success, but equally facilitate the emergence of more open, liberal and human working conditions. Thus, Senge stresses the organisation-wide participation in the diagnosis of learning disabilities, driven by team learning and shared visions (Senge, 1990, pp. 205ff.). Argyris and Schön (1996, pp. 3–30), too, emphasise the creation of what they refer to at as broadly spread critical reflections and communication skills.

The vision of organisational learning approaches discussed in this section thus remain within the tradition of ideas such as the human relations movement and the socio-technical systems approach. In this sense, it is assumed that with the creation of more possibilities for open communication and deutero-learning, the often conflicting personal, social and economic interests can be reconciled. However, in the next section we will show that – especially given the ultimate turn of intervention research away from organisational learning to the learning organisation – in common with deutero-learning, aspects of competitiveness and effective learning processes have also gained in significance. We will emphasise that the creation of learning organisations ought to be understood as a new 'one best way' of OD practice.

2.3.3 The Ultimate Quest of Intervention Research: Building the Learning Organisation

The intervention research perspective argues that only double-loop learning has the potential to free individuals from dysfunctional and self-sealing learning blockades. The literature about learning organisations recognises incremental and radical learning modes as valuable.[13] Both learning forms can lead to a higher degree effectiveness and competitiveness of business organisations (Edmondson and Moingeon, 1996, pp. 16–37). Contrary to the view discussed above about organisational learning, that sought to combine goals of humanisation and liberation with requirements of business organisations to be profitable, the literature about how to create learning organisation predominantly focuses on economic success. To put in the terms of Edmondson and Moingeon: 'We thus re-framed our inquiry, to ask whether and how learning organisations can gain competitive advantage ...' (ibid., p. 26).

The turn of learning organisation literature from attempts to develop compromises between efficiency requirements and chances for liberation in business organisations, to attempts to identify competitive advantages, has led to the emergence of various attempts by managers, practitioners, consultants and management scientists to present the best techniques or recipes for creating a learning organisation. Likewise managers have welcomed this idea because it is seen as a new operative tool to overcome the resistance or defensiveness of the members of an organisation against new managerial strategies. The concept is seen as an opportunity to detect previously hidden organisational slack resources, and as a way to get access to established informal work practices (Neuberger, 1994, pp. 238–69). When, following the tradition of intervention research as exemplified by Argyris and Senge, the intention to make tacit knowledge explicit was interpreted as an opportunity to develop interpersonal communication skills or to improve participation between and within teams, we now propose to pay attention to the economic success of effectively designed learning organisations.

In the following we will show how the model of the learning organisation is welcomed in management practice and science, and how it can be best interpreted as a new management tool, as a new 'one best way'. A first example can be found in an article by the management consultant Tom Sommerlatte, which addresses the question how managers can increase the capabilities of their firms to learn and how learning organisations can become high performance organisations (Sommerlatte, 1992). In general organisations are compared with organisms that can only survive by learning and by continuous change. In Sommerlatte's view, learning organisations are characterised by two features: 1) the creation of a corporate culture that is succinctly summarised by the motto 'all for the joint goal'; and 2) transparency of all processes that are relevant for competitiveness and efficiency (Sommerlatte, 1992, p. 118).

Another example of viewing learning organisations as management tools can be found in the work of a management scientist of the Technical University of Munich, Horst Wildemann who seeks to identify 'success factors of fast learning enterprises' (Wildemann, 1996, pp. 84ff.). He suggests to the establishment of evaluation criteria for improving the speed, the completeness and the efficiency of internal information-processing and knowledge development in the learning organisation. One feature of learning organisations he sees in the establishing of 'continuous improvement processes' (ibid., pp. 77–80). Thus, he conceives of continuous learning as an effective instrument for reducing costs and waste of resources.[14]

These two examples from the German debates on organisational learning clearly illustrate the tendency to see learning organisations as a new management dealing adequately with the challenges of new technologies and global markets. At the centre of these debates is the development of management recipes to create more efficient, flexible, economically successful, and competitive business firms. However, to be fair, not all advocates of the learning organisation concept have such a limited 'one best way' position as the one represented by Sommerlatte and Wildemann. The view which celebrates the creation of the learning organisation as a new management tool, might be seen as an extreme position in the literature. The mainstream discussions about organisational learning represent a more moderate position. Thus, Edmondson and Moingeon may well see organisational learning as a 'competitive advantage', but they also propose 'the learning organisation rubric' as a 'new framework' that ought to be clearly distinguished from other organisational learning approaches (Edmondson and Moingeon, 1996, pp. 6–37). But, contrary to the radical intervention approach, they explain lower level and higher level learning approaches, as learning modes with equal qualities in relation to economic success. In this sense, they seem to make a distinction between lower level learning and higher level learning. The former concerns the question *how* to learn, while the later has more to do with the question *why* to learn.

> We have defined 'learning how' as organizational members engaging in processes to transfer and improve existing skills or routines, and defined 'learning why' as organizational members diagnosing causality. We argue that these represent distinct organizational capabilities, which each can become strategic capabilities in different market environments (Edmondson and Moingeon, 1996, p. 35).

This argument refers back to our initial thesis that organisational learning has a dual quality reminiscent of earlier approaches in organisation theory, such as the socio-technical approach and the information-processing perspective.

Nevertheless, we agree with the authors to comprehend the appearance of 'learning how' and 'learning why' as a question of empirical research. This brings us back to the purpose of this study; the development of a comparative research framework for an empirical analysis of organisational learning in different social contexts. For this we will resume the above exposed form of argument.

2.3.4 Interim Summary: Some Key Arguments of the Intervention Research Perspective

In this section we will summarise some of the key arguments in the current debate about organisational learning and the learning organisation. Our intention is to use this interim summary to reformulate the arguments presented above in our own terms with the sociological interests of this study in mind. The outcome of the discussion in this section is a compendium of seven principal ideas in intervention research that will be used as indictors in the systematic comparison of the process of organisational learning in our three East German companies (chapter 5). In this comparison, we will critically examine these seven principles and reinterpret them on the basis of the enactment perspective, our concept of analysis which will be introduced at the end of this chapter.

We want to emphasise seven issues that we think play a central role in the reflection of *how* and *why* organisational learning takes place. Those issues include identity construction, the role of recipes in the way of learning, learning from the experience from others, the role of participation in the learning process, the ideal of a continuous organisational learning, the role of organisational slack resources in the process of learning, and organisational learning as a planned process.

1) Identity construction One of the basic ideas underlying organisational learning is that organisations develop a unique identity through which the inner processes of learning can be distinguished from an outer environment that is primarily defined in economic and technical terms (Argyris and Schön, 1996; Senge et al., 1990). As we saw above, intervention research focuses on the focal organisation as the learning unit. Scholars working in this tradition are primarily interested in intraorganisational learning processes. At the centre of their interest lie questions about when and how more or less open learning approaches are likely to appear. Their implicit assumption is that external pressures, caused by changes of markets and technologies, challenge the established intraorganisational learning modes. Traditional forms of learning that strengthen established routines and skills, as well as new learning patterns that lead to the emergence of new routines and core competencies, are construed as a problem of designing the focal organisation.

Intervention research assumes that organisations are intentionally constructed tools that are to fulfil particular tasks and goals. For this, they suppose further, organisations have to develop more or less organic design strategies which give room for more or less open learning approaches. In short, their basic assumption is that the structure of the focal organisation can reveal how and why individuals in organisations learn; and this in turn governs the learning capability of the complete learning system.

2) The role of recipes on how to learn   Students of organisational learning also assume that the organisational identity cannot be merely reduced to the structural design of the focal organisation. Beyond formal routines and espoused action theories, actors develop tacit and informal modes of dealing with, and avoiding of failures. The appearance of reinforcing defensive learning loops is seen as a consequence of tacitly developed recipe knowledge. Internal learning barriers are likely to arise because recipes are not identically with the organisations 'espoused' plans and goals. Learning recipes are understood as interpretation schemes, or as theories-in-use, which only indirectly structure how actors learn (Argyris, 1992a and 1992d). Intervention researchers are convinced that whenever actors reveal how implicit recipes limit their current learning processes, they are also able to correct their mistakes or moderate the impact of detected errors. This they consider to be a precondition for organisational growth and organisational success.

The aim of higher-level organisational learning consists of making implicit recipe knowledge explicit. Achieving such a goal is facilitated when individuals learn 'system thinking' in the terms of Senge (1990, pp. 95–104). Even when most students in this research tradition go along with the assumption that changing or making more explicit recipes generally does require the support of an experienced interventionist, some scholars claim that individuals are indeed able to improve knowledge about their learning system without external consultancy. They suggest to facilitate the development of new recipes in learning laboratories by using computer simulation (Isaacs and Senge, 1992).

3) Learning from the experience of others Unfolding the tacit nature of organisational recipes is not only seen as essential for creating new knowledge and for increasing the efficiency of learning results, it also improves the effectiveness of the process of learning itself. This argument builds upon the assumption that explicit recipes can easily be transmitted from one organisation to another. On the one hand, it is assumed that the better or the more accurate recipes are, the more easy it is to transfer them or the more easy it is for others to imitate them.

Recipes are seen as learning experiences that can directly be copied from others or that can easily be transferred to others. The idea is that managers can be educated to implement seemingly successful management ideas. It is assumed that not only deutero-learning, but also the learning of experience from others can be supported by moderation, coaching or mentoring of the interventionist (Argyris and Schön, 1996). In this perspective recipes are being compared with a computer software that can be programmed without much effort, and that can be easily saved and transferred from one place to another. Following the information-processing view, we argued that previously non-programmable recipes have to be transformed into deliberately programmed knowledge. The main purpose of such a transformation is to better control and to manage more effectively the learning from the experiences of others.

4) The role of participation in the learning process We saw that even the information-processing and in the socio-technical systems approach stressed the role of participation in the learning process. Role participation was interpreted as an organisational design strategy that seeks to involve more people in decision-making processes. Especially the improvement of more chances for open communication and self-organisation in teams is seen as sufficient to prevent the emergence of resistance (or defensiveness) to a planned change. Moreover, it also fosters the identification of employees with managerial decisions. In this sense participation is seen as a formal precondition for securing and improving the effectiveness of the decision-making processes.

However, this traditional role of participation in organisational change processes is not sufficient. Participative management often only leads to adaptive learning forms, because traditional ways of thinking are not being questioned. In that case, participation is little more than an 'espoused theory' and has no real consequences for the capacity of members of the organisation to look inward. Such a capacity not only would require open discussions about participation, but also a willingness to become more responsible and aware of what these actors say and think about this issue (Senge, 1990). Intervention research distinguished between two forms of participation. The newly defined role of participation had to involve, both organisational design strategies that provide possibilities to speak and communicate openly in a traditional sense, as well as the development of 'high quality inquiry' (Argyris and Schön, 1996, p. 284) that enable actors to learn how to learn. Only the 'positive synergy' between the two participation modes that are called 'participative' and 'reflective openness' (Senge, pp. 276–81) are likely to undermine the emergence of defensive routines and can be expected to empower the questioning of established ways of thinking and perceptions of others. In other words, participation in decision-making processes should be combined with the development of reflective skills to question the underlying values of the established modes of decision-making.

5) The ideal of continuous organisational learning The problem of developing continuous learning loops is central to the debate on organisational learning. Intervention research sought to develop the conditions for learning and to identify an environment that is likely to enable members of organisations to question and change their mental models. Actors were expected to become continuous learners, and such continuous learning was to be coupled to the detection and correction of errors. This was to allow for a better understanding of the actors' own ways of thinking. Continuous learning was also to lead to an improvement of organisational success, because the search for linear solutions and the blame of others for one's own failures could be avoided (Argyris, 1992d; Garrat, 1987; Senge, 1990).

Using such a perspective, it is possible to conceive of blockades as interruptions of continuous learning circles. Actors have to continuously search for such interruptions and have to correct them. Continuous organisational learning thus can be interpreted as a process that creates accurate solutions for a certain task. Those solutions in turn improve the effectiveness of the organisational decision-making process. In the tradition of the socio-technical systems approach, technical models such as computer simulation were combined with social ideas of 'personal mastery' and 'team learning'. For that purpose the creation of specific departments so-called 'learning labs' is suggested (Senge, 1990, pp. 139–73, 233–72).

6) The role of organisational slack resources in the process of learning We already alluded to the key role played in learning processes by organisational slack in the information-processing view. Organisational slack was part of a design strategy that sought to reduce the need for information-processing. Slack was understood as a surplus of unspecified resources that arises when environmental uncertainty increases. However, beyond this function, its role was also interpreted as a facilitator of 'self-organization' and 'creative behaviour' (Morgan, 1986 pp. 77–109; Grabher et al., 1994a).

Research in the tradition of the socio-technical systems approach made a distinction between redundancy of parts and redundancy of functions. Therefore in the debate about organisational learning approaches slack resources were seen as a main condition for support, enabling higher-level learning. The greater the uncertainty, the more adequately organisational design strategies have to be focused on extra material resources (in the form of an inventory and lead time or budget), and on extra immaterial resources (in form of extra-functional qualifications, inquiry skills or systems thinking). Organisational slack, thus, can be said to have two aspects: on the one hand, it is a kind of functional resource that helps to improve the adaptation to technical and economic requirements of external environment and on the other hand, it has the property to facilitate creative behaviour and more radical forms of organisational learning (Galbraith 1974, p. 433; Grabher 1994a, pp. 51ff.; Argyris and Schön, 1996, p. 20; Senge et al., 1990, p. 185).

7) Organisational learning as a planned process There are two underlying basic assumptions which are important. First, intervention researchers believe that higher-level organisational learning must start at the top (Argyris, 1992a, pp. 34–6; Garrat, pp. 122ff.). Secondly, they assume that, in contrast to traditional forms of planning in the learning organisation, the process of planning is directly linked with learning (DeGeus, 1996, pp. 92–9; Senge, 1990, pp. 187–91). They stress that the key criterion for the successful implementation of double-loop learning processes must begin at the 'highest levels of organization' in order to assure 'that individuals have enough power and autonomy' to achieve the intended outcome (Argyris, 1992a, p. 35). A similar idea can be found in the discussion about the 'building of learning organizations' in the context of 'learning as planning'.[15] The starting point is the 'new work' that has to be performed by managers in creating the learning organisation. In short, the new leadership style is seen as different from traditional manager roles such as administrators or authoritarian leaders. Instead new roles for managers are understood as: 1) designers responsible for the design of higher level learning processes; 2) teachers by educating them in 'system thinking' which is seen as a basic skill in learning organisations; and 3) stewards that are to assure that personal learning processes are worthy of the 'organization's larger mission' (Senge, 1996, pp. 292–8).

Besides stressing system properties, such as slack resources or the role of participation by involving a broad number of actors from different organisational levels in decision-making processes, planning is seen as playing a key role in the creation of higher-level learning. The planned learning processes are seen as a tool to question mental models, change established rules, and use playing as an instrument (DeGeus, 1996). The idea of planning by 'playing' is again an attempt to support learning in a technical way and for triggering double-loop learning through computer simulation.

2.4 Organisational Learning Revisited

Besides the problem of growing conceptual diversity in the current discussion about organisational learning there is another 'endemic problem': the problem of oversimplification (Easterby-Smith et al., 1998, pp. 260–61). There are two aspects to this problem. On the one hand, there are the normative claims of this perspective, in particular the desire for more human learning conditions and the wish for an increase in efficiency. In spite of the more balanced evaluation of the learning organisation view about the relation between incremental and radical learning, it seems safe to conclude that there is still an implicit assumption that radical learning continues to be the best way of organisational learning. Single-loop learning is often described in negative terms, such as defensiveness and risk avoidance, and antithetical to more effective and human learning approaches. Double-loop-learning, by contrast, is defined in a more positive language, because it involves and bring about more open communication, more participative management, and more team-oriented learning etc.

On the other hand, the conceptual models about learning and organisation, that practice- oriented researchers borrow from academic organisation studies, are often more complex than recognised (ibid.). The practical operationalisation of these models generates more simple theories about learning and organising, and results in rather trivial proposals on how to improve the effectiveness and the efficiency of intraorganisational learning modes.

However, for the purpose of this study we are not interested in a fundamental criticism of studies in organisational learning. We do not want to develop a comprehensive analysis of the conceptual ideas, nor do we intend to blame mainstream researchers in this research field for their practical orientation – as some more academic approaches tend to do. Instead we aim to develop a perspective in the tradition of organisational sociology. The choice of this approach appears to be advantageous with regard to the two main interests of our study: first, to develop and understand the social dimension of organisational learning processes and, second, to realise this aim by adopting a comparative research perspective. Our approach seeks to break new ground not only through a comparative analysis of organisational learning processes which is hard to find in the mainstream debate about organisational learning, but also through applying organisational sociology considerations which are rather uncommon, or just about to emerge in this field. Information-processing and systems models are still prevailing in the field, and they tend to neglect the social context of learning processes (Child, 1997, pp. 43–76; Gherardi et al., 1998, pp. 273–97; Weick and Westley et al., 1996, pp. 440–58). To put it in the words of Gherardi et al. (1998, p. 274):

> Learning is still mostly conceived in cognitive and individual terms, a sociology of learning at the present does not exist, and mainstream sociology has continued, in one way or another, to focus its attention mainly on the external conditions of learning, i.e. on such issues as the consequences of social differentiation, group formation and typification, while devoting only tangential attention to the social dimension of the learning process itself.

In the following we will pay attention to three crucial issues in the common debate about organisational learning that we consider to be problematic. After this we will use a neo-institutionalist concept to show how the neglect of the social context is rooted in a limited view about the role of institutions in the process of organisational learning. This will lead us to the last step in our conceptual part, in which we will introduce the enactment approach. This concept combines the ideas of organisational learning with institutionalist arguments and is the basis for our comparative empirical research.

2.4.1 Critical Questions Within the Mainstream Discourse about Organisational Learning

From the perspective of organisational sociology, it seems to be imperative to question the views of those scholars of organisational learning who tend to idealise radical organisational learning and who proposed rather simplified models for its explanation. There are three main problems that we will be addressing in the following section:

1) the problem of reducing the outer organisational environment to technical and economic aspects;

2) the problem of limiting organisational learning either to individuals who learn in an organisation or to the organisation which learns as a system;

3) the question of how goals and success criteria for organisational learning are to emerge.

The *first problem* refers to the previously discussed idea that the internal processes of organisational learning are to be seen as a consequence of economic and technical change in the external environment. If the degree of environmental uncertainty increases, traditional organisational design strategies are expected to fail and therefore should be transformed. The learning of new ways of thinking forms an important competitive advantage in relation to the growing challenges of new markets and technologies. Radical learning ideas and the improvement of the organisational adaptability are seen as the most efficient way to deal with the pressure of the environment.

However, from an organisational sociology perspective, limiting organisational learning to external economic and technical criteria is misleading. The idea of improving success and the chances to survive by making previously tacit knowledge explicit directly follows from the neglect of the wider social environment and the role played by institutions in the process of organisational learning. Organisations are to be seen as located in institutionalised environments and institutions. They are expected to influence internal organisational learning processes that should not be reduced to cognition and that have to be linked to isolated criteria of success (Child, 1997, pp. 67–8).

The *second problem* is closely related to the one-dimensional conception of the external environment and its separation from internal processes of organisational learning. We already saw that the focus of organisational learning research is mainly on individual or group learning in organisations. We discussed how individuals and groups can learn to question their mental models and learn systematically to improve the reflection about their own actions and about the properties of the system.

Likewise, it is less important to consider how and under which conditions learning is transformed into an organisational property (ibid., pp. 65-66). Individual learning activities tend to be overvalued and organisations are reduced to simplistic systems with either more mechanistic or more organic properties. The main problem is seen in the improvement of the reflexivity of decision-making. However, from our point of view, this rather implicit assumption about rationality in decision making has to be questioned. Organisations can not be simply understood as a '"container" for human activities' (Gherardi et al., 1998, p. 275), nor can individuals be seen as freestanding decision-makers in search of constant increases of opportunities to learn. Instead we have to ask again whether individual choices can be properly understood outside an institutional framework. In contrast to what studies about organisational learning tell us, institutions are not simply obstacles and constraints for learning. They also allow for the establishing of criteria by which individuals perceive and define the success of organisational learning (Child, 1997; Weick and Westley, 1996; Gherardi et al., 1998).

This aspect leads us to the *third problem* of common organisational learning approaches, the neglect of how actors or groups of actors develop their preferences and goals for learning. The criteria for successful organisational learning are just there, because actors as well as organisations are seen as instruments to achieve certain goals. Students of organisational learning are interested in the consequences under which actors fail to meet original goals or that prevent them from recognising or changing the underlying preferences of current learning tasks. But they tend to ignore to question where those goals come from in the first place, and how those goals are established (Child, 1997). Actors are expected to develop double-loop learning modes, and are able to stabilise those modes. An organisation that achieves those goals is considered to be more successful than others. This becomes visible when researchers introduce the idea of unlearning as a necessary precondition for radical learning approaches. The old routine-driven learning modes are interpreted as a blockage for the development of new rather action-driven learning approaches, because the latter are understood as a key requisite for survival (Swieringa and Wierdsma, 1992, pp. 64–70).

But, by failing to take into consideration the way in which the criteria for successful organisational learning emerges, it becomes problematic to understand how further development and change over time is to take place. This problem has two sides. On the one hand, scholars of organisational learning have sought to understand the linear link between higher-level learning and success, and how this link allows for identifying new 'one best way' criteria for creating learning organisations. On the other side, it seems to be the case that mainstream research in organisational learning is sporadic, less systematic and is linked to the experiences of students as interventionists, consultants or managers. The criteria for assessing the success of organisational learning thus tends to be externally set and evaluated.

All in all, we can conclude that the current debate about organisational learning is focused on the improvement of the reflexivity of action and on the adaptability of the entire system. This leads to a neglect of the social context and to a limited view about the role of institutions in the process of organisational learning.

2.4.2   Key Arguments of the Neo-institutionalist Perspective

In the last section we demonstrated that mainstream research in organisational learning has a rather limited perspective on the environment of organisations. Moreover, mainstream scholars seem to have problems explaining how the results of individual learning become part of the organisation. They display a distinct lack of interest in the origins of learning goals and setting up criteria for assessing the success of an organisation. Now we would like to consider how the critical questions exposed above in the common organisational learning debate can be resolved by adopting a neo-institutionalist approach. The purpose of this section is, first, to show how neo-institutionalists interpret the role of the environment for organisational learning processes. Secondly we would like to demonstrate how learning processes in organisations are understood. Finally, we are interested in the perception of the development of learning goals by the actors involved in the process. We will show that these ideas deliver some insights that may, in part, provide us with answers to our open questions about common organisational learning research.

Similar to the early ideas of the BTF, neo-institutionalism has problems with the idea of radical organisational learning. In spite of the growing popularity of the theme, neo-institutionalism seems to be rather reserved about the possibilities to initiate and manage organisational learning (Wiesenthal, 1995). In their introduction to a basic reader on the neo-institutionalist perspective, DiMaggio and Powell (1991a, pp. 15–19) have questioned the implicit instrumentalism of TOA research. Apart from trying to understand how to increase the autonomy of actors, neo-institutionalists focus their attention on the routines and taken-for-granted aspects of organisational life (DiMaggio and Powell, 1991a, pp. 1–38). They agree with scholars working in the BTF tradition that action is more routinised, less reflective and unintentional than practice orientated interventionists postulate. Significant cognition in organisations is not seen as a result of autonomous learning by individuals in organisations, but as emanating from what is institutionally embedded in society (Child and Heavens, 1996). It does not matter whether organisational learning is considered to be adaptive and incremental, the BTF view; or whether more radical and reflective learning is demanded, as is the case in current research on organisational learning. For neo-institutionalism, the behaviour within and of organisations can only be understood if it is related to the wider societal context. Organisations are seen as socially constructed and as bounded to external institutions that are considered to form the basis of modern capitalism.

One of the main differences between neo-institutionalism and the ideas about organisational learning we presented earlier, is that it 'brings society back in'.[16] If students of organisational learning were primarily interested in the learning by groups and individuals in organisations and were inclined to link the outcome of internal processes to rather abstract technical and economic aspects of the external environments, neo-institutionalists focus more on the influence of the wider societal context of management processes. Early institutionalism, very much in the tradition of contingency theory, still made a distinction between technical and institutional environments, but later scholars working in this tradition became increasingly interested in the influence of institutional environments on organisations (Meyer and Scott, 1992, pp. 1–5; Meyer and Rowan, 1992 pp. 21–44; DiMaggio and Powell, 1991a, pp. 1–38; 199b, 63–82). The change of focus of neo-institutionalism from an emphasis on the technical environment to an emphasis on the institutional environment illustrates its scepticism about the chances of an efficient adaptation by organisations to technical or economic demands. Organisational forms that are not efficient in technical or in economic terms are expected to disappear or fail. Instead neo-institutionalist argue that:

> The conventional answer to this paradox has been that some version of natural selection occurs in which selection mechanism operate to weed out those organizational forms that are less fit. Such arguments, as we have contended are difficult to mesh with organizational realities. Less efficient organizational forms do persist (DiMaggio and Powell, 1991a, p. 78).

Neo-institutionalists do not only cast doubt on the very possibility of measuring the effects of different organisational forms on efficiency and productivity as such. Whereas the perspective of the learning organisation interpreted organisations as tools intended to achieve specific tasks, neo-institutionalists stress that organisations also require support and legitimacy. In this sense neo-institutionalists focus their research on those aspects of the environment that mainly neglected in the common debate about organisational and managerial learning. They stress that organisations, beyond technical and economic requirements, have to respond to particular institutional environments. They assume that because organisations are in need of legitimating, they have to adopt specific structural forms such as cognitive schemes, organisational rules and work roles. The resources and staffing necessary for such a legitimation are to be provided by specific bodies in society such as the educational and the legal system.

The change of interests in organisational analysis from technical and market requirements to institutions has also had an impact on the explanation of neo-institutionalists about the idea of intra-organisational learning. The neo-institutionalist conceptions of organisation and action are quite different from assumptions prevailing in organisational learning approaches. Organisations are not seen as technical artefacts or as constructs of more or less rational decisions, but as institutionally constituted. Contrary to the mainstream view on organisational learning it is not the development of reflective modes of acting and learning that is at the centre of the analysis, but the ways in which routinised organisational practices occur and the reasons behind their emergence. Thus, the focus of research has moved away from the question how far incremental or radical learning approaches fit better with challenges of new markets and technologies, to the problem of adopting and imitating certain social practices.

> Institutional theory recognizes that those responsible for organizational practices may 'learn' these through a process of seeking to conform to what is accepted wisdom (cognitive pillar), normatively acceptable to the community or society (normative pillar) or enforced by regulations or laws (regulative pillar). Insofar as this applies, it means that significant organizational cultures and practices are not the result of an autonomous learning process, or at least not exclusively so, but rather emanate from what is institutionally embedded in society (Child and Heavens, 1996, pp. 5–6).

In this sense, organisational learning appears to be a process of adopting and imitation which is expected to improve the social legitimacy of an organisation in a specific organisational field. Indeed, the explanation of organisational learning is not limited to a single organisation in which individuals learn, or in which the organisation learns as a system. Instead, learning is seen as an interorganisational phenomenon. Organisational fields are conceived of as specific sectors in a society that are to be constituted by similar organisations. In this sense it is assumed that organisational learning in and between organisations leads to the emergence of a shared cognition, and as common rules and ideologies. The so-called institutional isomorphism appears as process where organisations adopt increasingly similar strategies in an 'organisational field', and therefore converge in terms of both their structure and their culture (DiMaggio and Powell, 1991b, pp. 63–82). Imitation of other organisations and the adoption of legitimised social practices is seen as effective for organisations because it allows them to realise an improved acceptance by other organisations and societal bodies. As such it can contribute to the improvement of their reputation and make it more attractive to get support from public and private sponsors.

All in all we can conclude that when reconsidering the open questions in the common discussion about organisational learning, one has to bear in mind that (Walgenbach, 1995):

1) whilst students of organisational learning stress the active role of individuals to improve the conditions for learning, neo-institutionalism stresses the preference of actors for socially legitimate expectations and practices. Instead of active learning strategies, passive reaction and conformity to institutionalised environments is considered to be the foremost form of learning;

2) whilst organisational learning approaches stress the pressure of organisations to fit with certain economic and technical environments, neo-institutionalism emphasise the inherent tendency of organisations to becoming more homogeneous. Thus, organisational isomorphism encourages organisations to see and respond to problems in the same way, to use the same procedures, to adopt the same routines, and to make the same decisions;

3) whilst organisational learning approaches have problems to explain the origins of the goals and of the criteria whereby the success of organisational learning is being assessed, neo-institutionalism has drawn our attention to the process of setting of goals for internal learning processes. In this sense what organisations are able to learn, is related to the very external bodies

which they depend on, and on the basis of which they can generate support and social legitimacy.

2.4.3 The Problem of Social Embeddedness

In the previous section we have demonstrated how neo-institutionalist approaches play an essential role in filling the gaps, left open by the common organisational learning literature. First, the one-sided interpretation of external environments as technical environments was replaced by the idea of the institutional embeddedness of organisation. Second, institutions were not only seen as one-sided obstacles to higher-level learning approaches, but as constitutive for organisational learning – irrespective of the fact whether such learning was interpreted as being incremental or radical. Third, neo-institutionalists tried to understand the origins if the goals and criteria used for the assessing the success of learning processes – something which in the past has been systematically underestimated or even ignored altogether. Institutional analysis of organisational transformation processes thus can be said to have had two main advantages that tend to be ignored in the main stream discussions about organisational learning:

1) neo-institutionalists are sceptical about the extent to which actors in organisations are interested in and able to uncover learning blockages. Instead of looking for how organisations improve their action rationality, they show how actors adopt new ideas, routines and rules, not simply because this is expected to improve efficiency, but also because this is expected to legitimate an organisation in a particular institutional environment. Organisational behaviour thus should not simply be interpreted in instrumental terms, nor should it be limited to the improvement of the learning capacity of a single organisation. Instead it is important to link it back to a society in which organisations are institutionally embedded;

2) an institutional perspective also has methodological advantages, because it allows for comparative studies of organisational learning. Thus, compared to the more popular intervention research tradition, this perspective seems to be more systematic in its comparison of different forms of organisational learning. Intervention research was more speculative and at best based its arguments on the description of nonrepresentative empirical material and on consultancy experiences.

Nevertheless, the two traditions resulted in similar conclusions about the role of actors and their possibilities to learn and improve the learning capability of the whole system. One can also observe some similarities that have led the two approaches to a failure of understanding of the social character of learning processes. Both approaches see organisational learning primarily as a respond to external forces. When students of organisational learning emphasise mainly technical and economic forces that trigger internal learning processes, neo-institutionalists see the main problem in how society influences learning in and between organisations.

The basic ideas of both views fit with the distinction between an under- and an oversocialised conception of social action in sociology and economics (Granovetter, 1992). The undersocialised conception of organisational learning of interventionists, and the oversocialised interpretation of neo-institutionalism, are based on a rather static and mechanical view about the relation between organisations and their external environment, about the interdependence of structure and action, as well as about the role of social context. In both approaches, irrespective of the fact that actors are interpreted as rational decision-maker or as followers of social rules, the two approaches use a common concept of more or less 'atomized actors'. Contrary to this tendency of atomisation, Granovetter emphasises the social embeddedness of actions by suggesting that (1992, p. 58):

> Actors do not behave or decide as atoms outside a social context, nor do they adhere slavishly to a script written for them by the particular intersection of social categories that they happen to occupy. Their attempts at purposive action are instead embedded in concrete, ongoing systems of social relations.

It thus seems safe to conclude that organisational learning is not a freestanding decision-making process bound to a single organisational unit, nor can it be interpreted as completely forced by regulative, normative and cognitive features of society. These limitations can be avoided when we conceive of organisational learning as social process which is not determined by technical, economic or societal features, and which is closely linked to the idea of social practice. In this sense social institutions are not an external or objective force which block or enhance the actors' possibilities to learn, but they are continuously constructed and reconstructed during ongoing processes of interaction (Granovetter, 1992). This idea of social institutions is different from the understanding of common organisational learning, as well as from neo-institutionalism, because institutional arrangements are not seen as an efficient solution for a certain problem, nor thought of as being societally determined. Instead, institutional arrangements are interactively established in a particular context. Social institutions are not static obstacles to acting and learning, but both shape institutions and are in turn shaped by them.

This leads us to the concept of enactment developed by Weick (1995a). His view is very close to Granovetter's idea of social embeddedness because it gives up the inherent assumption of organisational learning research and neo-institutionalism that the environment, be it defined in technical or social terms, forces organisations to adapt and influence how actors in organisations learn. The enactment perspective can rather be seen as an intermediary position which combines radical ideas of the interventionists with the sceptical ideas of the neo-institutionalists.

2.5   Towards an Analysis of Organisational Learning Processes in Different Social Contexts

2.5.1 *The Perspective of Enactment Theory: The Focus of Analysis*

In the following section we want to show that neither the one-sided idealisation of unconstrained and reflective learning forms stressed by mainstream research in organisational learning, nor the pessimistic picture about the weakness of actors to develop their own organisational learning strategies stressed by neo-institutionalism, are sufficient to understand organisational learning as a social process. Both sides have a rather inert concept of institutions which again lead to rather optimistic or pessimistic scenarios about the chances for actors to develop innovative modes of learning. Institutionalised organisational practices are either seen as impediments to deutero-learning or are understood as a necessary response to overwhelming social influences. However, the enactment perspective takes both arguments seriously by developing a combined view. Thus, this idea allows a closer comprehension of the complex relationship between the process of organisational learning as a social process and the role of institutions.

The focus of the enactment perspective is on interactions of various actors and groups of actors, inside and outside the organisation. In this sense the focus of research moves from seeing actors as therapists or rule-followers to viewing them as practitioners. At the centre of our research is the practice of learning; how actors socially construct their environment through various intraorganisational and interorganisational interactions. Thus, compared to intervention research and neo-institutionalism, the focus of analysis moves from questions of how internal learning blockages or disabilities can be overcome or how organisations respond to social influences, to the practice of social learning.

The enactment concept understands organisational environments differently. On the one hand the deterministic argumentation that organisations must adapt to social influences, which is common to neo-institutionalist approaches, is avoided. On the other hand, the enactment concept is different from the intervention research perspective which explains environments as something which can more or less be perceived perfectly. As we have seen, this refers to the individuals' ability to avoid the faultiness and improve the correctness of their perceptions. However, in spite of the conceptual differences, both views stress the importance of outside influences, either technical and economic or institutional, as being responsible for the outcome of learning processes. From an enactment perspective, organisational environments cannot be separated from the process of organising. It is assumed that actors in organisations 'enact' their environments (Weick, 1995a). This idea combines both the assumptions of interventionists about the consequential role of actors to develop broader prospects for future learning, as well as the arguments of neo-institutionalism that organisations are not closed systems, but that institutions bring society back into the organisational context. Enacted environments are understood as entities which are actively created by members of organisations. They can select, decide and can make happen what belongs to the their organisation (Weick, 1995a; Orton, 1996). Thus the distinction between organisation and environment appears to be ambiguous:

> It is the organizational actors themselves who, through the process of bracketing and still another aspect of enactment – that of reality construction – decide what belongs to their organization and what does not, as well as what entities or even events outside their organization are relevant as thus to be classed as environment (Czarniawska-Joerges, 1996, p. 3972).

Through the redefinition of the role of actors and the introduction of the idea of enacted conception of environments, the concept of organisation has to be reconsidered. The idea that organisations are socially constructed is different from seeing organisations as an information-processing system that enables individuals to perceive their environments more or less correctly. Nor can organisations be directly influenced through external institutions. The focus of analysis thus cannot be reduced to the question of common organisational learning research, namely how individuals overcome learning blockages and disabilities in organisations. Equally insufficient would appear to be how neo-institutionalists stress that learning through adoption and imitation is a consequence of the institutional environment. From an enactment perspective, organisations cannot simply be characterised accordingly to more or less accurate organisational designing principles or how ideas, rules and routines are adopted in response to their institutional environments, but as should be viewed as a 'community of practice' constructed through social relations (Gherardi et al., 1998, pp. 275–9). This view has consequences for the conception of organisational learning. It can neither be reduced to the successful improvement of individual cognition and information-processing capacities of the whole system, nor to the extent of adoption and imitation for the purpose of increasing the organisation's social legitimacy. Rather, organisational learning as a social practice occurs through interaction and participation in social relations, inside and outside of the organisation.[17] See Table 2.3 for the summary about the comparison of the conceptual background and the focus of analysis.

There are two ways in which enactment is interpreted in the literature. At first it is important to stress that enactment means that actors necessarily respond to their subjective definition of the environment. According to this, secondly, they socially construct the environments which are relevant for their actions. (Child, 1997, p. 53). However, there is an important aspect which is often overlooked which links the idea of enactment to grand sociological theory. It refers to Giddens' (1984) structuration dialectic that yesterday's structures constrain today's actions and today's actions shape tomorrow's structures. In Weick's theory of organising (1995a), it is the feedback loop from retention to enactment which suggests that the retained learning from previous enactment has influence on present enactments (Orton, 1996, pp. 186–7).

In this section we have seen that the enactment perspective has two advantages which are essential for the following, where our attention is focused on the analysis of organisational learning processes in different social contexts. Firstly, we assume that organisational learning, as a process of social practice, cannot be separated from its social context. Instead, it is assumed that actors produce the social context to which they interactively respond. Apart from the micro-perspective of learning organisational systems and the rather macro-perspective of neo-institutionalist approaches we want to introduce a middle-range concept for the analysis of organisational learning which focuses on learning as an interactive process where actors continuously develop both constraints which are bound to past learning experiences, and opportunities for further learning and innovation.

Table 2.3   The focus of the enactment concept in contrast to interventionist and neo-institutionalist approaches

	Organisational learning	Neo-institutionalism	Enactment concept
Main approaches	Argyris and Schön; Senge et al.	DiMaggio and Powell; Meyer, Rowan et al.	Orton, Weick et al.
Theories of actors	Individuals are designers and therapists	Actors are rule-followers	Actors are practitioners
Theories of organisation	Organisations are information-processing systems	Organisations are constituted by institutionalised rules of the society	Organisations are socially constructed
Theory of environment	Concept of technical environments	Concept of institutional environments	Concept of enacted environments
Theory of organisational learning	... occurs through individual learning and learning of the whole system	... occurs through adoption and imitation	... occurs through social interaction and social engagement
Focus of analysis	How do individuals overcome learning blockages and disabilities in organisations?	How do organisations adapt to their institutional environment?	How are interrelated constraints and opportunities for organisational learning socially constructed?

2.5.2   *Concept of Analysis*

The purpose of this section is to consider how we can analyse organisational learning from an enactment perspective. Hence we refer to the idea that organisations cannot really be perceived, because theories and metaphors about them are often misleading (Weick and Westley, 1996). As we have shown above, the models of organisation which are applied by organisational learning and neo-institutionalist approaches pay less attention to the question of how actors experience their organisation when they learn. Through the application of rather abstract metaphors such as the learning organisation or the interpretation of organisations as institutions, researchers become inflexible in how they perceive organisations and the outcome of related learning processes. Thus, the 'healthy tension' (ibid., p. 441) between theory and experience is neglected. However, despite our awareness of the fact that we are not able to solve this methodological problem, we agree with Weick and Westley (ibid.) that research about organisational learning should be more closely linked to the learning experience of actors.[18] That is why we focus our research on how organisational actors actually learn.

In this sense, we see organisational learning as a social phenomenon which occurs through interaction processes which can be both intra- or interorganisationally directed. According to Weick and Westley we define organisational learning as follows:

> By this we mean that learning is not an inherent property of an individual or an organisation, but rather resides in the quality and the nature of the relationship between levels of consciousness within the individual, between individuals, and between the organisation and the environment (ibid., p. 446).

Adapting this concept, we want to analyse the learning opportunities of actors which have changed over time. This means we want to study learning processes at different moments, t1, t2, t3, etc. For this have we developed a case study research concept. Here we are interested in such questions as how actors enact their internal and external environments, which social relations are relevant within the process of organisational learning, how intra- and interorganisational relationships and human resource patterns have shifted over time. This dimension of analysis will be illustrated within the case study reports (chapter 4).

Moreover, we want to compare the processes of learning on the basis of different dimensions. Thus, we return to the key arguments summarised about the surrounding debate about organisational learning and the learning organisation. We make use of these concepts to compare the differences within the process of learning in each company study. However, they will not be used as abstract categories, but will be critically linked to the concrete learning experience of the actors in each of the case studies. These patterns (indicators), introduced in section 2.3.4, are:

1) identity construction;

2) recipes on how to learn;

3) learning from the experience of others;

4) the role of participation in the learning process;

5) the ideal of continuous organisational learning;

6) the role of organisational slack resources in the process of organisational learning;

7) organisational learning as a planned process.

However, the application of these patterns will show that the neglect of the role of institutions is misleading. On the one hand, we will see that even when institutions do not determine organisational learning processes as neo-institutionalist approaches assume, they play a significant role in the micro-dynamics of organisational learning. On the other hand, in applying these patterns we will reconsider the key arguments of the leading ideas in the debate about organisational learning from the enactment perspective. This is the intention of the systematic comparison of the three case studies in chapter 5.

Our thesis that social context matters is based on the ideas about organisational learning and the role of institutions developed in the previous part of this chapter. We have shown that an organisation's environment neither directly constrains organisational actions, nor is it actually externalised. Our focus of research is on the institutionalisation processes when actors and groups of actors learn, rather than on structures and their institutional underpinnings. The emerging social practices and modes of organising are not universal, context-free or easily transferable organisational forms, but they are in fact related to a certain social context (Czarniawska-Joerges, 1994, pp. 1–5). Therefore, we assume that the emergence of learning opportunities is embedded in a system of social practices and work activities. Thus, chances to learn are closely related to a specific social context or, according to Gherardi et al. (1998), 'community of practice'. While interacting and learning organisational, actors become competent members of this community and develop certain opportunities for further learning. The general features of the social context are 'embedded in the general habits and traditions of community, and it is sustained and tacitly transmitted from one generation to the next' (ibid., p. 281). At this point we agree with neo-institutionalism that the environment has an institutional character, because people inside and outside a community of practice share institutionalised norms, values and relationships (Child, 1997, p. 55). However, these cultural and relational dimensions of social context are not rigid or invariant structures as neo-institutionalist approaches assume, nor are they more or less random as common organisational learning concepts suggest. Actors actively create the environmental constraints to which they respond. Therefore, we want to analyse how organisational learning processes are both shaped by, and in turn shape, social context.

The aim of this study is not to search for general features of organisational learning in the social and economic transformation of former East German firms, the empirical background of this study. Furthermore, we are not so much interested in the similarities in reorganisation processes which occur during the social and economic change of an entire society, but the differences. Our thesis is that societal change as a whole, such as has occurred in the former GDR or in Central and Eastern Europe, does not directly influence 'how' and 'why' certain organisational learning forms appear.[19] Instead, the rather macro perspective of societal change has to be related to the actual practice of organisational learning in a specific social context. Thus, at the centre of our analysis is the variance of organisational learning opportunities in each case study.

Although the background of this study is the social and economic transformation of formerly state-owned firms, our thesis is that the fundamental societal transformation had no universal influence on organisational learning processes in former GDR firms. The actual forms and outcomes of organisational change which these firms have undergone are seen as a problem which has to be empirically researched. We are interested in understanding how certain social and economic conditions, understood as community of practice, influence the learning opportunities, and, vice versa, how the openness of these learning processes influences the community of practices.

Although in the next chapter, the methodological part of this study, we use structural features such as the origins of the organisation, products and services, product differentiation and manufacturing type to describe the specific differences in learning situations in a certain community of practice, we want to close this section by again stressing that the focus of this study is the analysis of organisational learning as a social process. We will show that institutions are neither external realities which block higher-level learning processes, nor do they have determining influence on internal knowledge creation processes. Strictly speaking, our interest is in understanding those events that give the process of organisational learning direction and meaning. Once organisational actors start to make commitments (Weick, 1993) or strategic choices (Child, 1972 and 1997) they lay down the constraints and opportunities they face when they are learning. In this respect we agree with Weick (1993) when he emphasises that small events such as the decision to stay within an established market niche can have large consequences for the emerging organisational possibilities. Subsequently, we want to find out how specific starting conditions such as whether actors can refer back to traditional markets or not, whether they persist or change their manufacturing type, whether they develop customised products or just start to search for or create new markets, influence the ways in which organisational actors actually learn.

In this sense, we understand organisational learning as a social creation, embedded in more or less institutionalised cultural systems. According to the comparative research design of this study we will place our focus on whether organisational learning processes are more or less closely related to the traditional ways of thinking and acting and whether they consist of more or less homogeneous ways of organisational knowledge creation. Moreover, the openness and goal-specificity of organisational learning modes which actors develop within a particular community of practice will be examined. In conclusion, we want to find out about the differences and similarities in how actors enact their local cultural systems and thereby socially construct the opportunities and constraints for further organisational learning.

Notes

1 See for example Morgan (1986, pp. 77–109) who uses the metaphor of the human brain to illustrate the nature of organisational learning.
2 See Scott (1987) for the further discussion of this topic.
3 We will come back more detailed to this argument in section 2.3.
4 An idea was taken and developed further by contemporary systems theory (Luhmann, 1984).

5   Easterby-Smith et al. (1998, p. 264) identified six main clusters in the literature which have appeared in the last 20 years; psychology and organisational development; management science; organisation theory; strategy; production management; and cultural anthropology.

6   Prominent examples for publications in the English language are Dodgson (1993), Easterby-Smith et al. (1998), Miller (1996), Moingeon and Edmondson (1996). In Germany there have appeared an increasing number of surveys too, such as from Berthoin Antal (1998), Güldenberg (1997), Pawlowsky (1992), Wiesenthal (1995).

7   We use the term intervention research mainly in reference to the basic ideas: 1) developed by theory of action (TOA) with its leading students Chris Argyris and Donald Schön; and 2) developed by system dynamics approach (SDA) with its leading student Peter Senge.

8   For more details about the consideration on fundamental agreements and differences in both conceptions, see the essays of Chris Argyris and Miner and Mezias in *Organizations Sciences* (Vol. 7, No. 1, 1996, pp. 79–99).

9   As Swieringa and Wierdsma (1992) who added to conventional forms of single- and double-loop learning a third one in their proposal in *Becoming a Learning Organization*, so-called triple-loop learning.

10 The usage of terms such as programmable and non-programmable situations of learning indicates the closeness of these ideas to the above introduced information-processing perspective.

11 Pawlowsky (1992) gives an useful overview of the variety of such models.

12 Organisational structure is defined rather traditionally as channels of communication, information systems, the spatial environment, procedures and routines, and system of incentives (Argyris and Schön, 1996, p. 28).

13 Even Argyris made a step in this direction in conceding 'that in some cases single-loop interventions ... created liberating alternatives. Although they did not create double-loop learning ...' (quoted from Miner and Mezias, 1996, p. 89).

14 These ideas are not only abstract considerations of management science, but enjoy widespread popularity in the actual management practice in East-German firms too. As we will see later on, in the empirical part, in one of our three case studies the concept of continuous improvement process (CIP) was implemented to streamline the established organisational learning modes (chapter 4, pp. 67–86).

15 This is the title of the article of the former planning director of the Shell group Arie DeGeus (1996).

16 This is also the main message of the German volume which gives a general outlook about the state of the art of organisation theory, edited by Ortmann et al. (1997). See also Friedland and Alford (1991, pp. 232–63).

17 The concept of organisational learning as a social practice is also discussed in the essay of Geppert and Merkens (1999). The leading question of this comparative study was: How did the actors in two former GDR firms developed new social practices beyond institutional pressure?

18 Both authors also lay stress on the fact that there seems to be very little information about organisation in the existing literature on organisational learning (Weick and Westley, 1996, p. 441). As we have shown, existing studies about this topic mainly focus on individual learning processes in organisations.

19 This refers to our argument in 2.3.3. There we criticised the normative demand in the existing literature about learning organisations that the shift from lower level 'learning how' to higher-level 'learning why' and recommended seeing this problem as an empirical one.

3 Research Design, Company Cases and Methods of Investigation

3.1 Introduction

The conventional empirical research approach more or less relies on norms of rationality developed within the natural sciences. Ideally, the research process should be conducted as follows: The analysis should be guided by clear research questions specified in hypotheses which should be testable. A particular research design must therefore be chosen or developed. The whole research process, so to speak, is seen as something which can be planned and conducted according to plain and simple rules. It is assumed that data collection and interpretation will lead to a research report providing definitive answers to the initially formulated research questions. One prominent example for such more categorical research design is Yin's proposal to engage in 'case study research' (Yin, 1994), within the context of this kind of rationally orientated framework.

In contrast to conventional research methods, our research design resembles the focus of this study in the sense that its approach can be described as one of a process of learning. Our study must therefore be understood as an experience-based project. Our methodology is closely related to idea of Andersen et al. (1995) of 'doing intensive field studies'. There are several reasons for the application of these distinct research ideas. In the first instance, there are the interests of this study. As an alternative to traditional studies about organisational learning we are searching for context-specific explanations as to how actors learn and thereby stabilise and modify their institutional arrangements. The specific character of this approach requires, secondly, a quite detailed understanding of the complex social processes in the field and for this reason, the application of qualitative methods such as intensive case studies is required.[1] Thirdly, we have expressed our scepticism for quick simplifications of rather complex ideas about organisational behaviour by criticising the celebration of the learning organisations as a new 'one best way'. In addition, in the conceptual chapter we expressed our concerns about how grand theory tends to overrate the role macrostructures play in influencing the outcome of organisational behaviour. From the perspective of our research approach, actors are not the kinds of voluntary learners interventionists believe them to be and they do not behave simply based upon the way in which macrostructure institutions constrain them. Instead, we want to stress the consequences micro-processes such as interactions have on the macro-level and, and vice versa, and how macro-structural institutions influence the direction of the collective learning processes at the micro-level.

In contrast to the assumption of conventional research practices our experience-based methodology was not a systematic enterprise. Instead, re-conceptualising and modifying the research model had been a natural consequence of practising such an approach. Thus, the development of our analytical concept occurred through the integration of ideas and experiences which emerged while conducting the intensive case studies, discussing our ideas with colleagues and friends, and participating in academic discourses on this topic, etc.[2] And while we have not applied such an analytical model as recommended in the standard methodological literature, we have at the same time not only worked inductively. In the final analysis, we can illustrate that every part of this study has its own purpose in the research process. In retrospect, we can present a consistent picture of the methodology we applied, and this is the purpose of this chapter. The coherence of the research process is also the result of having developed a definite focus of research throughout the entire research process. The leading research question focused on the analysis of the role of institutions in the process of organisational learning. Moreover, qualitative methodology inspired by symbolic interactionism (Blumer, 1969; Schultz, 1995, et al.) was a consistent research guide from the very beginning of our project.

At the same time we want to underline that our study should be seen as an attempt to build theories from case studies in the sense of Eisenhardt (1989). Contrary to common research on organisational learning that mostly uses case studies to illustrate their normative models, we applied case studies to review these conventional ideas about learning in organisations and develop a new insight in the interdependence between organisational learning and institution-alisation. Thus, similarly to Eisenhardt (1989, pp. 532–4) we want to position our case study based theory-building in the larger context of social science research.

In the following section (3.2) we will briefly address the conceptual background and research interests of this study. Our research process can be divided into three main phases: The preparatory and selection phase, the intensive research phase and the phase of analysis. The task of the next three sections (3.3, 3.4, 3.5) is to describe these analytical stages.

3.2   Research Interests

When we stressed in the last section that our analysis goes beyond the objective research paradigm. We also want to disassociate ourselves from radical social constructivism that assumes that knowledge about social reality cannot be obtained from interviews because the interview situation itself is seen as an exclusive interaction between the interviewer and the interviewee (Miller and Glassner, 1997, p. 97). By applying an interactionist approach, we intend to learn about the social world and thereby develop a deeper insight into our main objective of understanding the role of institutions in the process of organisational learning.

In contrast to discrete case studies which deal with similar settings and topics, a comparative research strategy seems to provide a sufficient empirical base to show differences in how organisational actors enact their internal and external environment. We assume that each study in its own manner addresses similarities and differences in how actors and groups of actors learn interactively with each other and how these processes create enabling and constraining institutionalised conditions for further learning. In the conceptual chapter we had introduced the idea of analysing organisational learning as situated in specific 'communities of practice' (Gherardi et al., 1998) with their own institutionalised ways of learning, solving problems and organising. From an enactment perspective, in a sense both the relational as well as the cultural dimension of organisational learning processes will be considered. We want to analyse and compare the transformation of social relations and cultural systems in very different organisational forms. Both culture as well as social relations can be incrementally transformed or strengthened throughout these interactive learning processes.

3.3   Preparatory and Selection Phase

The reason for having selected three East German firms for the purposes of our research project was to do with former research experience in East Germany as well as with our involvement as we prepared this study in other projects which can be classified under the label organisational transition in the context of societal transformation in Central and Eastern Europe.[3] Moreover, our familiarity with the social context appeared to be essential in helping us to select suitable research subjects, as it was most convenient since it enabled us to forge close links to key actors in the firms. This was useful, because it facilitated a relatively unrestricted access to our enterprises and consequently provided more room for intensive field research.

Our comparative case study research was conducted on two levels. On the one hand, we compared how the actors in each firm transformed social relations and cultural systems. On the other, hand we developed an analytical strategy involving long-term studies to reflect on the nature of the process of organisational learning. The focus was on how interpretative and interactional practices had been modified.

The interest was to compare when and how in each of the case studies interaction patterns persisted, declined in effectiveness or changed. Strictly speaking, we focused our analysis on a comparison of how the actors in each firm transformed their ways of thinking and acting, their organisational concepts, their internal relations (such as human resource management strategies, organisational design or modes of participation) and external relationships (such as with customers, suppliers, owners, sponsors, local authority etc.) over a certain period of time.

Moreover, East Germany also appeared to be an interesting research field for our project, because it was assumed that the specific conditions of social and economic transformation would initiate organisational change. However, from our point of view, the empirically interesting question was to show the differences in how former state-owned firms dealt with the broad variety of 'triggers of organisational learning' such as the opening of markets, the dissolution of the collective combines, the privatisation of companies, foreign investments, and the introduction and use of new technologies in a company (Merkens et al., 2000). According to our argumentation in the former chapter, such social and economic characteristics of the transformation process at the macrostructural level of society should be considered in this study on the micro-level of organisational learning.

The selection of the three case studies is based on two principal assumptions. At first we decided to select firms with a broad variety in their institutional embeddedness at the macrostructural level. Our presumption was that what people learn, how they learn with each other and what this means for their prospects of further learning is influenced by the institutions which constitute and are constituted by a particular 'community of practice'. In this sense we searched for organisations which are socially embedded in quite distinct communities of practice for the purpose of analysing and comparing how interactive learning processes are represented differently in the local cultural systems. Secondly, we decided to select firms which have implemented reorganisation strategies or have announced plans to do so. In such firms organisational learning could be expected to play a critical role. At the same time, local managers of these firms seemed interested in learning more about their own strategies. For introducing new management ideas such as TOP or CIP as in firm A, profit centre structures as in case study B or job creation projects as in case study C. Even when the interests of management in some kind of action research was rather diffuse, their attention to this issue helped to create a relatively open research environment.

In Table 3.1 we want to highlight some key characteristics of the three case studies we have selected. Each firm belongs to a quite distinct community of practice with different resources, social competencies, rules and routines. Firm A represents an established international supplier of car headlights in the automobile market. Firm B represents an established producer of tools and machine tools which was transformed into profit centre organisation and in search of a market niche. Firm C represents a new founded job creation centre which had just started spinning-off new business activities and developing projects to establish long-term employment prospects through public sponsorship.[4]

Table 3.1   Key characteristics of the case studies

Key characteristics	Case study A	Case study B	Case study C
Key organisational tasks	assembly of standard price-competitive products	creation and production of customised quality products	job projects and spin-offs of small businesses
Construction of the organisational system	highly-structured manufacturing	medium-structured profit centre organisation	low-structured platform organisation
Focus of organisational learning	on the implementation of effective organisational design principles	on the development of customer-specific organisational forms	on the development of employment projects
Employment development	(reduction from) @ 1100 (1989) to @ 500 (1996)	(reduction from) @ 850 (1989) to 90 (1995)	(creation of) @ 200 jobs in the public and private sectors (1995)

The interesting question is how these quite different starting conditions in each community of practice, here characterised by key organisational tasks, social construction of the organisational system, and focus on organisational learning and employment development influenced the opportunities and constraints which emerged when actors and groups of actors learned from and together with each other. In line with Gherardi et al. (1998, pp. 279–81) we assume that the sets illustrated above of material, economic, symbolic and social characteristics of each case study structures as so called 'situated curriculum' both the content and contingency which actors face in their processes of organisational learning. Each of the before mentioned characteristics draws our attention to three quite distinct organisational domains with specific interaction, work and organising patterns which are the subjects of our analysis.

3.4   Intensive Research Phase

When we started our first intensive field research we had developed micro-theories for what might be important for the analysis of the organisational learning process. These micro-theories were based on conceptual reflections we had developed through literary studies, through discussions with colleagues and through experiences gained from the corresponding research projects mentioned above.

The first contact to the field was in the spring of 1993, when we began our case study research in firm B. The last intensive field research we conducted in the spring of 1996 when we interviewed some of the key actors of this firm after an official presentation about their organisational development and future projects.

In our project we applied the following research methods: participant observation, group discussions, intensive interviews and the analysis of documentation, both published and unpublished. We conducted intensive interviews and group discussions in all three case studies. Participant observation and documentary analysis were applied to varying degrees in each of the studies. In firm B intensive interviewing played the most significant role and documentary analysis and participant observation less so. The intensive research phases organised for each of the three firms were distinctive. In firm A we were employed as research trainees for one month. Next to intensive interviewing we therefore had more opportunities to observe participants and gain access to diverse official as well as unofficial documents.

In contrast to case study A, in firm C we worked together with a consultancy group for a time, and therefore had numerous opportunities to practice quite a broad mixture of intensive research methods. However, unlike for the other two case studies, we taped more interviews and interviewed the firm's key actors with a greater frequency and intensity in firm B. Table 3.2 shows that we actually carried out longitudinal case studies by having regularly visited all three firms over a period of approximately two years. Moreover, it becomes visible that we examined a broad number of interviewees, some of them several times. We marked the main period of our intensive research in italics.

Table 3.2   Brief overview about the intensive research phase

	Case study A	Case study B	Case study C
Number of interviews	37	20	41
Number of interviewees	22	14	22
Time table of the intensive research phases	1) *Survey: Spring '94* 2) Survey: Spring '96	1) Survey: Spring '93 2) Survey: Summer '93 3) *Survey: Winter '93/94* 4) Survey: Summer '94	1) *Survey: Feb.–Jul. '93* 2) Survey: Spring '94 3) Survey: Spring '96

However, what this table did not show is that the interviewees listed were not only organisational members. In each case study we also contacted relevant external key actors which had worked for or had close contact with or played a significant role in the development of our firms. In addition it has to be mentioned that in each firm we selected interviewees from different management levels, and from among both workers and the works councils. In the main phase of our survey we tried to interview as many interviewees as possible; in the other research phases we focused our inquiry on key actors who seemed to us to play an important role in the firm's organisational development such as strategic decision-makers, key players in crisis situations or critical actors. Most of these key interviews were taped and transcribed. Most of the interviews listed in the table were conducted in order to develop a deeper insight into the dominant interpretation schemes of each firm and to compare the opinions of different actors about some key questions with each other. However, when you compare the list of interview partners on page 10 with number of interviews in Table 3.2, you can see that some interviews apparently received more attention than others. This was regarded to our research strategy: We started with a broad number of interviews to get a broad picture of the ongoing learning processes on different levels of the whole organisation. Later on we concentrated more on the intensive interviewing of key actors that apparently seems to be highly involved in the organisational process of each enterprise.

Although we conducted our intensive case studies in a rather open and loosely structured manner, we did not just engage in narrative interviews. Instead, relatively early on in the research process, we developed a semi-structured interview guide (see Figure 3.1). The main reason for using interview guides was to discipline ourselves to structure the interviews in each case study in a similar manner. Furthermore, during the research process we learned that even during those interviews which had a more narrative and informal character, we implicitly referred to the structure of our interview guide which was developed according to our micro-theories that organisational learning is guided by key actors, can be characterised by specific modes of participation, is institutionalised in organisational concepts and reorganisation strategies, and becomes visible when unfamiliar situations or critical events appear. These micro-theories and the interview guide below are the outcome of a project seminar for graduate students offered at the Humboldt University in the winter term 1993/94 which dealt with both the conceptual ideas of this project and the first experiences from the field research in case B.[5] In this sense the interview guide can be seen as a product of intensive group discussion.

As already mentioned, in order to improve the conditions of our research process in each of our three firms we negotiated with the local management arrangements to conclude our intensive research phase with a presentation in which we presented our first impressions and some presuppositions about the observed reorganisation processes. These specific forms of group discussion provided us with a good opportunity to test or specify our micro-theories as well as our research questions about organisational learning.

3.5   Phase of Analysis

The main purpose of this of research phase was to interpret, reflect on and document our empirical data. Here we can distinguish between three steps which are documented in the next three chapters of this study. After the intensive research phase during which complex data material was collected, we set about to order our empirical findings.

The first step involved developing key interaction patterns providing evidence for our initial questions developed on the basis of our micro-theories about organisational learning. It was based upon the results of the interpretation process that case study reports were prepared for the concluding analysis.

Structure of the interview guide:

1) Reflections on the individual work situation

- Transformation of the individual work situation
- Transformation of formal qualifications required and training on the job
- Evaluation of the work climate

2) Reflections on organisational development

- Origins, concepts and structure of the firm
- Planned and accomplished reorganisation strategies
- Economic situation and future of the firm
- Transformation of human resource management strategies (including employment development)
- Participation in the decision-making process

3) Reflections on critical situations in the firm's development

- Dealing with crisis situations, unexpected and critical events
- Evaluation of these problems
- Suggestions to address and solve these problems

Figure 3.1 Interview guide

These reports are primarily exploratory and descriptive in nature, and reflect how the actors in each case study enacted their internal and external environment, and what this meant for participation and human resource management strategies. It is for this reason that the case study reports begin with a brief synopsis about the structure and history of the firm and then provide a detailed description of the most relevant transformation processes in each case study. In each firm the alteration of the collective learning patterns is described, and we have reconstructed how the actors observed and interpreted the processes of organisational development after the wall came down and up through the completion of our intensive research phase.

In a second step we have developed a comparative research design by bridging our interpretations of empirical data with the more theoretical questions introduced in the conceptual chapter. Here we translated some of the key assumptions in the debate about organisational learning into seven micro-patterns (indicators) and sought to test which role each of these issues would play in the social practice of organisational learning. Thus, our intention was to compare how each of these seven indicators had been enacted in each case study and thereby come to a closer understanding of the role of institutions in the process of organisational learning. Therefore, we compared how organisational learning processes in each firm had been given meaning on the basis of the following key questions:

1) How did the actors socially construct their corporate identity?

2) How and where had recipes on how to learn been developed?

3) In which way had the experiences of other actors been integrated within the processes of organisational learning?

4) Which role did participative learning approaches play?

5) How did the actors deal with the emerging discontinuities within the process of organisational learning?

6) How had organisational slack resources been socially constructed?

7) What was the meaning of planning in the development of each organisation?

By comparing the organisational learning processes in our three case studies we were able to show quite significant differences in how interactive learning patterns had been socially constructed. Moreover, we used the systematic comparison of the cases to continue our initial critique in the conceptual chapter of conventional organisational learning approaches. Our critical position on some of these key assumptions becomes explicitly apparent in the title of two sections, namely section 5.2.5. which we labelled 'Beyond the ideal of continuous organisational learning' and section 5.2.7. which we called 'Organisational learning as a planned and pragmatic process'. Both can be read as a data-based, critical redefinition of two key arguments within common organisational learning approaches where learning is seen as continuous improvement process and even planable. Our intensive field analysis has however shown that such interpretations can be misleading, because they only seem to be relevant in quite specific communities of practice.

The final step of our interpretative research phase is documented in the last chapter of this study and compared to chapters 4 and 5 is thus more reflective in nature. In the preparation for the concluding chapter, we applied research results presented previously in order to consider the role of institutions within the process of organisational learning in a more comprehensive manner. Above and beyond the critique of conventional students of organisational learning and particular neo-institutionalist scholars, we employ our research experiences to develop new ideas and provide suggestions as to how research on organisational learning could be developed further.

3.6   Concluding Comments

According to the purpose of this study, we aim to achieve a more profound understanding of the dialectical relationship between organisational learning and institution building, the discussion in this chapter should provide evidence which supports our initial argumentation: Through the application of an experience-based methodology, each of the following chapters of this study represents a different stage of our research process.

The case study reports in chapter 4 will give a compact introduction of each of our three firms. Preparing these reports was the first step in the interpretation phase. However, this chapter might conveniently illustrate our intent to develop a process perspective on organisational learning.

The comparative discussion of the empirical findings in chapter 5 represents the next stage of our experience-based interpretation process. In this research phase we compared and analysed the different modes of organisational learning between each firm and the role of institutions in this process.

However, the conclusion chapter represents the terminal step of our interpretative research phase. This chapter refers mainly to our interests in theory building expressed in the conceptual chapter where we introduced the enactment perspective and contrasted it with common organisational learning approaches and neo-institutionalism. Consequently, we focused our attention on a more comprehensive reflection on institutional tensions emerging in the processes of organisational learning and thereby revert back to one of the main concerns of this study of identifying the consequences of micro-level organisational learning processes on the macro-level and vice versa.

Notes

1   However, in contrast to Andersen et al. (1995) we prefer the usage of the established term case study research.

2   We thus received an opportunity to publish some of our ideas prior to the completion of this study (Geppert, 1996; Geppert and Merkens, 1999; Merkens, Geppert and Antal, 1999).

3   Our main projects included a single case study about the transformation of organisational culture in an East German industrial firm in 1990/91 (Geppert, 1991). Moreover, we conducted a study about the privatisation policy of the THA in cooperation with the Social Science Research Centre Berlin in 1993 (Geppert and Schmidt, 1993; Geppert and Kachel, 1995). In addition to this, we worked together with a consultancy firm on a job creation project in 1993/94 in East Germany.

4   A more comprehensive description about the background and social characteristics of each case study will be given in the next chapter.

5   With some of these students we have not only prepared the interview guides, but they furthermore participated in the intensive research phase and in the phase of analysis.

4 Trajectories of Learning in Three East German Companies

4.1 Case Study A: Integration in a Large Industrial Group

The Origins of the Organisation

- **Short introduction to the structure and history of the firm's organisational development**

Before privatisation, firm A was one of the largest suppliers of headlights to the automobile branch of the former CMEA (Council for Mutual Economic Assistance). It was part of a state-owned combine, a so-called *Kombinat*.[1] In 1990 approximately 1,100 employees worked for the firm.

The production of headlights in firm A was organised in a quasi-Tayloristic fashion in order to supply relatively fixed customer markets. The main task was to produce headlights for the automobile sector in the GDR, in the CMEA and beginning at the end of the 1970s in the West German market as well. Management activities were primarily concerned with organising the production process. R&D capacities were split between the headquarters of the combine (*Kombinat*) in R and the production site in B. All marketing activities were centrally guided by the Ministry of Foreign Trade. In short, managerial learning in this period was focused on increasing productivity in order to fulfil externally controlled goals, but without any entrepreneurial responsibility.

Indeed, from an organisational development perspective, firm A's entrance into the Western market in the late 1970s was significant for two reasons. First, the firm had the opportunity to invest in modern technology with foreign currency before 1989 and, secondly, became exposed to Western quality standards. At the level of material organisational resources, both proved to be important benefits within the context of a changed environment.

After the Wall came down, the management of firm A enjoyed a short period of relative freedom to search for its own organisational development profile. The former combined as a whole was in decline and at first relatively passive in its decision-making processes. Nor did the Ministry exercise direct external control. Added to this, the central governmental privatisation agency – the *Treuhandanstalt* (THA) – was, initially, less capable of acting during its early stages.

At this point in time the local management declared 'the salvation of firm A and employment at site B as its first task'. The path to salvation was unclear. Management considered three options: First, to remain within the combine; secondly, cooperation with a potential investor; and thirdly, the development of their own survival strategy. However, the last perspective did not get the same attention as the others.

A passive salvation strategy was preferred to more proactive forms of reorganisation. No-one in management was interested in risking a more self-oriented strategy. They only defined a narrow strategy to maintain the established access to the Western customer market following the decline of the GDR and the CMEA market. The search or creation of new market segments was not seen as a management task.

The main part of reorganisation began under new ownership. Local management was not involved in the negotiations about the firm's privatisation. A multinational company with its headquarters in West Germany, supplier of parts to the car industry, took over firm A on site B, together with other production lines of the old combine. The rest or less attractive parts remained under the administration of THA. The new owner built up a new industrial green field site in E for other manufacturing lines, but the production of headlights continued in firm A at its traditional site in B.

4.1.1 Organisational Learning Problems

1) Challenges of enacting an external relations environment In contrast to the other East German enterprises for which the privatisation agency had difficulties finding interested buyers (Geppert and Schmidt, 1993; Geppert and Kachel, 1995), right from the start beginning in 1990 firm A attracted two possible investors. They were a large multinational with its headquarters in West Germany and a medium-sized West German firm, and both the automobile market suppliers.

Before the final decision about the future investor was made, there was a minority of actors to be considered who wanted independence from the former central administration of the combine's headquarters and to develop their own position about the future of the firm. But the local executives did not support such tendencies. The former senior manager – today he is responsible for manufacturing – explained as follows why the option for an autonomous organisational development was not seriously considered:

> The question arose: What will happen when the market comes? And we came to the following conclusion: the local markets, like Truant and Wartburg, had already collapsed. The Eastern European market was unpredictable. So, after two visits in competitive West German firms we thought about spinning-off. But then we stopped for a moment and saw that future profits would only be possible with low wages. On top of this, our technology standard was inadequate. With the same currency [after monetary unification in July 1990] we would stand no chance. By our calculations we would have had to invest 70–80 million DM in technology and equipment to modernise our firm and have it meet Western standards (Interview, 1a/2).

Besides doubts about the possibilities for a self-organised restructuring of the firm, there were few initiatives coming from local managers about participating in the negotiations about ownership. Instead, the local management waited for the outcome, the future investor. Only after the announcement that a multinational would be the future owner did the local managers see the need for negotiations in order to avoid the closure of firm A and the integration of its functions – the production of headlights – at the planned new location. Looking back, the local managers interpreted the retention of firm A and its labour at the traditional base as a successful outcome of their bargaining with the new owners. All in all, the local managers seemed to be satisfied with the new ownership situation, especially because there was less certainty about the intentions of the other possible investor:

> At that time the decision was between the multinational X and the medium-sized firm Y. Both had know-how as well as markets. Our staff was divided into two parties. They argued against X because of its reputation for being an inflexible giant. And against Y they argued, because of its low capacity to invest, which meant less employment ... We also feared that Y wanted to eliminate us as a competitor (Interview, 1a/2).

However, besides the boost in confidence which the actors got following the takeover of firm A by the West German multinational, there also seemed to be scepticism about the new owner's flexible management capabilities. Organisational behaviour of the multinational was compared to the administration of the former state-owned combine.

In an interview with one of the new Western managers, it was said that although not all parts of the combine were interesting for the multinational, the East German group of suppliers was seen as an 'Eastern equivalent to the Western multinational' (Interview, 3a/1). Against this backdrop, the potential investor was not interested in the combine as a whole, but in complementing their own production profile. In this sense, the integration of firm A into the multinational's general structure was achieved by making it one of the three bases for the production of headlights for the whole conglomerate. The company was thus able to concentrate the production of headlights at three sites, two in Germany – one in West Germany and the other East Germany – and one in Malaysia. Two other manufacturing locations in Europe had been shut down.

What were the interests of the multinational in taking over the manufacturing of car headlights in East Germany?[2] According to the interviews, the main goals of the company prompting their takeover of firm A were as follows:

- to gain a competitive share of the Eastern European market;
- to profit from its establishment near a large automobile firm;
- to benefit from state subsidies for investment in East Germany;
- to gain long-term advantages through lower production costs (especially wages);
- to tap into a source of skilled labour (Geppert, 1996, pp. 254–8).

The integration of firm A into the multinational was carried out with the intention of focusing the processes of organising on the 'core business'. The range of products was reduced because the manufacturing of headlights was seen as the primary task now. Based on past experience, the established market relations in Eastern Europe as well as in the West were viewed as relatively stable and with a growth potential that could be further served by large-batch and mass production. Similar to the experiences of the multinational, the employees within firm A were accustomed to producing for stable markets, where bulk buyers and bulk orders were dominant. As in the past, customer relations were centrally organised and separated into specific functional tasks such as purchasing, quality management, marketing etc.

Another important aspect for the enactment of the external relations environment was the decentralisation of the whole firm and the reorganisation of former supplier structure. The management focus on decentralisation required decisions about the outsourcing of previously integrated functions.

Some of them, such as the maintenance department, became external suppliers.[3] One of the two newly appointed senior managers from West Germany explained this task:

> First we had to decentralise the manufacturing process. For instance, we outsourced the galvanising process and the production of synthetic parts ... We decentralised different production lines which now work as our suppliers. They took over some of our employees too (Interview, 2a/1).

Besides the creation of new external supplier relations, the multinational also transplanted its well-established supplier relations for primary headlight parts to East Germany. At the same time, the firm's traditional supplier relations in East Germany declined primarily because of the unreliable delivery terms of former suppliers as well as their insufficient quality standards; by this time a special quality certification was required before awarding a contract.[4]

The following section will analyse: 1) how management perceived and dealt with unexpected environmental changes and the challenges of the intensifying competition within the global car supplier market; and 2) how they defined and reorganised the firm's core business activities.

2) Challenges of enacting an internal relations environment The takeover process of the former GDR firm was centrally organised by the multinational. It took over the firm with its staff, technology and products. According to the tradition of the multinational two senior managers were newly appointed: a manager responsible for manufacturing and technology and one responsible for commercial and accounting tasks. Nevertheless, the experience and social competencies of the former executives and middle managers were not disregarded. Most of them were retained and became responsible for tasks within the manufacturing process. However, some of them lost their former status and position. The differences in job design between the former East and the new investor from the West were mentioned as one of the main reasons for this:

> In the white-collar sector there have been tremendous changes. We had to reorganise it based on a long-term perspective. Today there are still 220 employees, but we need only 160 (Interview, 4a/1).

In other words, the alteration of white-collar workers into blue-collar workers often meant receiving lower wages and often less- skilled jobs for the individual employee.

Looking back on their primary activities in East Germany, the two senior managers chiefly stressed the desolate state of the firm as a whole and the problems they had with the mentality of the employees. One of the senior managers gave the following description:

> After my first visit to the firm I was really shocked, especially by the working conditions, ecological situation, the design of the building, the offices, the plant, the logistics. I had not seen such a ravaged location even in South America, where I worked for some years ... The group mentality of the people here pervaded the whole process of organising. Everywhere one used to smoke. Nobody wanted to be responsible for their actions. At the beginning I felt like a father, who was asked about everything and I had to endorse every decision (Interview, 3a/1).

The interesting point is that despite stressing the mental problems with the staff, the initial reorganisation activities were perceived as administrative and technocratic tasks rather than as a challenge to transform established human resource management practices. It was in this sense that the commercial manager stressed the importance of technological and functional reorganisation directly after the takeover:

> We first improved the technological conditions. Our focus was on the manufacturing process. And we introduced a modern logistics system. The aim is to have an economical product of high quality (Interview, 3a/1).

All in all, the process of reorganisation was carried out under the motto: 'Concentration of all activities of the firm into the core business' (Interview, 2a/1). However, as we will discuss below, the definition of and attention paid to the 'core business' were shifting over time.[5]

The first stage of the firm's reorganisation was characterised by the adoption of the multinational's well-established institutionalised routines and rules. The basic organisational design principles of the West German plant served as a blueprint for what was assumed to be needed for the organisational change. The whole process of organisational change was always discussed in terms of comparison to the West German equivalent. However, the adaptation of the new East German location to the West German blueprint was facilitated through the cultural similarities of both, their deeply rooted tradition of producing with a comparable production system.

Management understood that the modernisation of the former state-socialist firm was the primary task after the 1990 takeover. The initial reorganisation attempts were directed at the functional integration of the firm within the structure of the industrial group. The future core business of firm A would be focused on the manufacturing and assembling of car headlights. However, these reorganisation activities in turn had to increasingly contend with massive shifts in the well-established market relations. In turn, the question was: Whether and how managerial efforts to modify the established organisational design were affected by the emerging environmental turbulence? Another question to consider was whether the managerial focus on the reduction of the firm's manufacturing costs worked against these attempts to transform its traditional processes of organising, and if so, why?

3) Challenges for human resource management and participation There were two main challenges for human resource management within the firm. Like in other East German firms there existed two problems: Reducing personnel and adapting or developing the staff's skills to the new challenges of a modern capitalist economy. The first task, the downsizing of employment numbers, was closely coupled with the positive expectations about the development of the future market. Particularly the hope that the traditional Eastern European markets would be growing encouraged one to overestimate future employment. The works council referred to this situation as follows:

> The takeover did not oblige the investor to maintain a specific number of employees. One hoped that the employment numbers would hold stable through the solidity of the established mass markets, especially in Eastern Europe (Interview, 5a/1).

This statement shows that the evaluation and development of workers' skills was at first seen as a function which relates to the output. The quality of work was understood as a secondary issue, first came the salvaging of the firm and thereby supporting the employment of as many as possible. Like management, even the works council was much more inclined to consider employment numbers rather than the development of human resources.

According to the multinational's strategic orientation of concentrating its 'core business' activities on the manufacturing of headlights, a lot of the previously internalised functions were outsourced. Moreover, the multinational could fall back on its established internal institutions, like occupational pensions, which allowed them to lay off elderly employees earlier and pay them retirement pensions. Besides, they also used the governmental retirement schemes for laying off elderly staff earlier.

One can find a difficult hierarchical system of subordinated management functions there. Although the firm's manufacturing functions are subordinated to the West German location, the personnel and commercial functions respond directly to their corresponding management departments within the newly established plant. This seems to be the case for two reasons. On the one hand, with a corresponding personnel policy in the East, the firm was able to improve on staff exchange depending upon manufacturing capacities. On the other hand, there existed obligations to administer joint budgets in East Germany because the investor was receiving government subsidies. Moreover, there were conflicting differences between the established basic routines of firm A to its counterpart in the West and there were many more similarities between the two new East German locations. For instance the wages or the internal subsidies for employees differed between the East and the West.

Nevertheless, there are more similarities than differences between the essential organisational design principles of the past and under the new ownership. However, against the social practices of organising in the West, in the former GDR firm there existed qualitative differences in job design. On the one hand, the interviewees emphasised that the number of white-collar-workers was proportionally higher than in the West. On the other hand, the amount of skilled workers in the former GDR firm was also greater than in West Germany.[6] In this sense the established job design could be interpreted as a potential for the shifting of the traditional organisational design principles to more organic ones. In the literature, the broadening of workers' skills is understood as a precondition to develop team learning and self-organisation capabilities (Morgan, 1986, pp. 77–109; Grabher et al., 1994a).

Besides the possible connections between organisational design strategies and human resource development, there is the question of participation. How do the employees of firm A became involved in the integration and reorganisation processes within firm A after the takeover? The chairman of the works council mentioned fewer possibilities to participate in decision-making processes shortly after the takeover and for future organisational development stressed mainly the importance of personnel stability, especially in the main management functions:

> The whole manning agreement was implemented through the [multinational's] central administration. The works council was only informed about it. However, we have more of the old managers here than at the new site in E where more Western managers were appointed. I would not say that this [personnel continuity] impacted negatively on our development (Interview, 5a/1).

This statement documents again that active reorganisation attempts of the previous East German managers ceased after they could make sure that their aim had been achieved: to salvage the firm and its labour. In this sense the first steps of integrating the human resources of firm A follow the centrally administered strategy of the multinational to develop a new location for the manufacturing and assembling of headlights for the established markets in Eastern and Western Europe. All in all, they should succeed in doing so with lower unit costs than in other European locations, especially in West Germany. The question here is: How such detailed planning activities influenced the possibilities for direct participation? Or, to put it the other way round: What were the possibilities for direct participation when originally planned strategies had to be corrected?

4.1.2 The Process of Organisational Learning

1) Enactment of the external relations environment The original assumptions of the multinational about the future market development had to be corrected. The early optimism about the future possibilities to supply the Eastern European and domestic markets from their new base in East Germany proved to be more problematic than originally supposed. In interviews the local managers characterised the market development since the takeover in 1990 as follows:

1) the decline of the Eastern European market, especially in Russia, was interpreted as a grave event for the further development of the firm. The problem was that the previously steady orders from there now came very irregularly. In the beginning, the firm's deliveries to Russia were supported by credit guarantees from the government. However, the Russian customers 'began to stop their orders or they only ordered when they were able to pay' (Interview, 3a/1);

2) the expected advantages arising from the group's investment in the vicinity of a multinational car producer also proved to be a miscalculation. The reason for the cancelling of the large-batch contract was perceived to be the result of the tight cost management of the car producer. The local management blamed the car producer for the pricing out of their firm in favour of less expensive competitors. However, in other discussions some of the interviewees emphasised that the loss of the local market had not so much to do with 'hard economic facts' than with 'personal' dissonance between the responsible managers of the two firms;

3) however, one could also understand the loss of market share in the latter as a direct impact of the increasing international competition within a more globalised automobile sector. The works council compared this situation to the metaphor of 'playing cards': 'The pressure from the competition becomes ever harder. It is like playing cards. The competitors play for high stakes with the prices until somebody has to pass. Our company has thus lost some bulk orders' (Interview, 3a/1).

One of the two chief executives who has been running the firm since the takeover has for this reason demanded that the firm become more competitive. In comparison with the firm's international competitors he saw the issue of cost reduction at the top:

> The prices on the headlights market are very tight. Our firm has always reacted to this problematic situation by focusing on our core activities (the manufacturing of headlights) … We now have new competitors in Spain, a new base was opened in North Italy and Y, our competitor in Germany, took over a Czech firm. That is why competitiveness is the priority, otherwise the production will shift further to the East (Interview, 2a/1).

This line of argument gives an interesting insight into the process of interaction with the firm's external environment. The existing customer relations are interpreted as more or less impersonal constraints with their own logic. The use of the term 'we have always reacted' by the senior manager indicates that he has not considered an applicable enactment of customer relations. Instead, the reactive adaptation to unknown and powerful economic pressure is stressed. Moreover, the improvement of their own cost management was mentioned to prevent a further decline in the established market share. In this sense a one-dimensional relationship between the existence of the firm at the new East German base and the reduction of production cost to attract the established and potential new customers has been constructed. This definite strategic adjustment influenced both the external and internal processes of organising.

Externally, the multinational immediately began to compensate for lost orders by transferring production lines from their traditional West German base to their new location in East Germany. Here it was a question as to whether or not this shift of traditional manufacturing capacities to the East would produce conflicts between the two locations? It did in fact and the main strategy of local executives was to lower the resistance of the West German managers by proving the benefits of lower manufacturing costs in the East for the multinational as a whole.

Another form of external compensation for the pressure arising out of competition was the outsourcing of previously functionally integrated processes and the shifting of pressure by the car producers to their own suppliers in order to reduce costs. The relationship between customer and supplier can be heedful or heedless (Weick and Roberts, 1996). In this sense the latter are based on quite formalised and calculated operations and the former on mutual and interactive processes. Observing how our firm inter-related to the suppliers of certain – so-called – know-how parts for their end products is an interesting question. Here as well heedless low trust interactions were preferred to heedful high trust cooperative relations. If the relations to such a supplier became problematic because of emerging difficulties in delivery terms, product quality etc., or because of the suppliers inability to fulfil the expected price reductions, firm A enjoys the right to cancel the established contract of sale. Moreover, the firm as the owner of the tool for the produced supplier part can easily transfer it to another supplier when problems emerge. This can be for cost reasons, low quality etc. Thus, it can be concluded that the establishment of more ceremonious and cyclical price negotiations between firm A and its suppliers in order to reduce production costs made this relationship more heedless. The establishment of cost efficient results became more important than the development of mutually cooperative relations.

According to the firm's outsourcing activities, what became visible was that the definition of what the 'core business' should be shifted over time. On the one hand, the modernisation and reorganisation of the firm's logistical system was celebrated as a successful event. Later, the outsourcing of this expensive investment was seen as an inevitable prerequisite for focusing on the firm's core activities. On the other hand, because the firm had increasing quality problems with a supplier of a know-how part, the local management decided against its current decentralisation strategy and wanted to reintegrate this function. However, both the disintegration of the logistics function and the reintegration of the supplier function were justified as necessary to reduce costs through the firm's 'concentration on its core business': the manufacturing of headlights. In this sense, marketing as well as research and development were superior organising activities. The first is centrally guided by the multi-national. The latter activities are divided. The research department is centrally organised at the West German location. The local development department is more or less responsible for assisting in the manufacturing process.

The processes of organising in firm A can be characterised as 'functionally crystallised' (Sorge, 1985). The idea of this organisational design is that all the different functional units of the firm should be well coordinated so that the firm as a whole can guarantee a continuous output to the established mass buyers. However, the logic of this organising principle becomes problematic when the wishes and needs of customers become more specific. In our case study, the official management strategy still assumed the stability of traditional customer wishes. That again serves to legitimise the maintenance of the traditional organisational design strategies. Here the question arises: Are the perceptions of leading managers consistent?

However, the observations of the managers within the purchasing division who had to be sensitive to the ordering policy of the car producer left room for doubt. The interviewees mentioned not only that the ordering behaviour of the customers had changed in comparison to previously:

> The planning behaviour of the customers became very different. There are two tendencies. On the one hand the orders of the customers are very precise and long-term. On the other hand, we have anarchic customers who announce new order quantities every day (Interview, 6a/1).

Moreover, the leading manager of this department claimed that the number of 'anarchic customers' is growing, making the traditional forms of long-term planning and large-batch production more difficult. The management strategy to deal with these challenges was more traditional than attentive. To the question what possibilities did he see for managing this situation he described three scenarios:

> 1) Manufacturing has to compensate for the variation in orders. 2) Another possibility is to restore our warehouse facilities. But that is against our plans to reduce storage capacity. Nevertheless, it is necessary to have storage capacity for specific customers. And 3) we should be able to organise our manufacturing just-in-time. Yet this would only seem to be a workable concept were we to have more regional suppliers. Here you must take into consideration that we have suppliers from Malaysia where only the transport of the parts by boat takes 4–6 weeks. That again needs long-term planning (Interview, 6a/1).

If one would take all three mentioned possibilities together, one comes to the conclusion that the firm needs a more holistic concept for reorganising. However, as we will discuss later, the traditional 'functional crystallisation' was not questioned.

Another member of this department underscored the descriptions of her superior. She emphasised the increased dependency of the firm on the will of the car producers: 'The pressure for short-term deliveries has grown' (Interview,

6a/2) and she gave an example of their increased dependency on customer orders. Furthermore, the firm has the legal right to sue the car companies for breaking agreements, but one has ignored such conflicts thus far out of a fear for losing customers forever. On the other hand, she called attention to the problem that the firm is not flexible enough to compensate for shifting customer demands. The reduction of stock levels within the firm and its suppliers extends the problem and demands a transformation of the established organisational design strategies:

> To deal with bulk orders is no problem for our firm. The problems arise when customers want small quantities or – much more complicated – small quantities of a complex and expensive product. If they are in stock we have no problem, but if there are no parts or end products in the warehouse the question is: How long will it take our suppliers to deliver? Do they have parts in stock? (Interview, 7a/1).

It thus became apparent that the past stability of ordering – in its quantity and in its specificity – shifted, but that bulk orders from bulk purchasers still exist. In the next section we discuss how the firm dealt internally with this shifting environmental context. Externally, the actors perceived a greater pressure from buyers to supply their product at lower cost and to react more flexibly to their demands. According to this, the management strategy was to delegate this coercion to its own suppliers. Cooperation with their suppliers and with their customers too was mainly discovered as an inherent necessity, rather than as a possibility to create more heedful interrelations that would enable the emergence of more active strategies for change, like opening new markets or the creation of innovative partnerships with suppliers or customers. The growing ambivalence within the established market was not understood as a challenge for an active enactment of the environment. Instead, the fear that the manufacturing capacities from East Germany could be moved further to the East served as an excuse for increasing strategies of cost management both internally and externally.

2) Enactment of the internal relations environment The modification of internal processes of organising became a new task after the initial reorganisation phase of functional and technological modernisation. The pressure from the customers was not only focused on the price and the quality of the supplier product, but even the organisational design principles of their suppliers were monitored as well. For this task, the car producers principally used the regular quality auditing. In these meetings it was important for firm A to prove the application of new management concepts such as team orientated production (TOP) and continuous improvement processes (CIP).[7] As we will see in the following, the new management objectives did not encourage an essential shift of the traditional ways of perceiving, thinking and organising.

However, the awareness of the modification to the well-established organisational design principle was not simply an outcome of indirect pressure from the automobile producers. Rather, it was used to underline their strategy of cost management. For that aim the management espoused the human potentials of the two main management concepts which were implemented. So they stressed the impact of the realisation of TOP as follows:

> With TOP, a large part of the decision-making processes can be delegated to the shop-floor ... Before we had a high degree of technological centralism here, but TOP is directed to the people (Interview, 2a/1).

> TOP means that specific decisions were delegated to the bottom and specific goals of the firm were divided up between the teams (Interview, 3a/1).

The interesting point is that both statements refer to the inherent potentials of teamwork to delegate social competencies from the top to the bottom. However, even the meaning of the term 'team orientated production' indicates that the original idea of teamwork which was to create the social conditions in which the actors would have general opportunities to self-organise their work was not really intended. The description of the responsible coordinator for the implementation of new organisational concepts indicates that the label TOP was chosen consciously to limit the new concept's impact on other functions of organising: 'What we have here is not really teamwork. TOP is rather a system with a certain hierarchy. The leader of the team is the head' (Interview, 8a/1).

Not teamwork, but 'team-oriented production' should be and was in fact realised in firm A. The former is more concerned with self-organised processes, but the preference for the latter did not leave much room for more time and human resource intensive shifting. Instead, the implementation of TOP was initiated from the headquarters in West Germany and guided from the top. The management chose the leaders of the team. Traditional manufacturing at assembly lines with different wage groups was maintained. The former work groups at the assembly lines were renamed and referred to as teams.

As a supplement to the individual performance-related wages, the workers now receive a collective wage bonus based on the performance of the whole team. This means that the individual performance of one team member has a direct influence on the monthly and annual wage level of others. To the question whether this produced new conflicts because weaker team members were thereby responsible for the loss of income of high-powered workers the works council answered:

> We do not have elite teams here, but mixed teams. That means weak and strong workers work together. From it results two tendencies: Tolerance and mutual support between the worker within the team and, secondly, the opinion is also emerging that one does not want to work with the weaker employees. The latter tendency is increasing (Interview, 5a/1).

On top of this, one must also note that the speed of some of the assembly lines was increased. Thus the pressure to shift from 'mixed' to 'elite teams' became greater. Employees who had problems dealing with the increasing pressure to perform were delegated to the low-level jobs, for instance in the packing department. However, the managers cancelled their earlier practice of employing less productive workers such as those with health problems in the small-scale manufacturing department. For that increasingly complex task we were told by the interviewees, one could not use unskilled or disabled workers. Here one needed skilled workers with broad competencies for complex and varied manufacturing processes.

However, the main business of the firm was still seen as being in mass production for mass buyers. For this reason the automation and rationalisation of the assembly lines was seen as the primary task. Whether from a long-term perspective an essential modification of the Tayloristic forms of production would be more practical, one of the senior managers replied:

> Nobody talked about that for ten years. The modification of Tayloristic organisation of work has its limits. Mass buyers need mass production ... I can express our work performance in seconds. The reduction of mass production has to be technologically feasible. That is why only 20 per cent of our business is in small-scale production (Interview, 3a/2).

This argument was perfectly suited to justifying an increase in cost management within the firm. Against early management assumptions that the continuance of traditional modes of production with lower costs was sufficient for the future development of the firm, it seemed management was becoming more uncertain about that:

The pressure of costs is increasing. The wage difference between Germany and countries in Eastern Europe is enormous. A worker in the Czech Republic earns 1.80 DM compared to 18.20 DM per hour here. We have to outsource simple functions and implement new technologies. Thus we are able to assemble headlights in East Germany (Interview, 2a/2).

This argument shows again that the announced application of new organisational concepts does not in and of itself lead to an essential shift in the long-established forms of organising. Moreover, increasing cost management hindered the emergence of the creative potentials in teamwork. The management focus on the 'core business' of the firm encouraged the limited perception of inefficient organisational functions or parts that had to be outsourced, integrated, automated or streamlined. As we will discuss further, the employees were thus understood as parts rather than as human resources capable of participating in the whole process of organising.

Like TOP, the idea of CIP was used as a management instrument to support the established cost management activities. To the question what does CIP mean, the manager responsible for its implementation argued: 'CIP means the solution of problems at a low cost which can be quickly realised' (Interview, 8a/1).

Beyond the assumed outcome of multiplying the firm's cost-efficiency, there seemed to be less managerial attention paid to the cultural blockages on the development of human potential in the processes of 'continuous improvement'. Especially the preservation of the deep culturally rooted partition of mental and manual labour proved to be a major barrier for the evolution of intrinsic and participative effects that are stressed in the current management handbooks. Complementary to the implementation of the TOP-concept, management did not really intend to shift the established forms of hierarchical cooperation between senior manager and middle manager, manager and worker, worker and worker etc. The main reason for initiating the reorganisation processes was to reduce production costs and to demonstrate to customers that firm A has recognised their demands to modernise the organising process. The following statement by a manufacturing engineer documents that an essential shift of the traditional forms of organising is not only a question of the introduction of new organisational concepts. More important seems to be how the implementation of these ideas encourages the modification of traditional ways of perceiving, thinking and acting. Obviously that seems to have been the problem for the interviewed engineer. He defined CIP more or less as an affront against his profession and the quality of his work, and not as a concept that could improve the mutual cooperation between different actors and groups of actors:

> CIP, that is only a slogan. They (the managers) create a lot of trivial pin boards, like in the former GDR. What is instead necessary is that a manufacturing engineer recognises failures. And if he is not able to do so, he is a poor engineer. And the poorer an engineer is, the more apt he is to have a lot of CIP procedures in his territory (Interview, 9a/1).

In the organisational learning debate about this issue, there is a discrepancy between the 'espoused' management theory and 'theories-in-use' (Argyris, 1992d). The espoused idea of CIP was twofold: to motivate the employees to develop new ideas and to encourage their rapid realisation. However, in practice these intentions were rarely observed. All in all, the management did not seriously consider alternatives to reduce the gap between theory and practice. Against its original potential, CIP have not been used to improve participation at all levels of the firm's decision-making process. Instead, 'continuous improvement' processes were initiated and managed from the top as a supporting instrument to rationalisation.

3) Human resource management and participation   Although the original idea of teamwork stresses the emerging chances to develop self-organising capacities, in our case study only a few possibilities for such holistic forms of mutual learning are perceptible. On the one hand, here teamwork is primarily understood, as a management instrument to increase performance on assembly lines. On the other hand, by moving some of the planning managers from their individual offices to offices on the shop floor, it is hoped that the coordination between planning and manufacturing functions will be improved. However, while straight contact might help to improve mutual communication processes, the potential for broadening workers' skills through classic human resource methods such as job rotation, job enrichment and job enlargement were not promoted. Instead, in order to increase output the work pace on assembly lines was intensified and the job accordingly became more stressful. A team leader described the situation as follows:

> The length of the assembly lines were reduced, because every meter of the line is now seen as a cost factor. Before that we were able to continue our work, when something happened, when a team member had problems or when there we experienced technical failures. Now we are unable to do that, we have to stop the line (Interview, 10a/3).

The team leader emphasised on the one hand the increasing stress emerging from the monotonous work tasks. On the other hand she mentioned that because of the increasing types of headlights, the shrinking storage capacities and the less time available to plan in advance, the refitting time has grown. The latter argument is again contrary to the traditional management orientation that no recognisable alternative exists to the traditional continuous production line.

Moreover, because of the strict sharing of wage brackets, existing possibilities for job rotation are not exploited. To give an example: If a worker in a lower wage group shows that he/she is able to work for a specific time in a higher one, the wage group has to be increased. This is a fixed rule that was transferred from the West. However, in our case study this is understood to be too costly, which is why the local managers instructed the team leaders to restrict such possibilities.

In this sense one can conclude that the implementation of new management concepts guides the perpetuation of traditional organisational design principles. This opinion is not expressed by the leading managers. One instead hears arguments that are more sceptical about the realised organisational change. One East German production manager who criticised previous attempts to effect organisational change and demanded a more holistic management orientation:

> It became clear that whereas teamwork had been implemented, such a halfhearted setting was not sufficient. On the one hand, the whole organisation of the multinational has to be modified. On the other hand, the transfer of responsibility has to be combined with the adoption of competencies. For that one needs much more sensitivity. It is not enough to create teams and arrange their formal coordination with the planning functions without transferring the essential competencies to the teams (Interview, 1a/3).

Here the employees are not seen as valuable human resources whose development could improve the firm's flexibility. Instead, most of the actors, especially at the shop floor level, are treated as parts which can easily be exchanged with others or replaced by automatic machines. Those situation influences established industrial relations between management and works council. Their relationship could be characterised as an ambivalent one. The management seems to accept the works council as an institutional obligation that has to be considered in the decision-making process. However, often the works council is consulted at the end of this communication process. In this sense the works council is understood as a respected counterpart, but not as a potential partner. One of the senior managers characterised this relationship as a formalised role play:

> The works council has a specific responsibility within our enterprise, according to the Works Constitution act. But it should restrain itself when it comes to economic issues. Every side has to play its part, the management and the works council (Interview, 3a/1).

The works council wanted to have more influence, but found itself in the end in a weak position. The leader of the works council was critical of the rigid cost management of the firm, but saw less room for enacting his own strategies. One of the standard management justifications for their strict cost management was that as long as lower social standards and wages in the East could be maintained, the transfer of manufacturing capacities from the West German location to firm A could be easily legitimised. According to this management position, all attempts by the works council to demand the adjustment of the social standards to those of the West, or other attempts to influence the human resource management can be interpreted by the management as risky with regard to protecting existing labour. The leader of the works council gave one example for his locked-in position:

> For the implementation of new organisational models, like the new shift system, blackmail often played a role It took the form of the following argument made by managers: If you are against that, the future manufacturing capacities in our firm are in danger (Interview, 5a/2).

In this sense, the existing institutional deviations from the West German blueprint within firm A were mostly used to support the local cost management strategy. The chance to create an organisation with more human resource related processes aimed at increasing the self-organising capacities of the actors or the groups of actors received less attention in the established management processes.

4.1.3 Organisational Learning: Starting Conditions, Enacted Conditions and Possible Perspectives

The initial phase of integrating the former GDR firm within the multinational was understood as a functional task. The reorganisation process was focused on the technological renewing and functional adaptation of the firm to Western standards of manufacturing. As a blueprint it served the West German location in the manufacturing of headlights.

However, the planned organisational change was disturbed by an unintentional shift in established market relations. The firm was confronted with an enormous shrinkage of its market share and with a qualitative shifting in customer behaviour as well. However, the latter was not recognised as a challenge to attempt more qualitative and organic concepts of organisational change. Rather the reaction to the external turbulence was an increase in cost management and an expansion of traditional basic routines to the new firm in the East. On the one hand, the multinational transferred manufacturing capacities from the West to East and searched for possibilities to replace labour at the assembly lines through automation. On the other hand, it organised an intensive internal and external exchange of the workforce from one workplace, one position and/or firm to another. In this exchange cycle the development of human resources focused primarily on the managers concerned.

The definition of the firm's 'core business' repeatedly became an important task for management. According to this, the question of how to reduce production costs could simultaneously guide the outsourcing of manufacturing functions or the integration of former supplier functions and similar product lines.

In reaction to the environmental shift attempts were made to make the process of organising more flexible. Contrary to the original idea behind such concepts, like TOP or CIP, their implementation has not improved the self-organisation capacities of the work groups. The tight coupling of both organisational concepts to narrow aims of cost reduction yielded less room for the development of human resources and more direct participation. The works council could only partially compensate for the latter, because its participation in the decision-making process was more formalised and rather defensive. One can note that rather adaptive and reactive collective learning sequences characterised the organisational development in this case. Experimentation and scope for learning to self-organise were not as readily available in the established management processes. Instead the management focus on tight cost issues led to searching for and the streamlining of insufficient organisational slack resources in the process of organising.

In the end one possible outcome could be that like the previous West German location, the manufacturing capacities of firm A could be transferred to cheaper sites in the East. The first step in that direction has already been taken. Six years after the takeover of the East German site the multinational founded a joint venture for the manufacturing of car headlights with a Russian partner firm. The managers now responsible for building up the new businesses are East German managers.

4.2   Case Study B: Searching for a Market Niche

The Origins of the Organisation

• **Short introduction to the structure and history of the firm's organisational development**

Before privatisation, the current firm B was a specific division of a large combine producing electrical and electronic products primarily for the local and CMEA market. The division – a production engineering centre (*Rational-isierungsmittelbau*) – was situated in the headquarters in Berlin. The task of this special division had emerged as a specific outcome of the centrally planned economy. The dominant and increasing uncertainty of getting essential services and deliveries on time and in the right quantity and quality to maintain the manufacturing process generated the need to create a special division which would be able to compensate for such problems. So, its main functions were to produce machines, tools or spare parts which were hard to get under the conditions of the centrally planned economy, and to sustain a continuous production process. In former times more than 850 people were employed to supply products that ranged from a simple mechanical tool or spare part to a complex automatic machine. In this sense they only produced for the internal market of the combine. Nevertheless, they had relatively constant orders from other divisions and were able to react flexibly to the wishes of the internal customers.

With the societal upheaval of social and economic transformation in East Germany the whole combine was confronted, both in local and international markets, with an immense loss of their market share. Consequently, the established forms of social and institutional embeddedness eroded.

The central governmental privatisation agency, the THA, was instructed by law to administer the former combine with its 8,000 plus employees. The top mangers were exchanged and a new *Treuhand*-manager was appointed. The formal structure of the combine was turned into a so-called industrial holding. The former divisions were transformed into four profit centres. One of them – the former integrated division – became the profit centre *Werkzeuge-und Sondermaschinenbau* (tools and special mechanical engineering). The relations to the other divisions were reorganised on quasi market principles. The previous production units of the combine that had been organised on bureaucratic principles now became profit centres that had to learn to cooperate as independent market agents.

For firm B this meant having to reorganise all social relations with other divisions, renegotiate traditional supplier relations, search for new suppliers and, above all find new customers. The processes of organising that had been socially and institutionally embedded through different and separate internal relations to administrative and other production units now was taken into their own hands. Former excluded or centralised production functions like purchasing, accounting, sales and marketing were now integrated and had to be organised separately. Other functions, such as maintenance, were outsourced.

However, the privatisation of the firm appeared to be a relatively complicated process. Although local management made some attempts to leave the industrial holding and set up their own independent business unit, they ultimately decided to stay. Thus, after the privatisation of the holdings, various conflicts of interest emerged between local management and the new owners. The latter seemed primarily interested in profiting from the development of the real estate and less so in the business of the firm.

4.2.1   Organisational Learning Problems

1) Challenges of enacting an external relations environment   With the foundation of the industrial holding, the formal status of firm B shifted from an internal division into a semi-autonomous business unit. The formal shift of organisational form went together with massive personnel reductions in all profit centre organisations. There were different interpretations about its consequences for the process of further organisational development. One relatively confident interpretation of the situation came from a local manager of firm B. He said:

> We were 800 employees in tool engineering. Now we are 90 and you can imagine, that the best are still here, but the oldest too. With the latter I do not want to say that the older workers are the best. However, that has to do with the social plan (Interview, 3b/1).

The social plan was negotiated between the *Treuhand*-management and the holding company's central works council. In this legal document both sides committed the local managers to take into consideration the social situation of their employees in their decisions about lay-offs.[8] However, another leading local manager interpreted its consequences more problematically:

> We had to lay off young people which should be the performers of the future...
> In an established enterprise it is consequently right to retain people who worked
> there for more than 30 years. But in the enterprise that I plan to rebuild, that was
> a totally wrong decision (Interview, 2b/1).

The formal shift of the former combine into an industrial holding and the
administrative decisions for downsizing seemed to be the most important direct
coercive institutional influences of *Treuhand*-administration on firm B's
organisational development before privatisation in 1993. There arose indirect
problems from the lengthy process and specific details of the privatisation
situation of the whole holding company which then influenced the further
organisational development of firm B. The THA wanted to sell all profit centres
of the industrial holding together. It was planned as a 'package privatisation':
One reason for that appeared to be that they saw the privatisation of the former
combine not only under the aspect of saving the existence of the companies'
established business activities, but also as a financial deal. In spite of these
uncertainties firm B saw the *Treuhand*-administration not as problematical as
other former GDR-firms (Geppert and Schmidt, 1993; Geppert and Kachel,
1995). One reason for that – to be discussed in the following section in greater
detail – was certainly the investment opportunities of the firm before
privatisation. However, for the issue of organisational learning it has to be
mentioned that within the management group there existed some differences
over the question of whether to stay under the roof of the holding company or
to develop an organisational concept for an independent firm.

Besides the vague ownership situation, the most important challenge for
the firm's organisational development was the change of interorganisational
relations after the foundation of the industrial holding. The interrelations with
the other profit centres shifted from bureaucratic to contractual forms of
coordination.

> Cooperation with the other profit centres of the holding company is now based
> on contracts. Now the other firms are external firms. However, we still work
> together closely. And the other firms of the holding company have to ask, if
> they award a contract to an outside firm. They have a duty to do that (Interview,
> 1b/2).

However, the transformation of interorganisational relationships from
administrative into market-like was not the main issue. More problematic for
firm B was the successive decline of the demand from the other profit centres.
The market share of internal customers within the industrial holding shrank

from 40 per cent in 1990 to 15 per cent in 1994. The main reason for that was seen in the crash of traditional markets in Eastern Europe. These and the domestic market had been the main channels of distribution in the past.

These problems arose from the need to find external customers as the following explanation of two managers illustrate:

> After the change [in 1989] we took quick a blow. We worked only for the Eastern market before (Interview, 1b/2).

> Before the change [1989] we were used to getting out extra orders, but now we are permanently searching for customers (Interview, 4b/1).

Both arguments indicate one of the paramount problems for further organisational development, the search for customers. There are different reasons for this in all the interviews with the managers. However, for our purpose it is important only that the managers see a desperate need to search for customers. That was the main task for other former state-owned firms too. Our purpose is to ask, rather, how the actors changed the existing social practices and forms of the interrelations to deal with this completely new situation. Here we come to the question of social embeddedness of organisational learning and its inherent logic of efficiency. Firm B does not have to find markets in general, rather the organisation is embedded in a fabric of social relations from which emerges a specific kind of market relations.

2) Challenges of enacting an internal relations environment The chief task of firm B in the past was to find technological solutions for a great variety of problems. They were specialised to manufacture a spectrum of products that ranged from particular tools to automatic machine tools. These were no mass products, but specific products for specific tasks. So, on a large scale the past organisation of work within the former department had an artisanal character, but the fixed division of tasks, hierarchical supervision and detailed rules within the combine as a whole prevented a more holistic view of the process of organising in firm B. With the foundation of a profit centre organisation for the actors, more holistic concepts of organising became essential. Now the actors had and wanted to learn to self-organise their processes of organising. Looking back, the leading manager defines this 'learning problem':

> The division primarily built tools and special machine-tools for the whole combine, not for customers. Sometimes somebody who needed a specific tool came to us spontaneously and asked for help. But there was also the

administration which normally ordered the production of a specific tool ... However, customers were not there. There was only the combine for which we built tools. There was no marketing, no acquisition, and we did not have to make price bids. All these new tasks we had to learn (Interview, 1b/2).

The specificity of the past development was that the department had to be able to fulfil fixed demands from administration and react flexibly to emerging problems as in the examples given where actors had to construct and manufacture instantly the model of a particular tool. This story sounds really strange and would be an inconceivable task for a firm or division that produces mass products under pressure of cost-efficiency like firm A. Instead, firm B had be able to react flexibly to very specific and often difficult orders. They had to be able to find solutions for nonstandard products. One manager underlined the value of the past experiences where they learned to experiment:

Please note that in the past we had to improvise a lot. For me that is one of the reasons for the existence of the so-called East specific skills. There existed no perfect solutions. I was unable to buy the right thing at the right place. Every day I had to improvise in my decisions, had to find out how something could work. That was our schooling (Interview, 2b/1).

What this documents is that beyond the bureaucratic forms of organising there exist social practices and interrelations between actors and groups of actors that inspire experimentation. In relation to the debate about organisational learning, we can conclude that the firm had developed complex learning capabilities in the past. The question now is whether the firm was able to develop their flexibly specialised organisation of work further, under the condition of unfamiliar competitive markets and an unstable ownership situation. In contrast to the past where cost efficiency was less important and special wishes of 'customers'[9] could be more easily refused or delayed, under new conditions it is necessary to analyse how such distinct alternatives like cost efficiency and differentiation of the product range or flexibility and productivity improvement (Sorge, 1991) can be combined in such a way that further organisational learning is feasible.

3) Challenges for human resource management and participation In interviews the managers emphasised that the employees' skills to improvise have to be valued like 'gold' for the further development of firm. Nevertheless, there existed claims about disadvantages in the development of employees' skills too. In particular, the strict division of labour has been understood as a main handicap for creating more flexibility of workflow. One manager summarised this problem:

> There existed very unilateral qualifications. That means we had (in the past) a workshop with turning lathes, one with milling-machines and one with block levellers and so on. And the workers were either turners, millers or planers and so on (Interview, 1b/3).

And he mentioned further that the search for customers on the market not only requires a flexible work organisation, but a staff with broader skills. In this sense he argues:

> For me it is important that the employees are flexible and that I can employ them flexibly. In the end I say, if we go down ... it is only those workers who are the most flexible who will find new jobs (Interview, 1b/3).

The latter argument indicates that flexibility became an important issue for management. However, for them flexibility involves a different understanding of the worker's own risk taking and a readiness to work overtime. The latter often conflicts with the institutionalised system of industrial relations. It was assumed that this would cause conflicts with the central works council of the holding company.[10]

For our purposes we are interested in analysing how the existing flexibility of human resources can be developed further. Moreover, there is the question of whether the broadening of skills was seen only as a question of formal qualification, or whether it was interpreted as a question of more participation too.

4.2.2 The Process of Organisational Learning

1) Enactment of the external relations environment In the attempts by firm B to attract customers, such questions needed to be considered, like which products are needed in the market and how they can be attractively presented to their customers. It was necessary to develop new pamphlets to attract customers. The problems associated with this new situation are documented by this reflection of the leading manager:

> I always say that we are invaders. We take off orders from other firms. Before the wall came down Mercedes-Benz did not need us. They had their traditional suppliers (Interview, 1b/1).

This argument shows exactly the conflict that managers have to deal with which is the new situation of being in competition with others to attract customers. The firm had to develop a strategy that convinced customers to buy products from firm B and this often involved a shift in their well-established traditional supplier relations. Coming into the established Western markets was one of the main problems of many former GDR firms.

Firm B handled this difficult task in some respects unconventionally in comparison to its competitors. One manager gave an example:

> We go to firms. That is something we have over our Western competitors. They often do not have a marketing department, because the customers came to them and asked them whether they were able to build something. We turned the table and asked the customers whether we could be allowed to build something for them (Interview, 1b/2).

From this statement one can recognise what it means when one refers to the emergence of market interrelations as being socially constructed. Firm B started to make personal contact to potential customers in the local context. For that, management expected and got support from their employees. The following statement of a manager emphasises the handling of critical order situations:

> Fewer orders, this is really a problem. Then we do the following: We take the whole team, the whole department of planning, that is 14 I think, and go looking for customers. Then we send them directly to firms and we have got the power. Sometimes we saw ourselves as clowns, but that is not so important (Interview, 3b/1).

However, this statement shows the inexperience and the mental difficulties of the local managers to create close social as well as lasting customer relations. However, the less formalised organisation of work was open enough to encourage even subordinate staff to support the search for customers. So for instance, an attractive contract with a renowned automobile producer that ordered tools and machine tools developed out of an informal relations had by an ordinary worker with an employee in this enterprise. Such kinds of networking could only emerge because the processes of organising were loosely coupled, which again yielded the development of narrowly coupled social ties.

> The first contact to Mercedes-Benz emerged through the personal relation of one of our employees. He knew someone at Mercedes who arranged an interview. After this Mercedes came to us to audit our firm (Interview, 1b/1).

According to this positive example, one has to notice that some managers had the vision that every employee should be able to work in marketing in critical situations, but they underestimated the necessity to develop the appropriate competencies for that task.

Most of the jobs at firm B were local ones, but they also created connections with foreign customers.[11] They acquired, for instance, an attractive job with a large Chinese enterprise. Here again the talents of managers to develop social relations that are not just short-term market exchanges become visible. Firm B not only got the supplier of tool-machines that were constructed according to the first (rough) construction plans of the Chinese company and developed further in the process of manufacturing, the firm was also responsible for training the Chinese workers who were to work on the new machines in future. This kind of organisational behaviour firm B learned about through its own experience with suppliers of CNC-machine tools that they bought together under obligation by the supplier to train the users.

However, for the creation of markets, the development of networking relations to customers was only one issue. Moreover, it was public programmes and the financial support from the privatisation agency which enabled firm B to get the necessary resources for its further organisational development and learning. They learned to bring themselves into such a position where various organisations, like customers, the THA and public institutions were attracted to cooperate or give them public support. The leading manager gave two examples showing how they learned the game of applying for public subsidies:

> We had to work with technologies in the last years (before 1989) that were unfavourable. (In the past) We did not get much investment ... Due to the fact that we were very successful, we got the authorisation from the Treuhand-managers, the board of supervisors and the privatisation agency for some investment. There are other profit centres which need urgent investment too, but they do not get any subsidies, because of their bad order position. However, we have really promoted ourselves and have invested 5 billion DM. I can show that I have a full order book (Interview, 1b/1).

> Every product we produce is an innovation. We can get public subsidies for product innovations as a small firm. That we can only do because we are not a large firm and because we have an acceptable turnover (Interview, 1b/2).

Both arguments speak for themselves. Firm B learned to write such pamphlets which put them in such a position that the bureaucrats who manage public programmes were able to imagine that firm B was one of the clients which they wanted to or should support. The latter statement especially sounds a little bit macabre, when one thinks that they had fulfilled the criterion of the public programme because they downsized from a large to a small firm. Nevertheless, it was clever to announce some of their normal products as specific innovations. It indicates both the talent of management to acquire necessary financial resources and the specificity of their products – no mass production – that needed both specific forms of organising and broadly developed human resources.

Both the successful development of the firm and the pattern of budgeting under *Treuhand*-administration seem to be one of the foremost reasons that the management stayed within the industrial holding. Nevertheless, from time to time some efforts were made by different managers to leave the holding company and to lay the foundations of an independent private firm. But the leading manager could make sure every time that firm B continued to be a member of the holding company in the future. And what were the reasons why some managers wanted to leave the holding company and why they at least remained within the industrial holding? The reason for leaving the industrial holding had to do with the uncertainties that emerged from the fact that some of the new customers feared that without transparent ownership relations, interorganisational cooperation was not secure from a long-term point of view. That is why some of the managers argued for the establishment of a private firm. However, the leading manager supported the *Treuhand*-strategy of selling the holding company as a whole. He thought that a large industrial investor would buy the firm. In the end, as it became obvious that the THA would not find a prospective buyer with an industrial background, the influence of the leading manager shrank: 'Yes, that was when Mr. M. became inconsequential. We could change his opinion and he said: Now I am fed up' (Interview, 2b/1).

The organisational concept to develop their own spin-off which they had prepared was then presented to the privatisation agency. But it was too late and in the end too modest. The *Treuhand*-managers did not accept the concept. Interesting is why the leading manager became inconsequential. To this one manager replied answered:

> We said to him: Please stop it, you are naive. Do not believe all they [the *Treuhand*-management] say. Today he is at the point where he believes none. Before he was so naive and said: They want only to do the best for us (Interview, 2b/1).

The statement shows that management and organisational learning are discursive processes which involve conflicts and do not always have a positive outcome. The mistrust which the leading manager developed after privatisation emerged occurred when a real estate group took over the industrial holding and began to establish a new regime of fiscal control. Prior to this he was loyal to the THA's privatisation policy and the loyalty had grown in large part because he and his subordinate managers could design the process of organising themselves without fearing that failures would lead to the closing of the firm. In this sense the 'soft budgeting' of the *Treuhand*-administration inspired the firm to learn and experiment. The reasons for that we will discuss in the next section, where it will be shown how past flexibility of organising was developed further and how and where institutional restrictions appeared.

2) Enactment of the internal relations environment As discussed before, there existed management interests to invest in new technologies and rationalise the work organisation. First it is necessary to discuss how managers justified the change of organisational design and how this influenced the established processes of organising. According to the analysis of managerial attempts to transform organisational design strategies, it is also necessary to take into consideration how the privatisation of the industrial holding as a whole influenced the initial process of organisational change. The latter refers again to the social embeddedness of the process of organisational learning.

Nevertheless, there seemed to exist an awareness within the management group of the importance of the skills of their employees to improvise and react flexibly to new situations, They also felt that these human capabilities had to be organised more efficiently. In the analysis of managerial aims for organisational change, it became evident that what emerged was a conflict over how to combine the opposing concepts of being efficient on the one hand, and remaining flexible on the other. As discussed before, the emergence of such a conflict seems to be a typical problem in organisational learning. The question was how they could combine their capabilities of acting flexibly and creatively with the increasing economic requirements of the new market environment.

The handling of this conflict became visible with the decision of the local management to reorganise their intraorganisational processes. According to the reorganisation of the industrial holding, they wanted to establish the profit centre principle.

According to profit centre organisation, within the holding company as a whole the local managers implemented three different profit centres. They were organised more or less as product specific divisions (with three managers at the top) responsible for coordinating all organisational functions[12] from order processing to the marketing of the end product. In the interviews it became clear that the chief task of the three local profit centres was seen to be increasing the rationality of work organisation. Based on their experiences in the GDR, the local managers wanted to be able to control who – meaning which employee, group of employees or department – was responsible for failures or increasing costs. They wanted to avoid a continuance of traditional behaviour where an impersonal bureaucracy was the scapegoat. One of the managers explained the profit centre concept:

> So we said, let's keep all decisions about receipt of orders, including negotiations about the modes of delivery, in one hand. And this under the direction of the three profit centres. Because we say by doing so, we are able to increase the flexibility, throughput, etc. I am responsible and in terms of how I organise the point is this: I cannot blame others as was the case in the old hierarchy (Interview, 3b/1).

But the managers underestimated the coordination problems which continued to emerge, leading to new conflicts. It was their understanding that their work organisation was different from producing mass goods with a high degree of automation where the coordination between actors could also be easily formalised. Instead, firm B offered specific products whose manufacturing contained a high degree of practical knowledge and which required intensive face-to-face cooperation and communication. Looking at the interviews it becomes apparent that a strict allocation of costs between profit centres did not work and in fact hindered heedful cooperation. So, managers themselves and workers too claimed that under the high pressure of order fulfilment the preferences for which jobs were more important and which ones could be done without had to be negotiated between the separate departments. And the negotiated preferences about organising the jobs again influenced the usage of particular machines which had to be shared by all three profit centres.

Another example for the enlargement of internal cooperation issues is the mutual exchange of jobs between the departments in situations where one profit centre has too many and another too few jobs. For such coordination processes specific skills of managers and workers are necessary which would be neglected if the espoused cost centre concept of managers was realised in practice. The pure orientation of local managers to minimising costs and maximising profits of their own department would hinder a free exchange of information and mutual knowledge creation between different actors and groups of actors.

In this sense the profit centre organisation appeared to be a considerable part of the 'espoused' rather than practised theories of managers (Argyris 1992d) where the intention was to rationalise the work organisation on the one hand but which on the other was also used to demonstrate efficiency to outside observers, like the privatisation organisation. After various discussions with the management it is assumed that the espoused organisational concept for firm B was an essential script to stabilise the organisation after a large number of lay-offs. In practice the organisational structures seemed to be enacted much more experimentally. The explanation of the leading manager to questions about how they developed the idea to structure their firm and how they realised their original ideas underline this interpretation:

> The consultancies have made some recommendations about how to organise our work. They said here and there you must do more ... But in the end this has to do with coercion. To allow the emergence of a structure is much better than to plan a structure and to employ people to produce such a structure. The organisational structure in our firm emerged within the process of working. We produced and, by the way ... we shrank. We started with 175 employees in 1990 which we could not all stay ... Now we are less than 100 people. So, the structure always had to adapt. There existed a structure which suddenly disappeared (Interview, 1b/2).

We had the opportunity to observe organisational development at different intervals. It became clear that in the end the whole profit centre organisation was put into question because its social effects did not fulfil the expectations of managers. Especially interdivisional coordination seemed to suffer from the emergence of attempts at separation within the profit centres which led to egoism and disturbances of past intrinsic forms of mutual support and cooperation. After the movement of the production site of firm B the problem became evident:

> In Treptow [the old production site] it was alright with the profit centre organisation because of the construction of the plant. In the new plant I could see this was different. We shrank again from 100 to 92. Now we should forget the profit centres. We have always set up our machines differently, because it is now easier to manage. The profit centre of course has deficiencies. It is not so flexible that other profit centres could assist if there is a need. The existing reserves are not used optimally (Interview, 3b/1).

However, the shift of local management to more control of workflow has to be discussed in correspondence with the change in the ownership situation at the beginning of 1993. With the change of ownership, the *Treuhand*-policy of low budgeting was over. The new owner, a West German real estate group, bought the entire industrial holding. However, the business strategy of the new owner was not clear, but it was forced by contract to guarantee employment for the 1,300 employees for a limited time. As a consequence of the privatisation, all profit centres of the holding had to leave the attractive industrial site on the river Spree. As for the new owners' interests, it became obvious that its business strategy of marketing the real estate on the riverside conflicts with the specific business interests of firm B.

> The new owner is a real estate group. They bought mainly the real estate. It would be much better, everybody would say here, of course, had we been bought by a company from the manufacturing sector suited to our profile or where our profile could be complemented (Interview,1b/2).

However, new ownership meant now mainly cost management and budget control. Every profit centre of the industrial holding got a second executive manager with the task of cost control.[13] The leading manager compared the owners' cost management with his past experiences in the former GDR and with the *Treuhand*-administration and came to the conclusion:

> I found it very good before (under Treuhand-administration) ... One could decide independently. I had to inform the administration, but I did not have to have every decision countersigned. We were a profit centre, like the concept intended, but now we will be really patronised. We say often: That is harder than in the former East (Interview, 1b/2).

The new owner did not seem to be very much interested in the production profiles of the firm. The executives of the investor pursued a strategy that was often summarised by local managers under the slogan 'make profits or perish' So the established flexible forms of organising lost their flexibility not only because the owner's strategy was to cut all future investments and force all firms of the holding to leave the old industrial site with the obligation to pay for that with their own profits. However, the traditional strength of the firm to deal with problematic situations also appeared under the conditions of new ownership. They refused to move to the much more expensive new industrial site of the owner offered to them and searched themselves for another production plant with lower rent costs. Nevertheless, firm B showed that it was able to fight for the right to have a future, but the local management again avoided the use of a critical situation for a spin-off decision. Instead claims about the problems of new ownership were dominant:

> I think it would be better to have an industrial company behind us. The communication with the new owners costs us energy and time. They want reports, they want to be informed about everything. A firm that is independent does not need to provide reports about turnover and costs etc. They want to have figures weekly and this is a burden (Interview, 1b/3).

At this point a researcher could reach the conclusion that management indirectly compensated for the cost pressure of the new owners through the enforcement of their own control claims. As a solution to the manager' claims that employees identified poorly with the firm, the implementation of identical clothing for all workers to enforce more loyalty was considered. Here the inconsistencies of management's developed strategy of human resource management becomes manifest. This will be discussed in the next section.

3) Human resource management and participation It was noted that human resource management became an important issue in the organisational development of firm B before privatisation. The management used the possibilities of public sponsored training programmes to increase and broaden the skills of the employees, as well as to improve their own management knowledge. The reason for the enormous need for qualifications and the broadening of the employees' skills derived from the difficult situation that less workers had to develop the social competencies to act flexibly in time and in different jobs. The leading manager explained this situation:

> Qualification we take very seriously. You have to notice that our people were quite specialised ... Then we began to organise training courses. Today we have no rotary grinder who cannot drill. The grinder can work there to, but they can turn too. We do not need top workers, but they have to be able to deal with bottlenecks. When we need somebody for drilling or turning, then they must be able to move (Interview, 1b/1).

Besides the public training courses for workers and managers under the *Treuhand*-administration, the firm used the investment proceedings for workers' training too. They contacted the supplier of new technologies to train the future operators.

We bought one machine with the option to train our workers there. However, the first machine we did not get so conveniently. Here we were too much Ossi-like.[14] For other technologies which we bought this year, we got the training course at a discount (Interview, 1b/1).

However, the need to broaden the workers' and the managers' skills depends directly on the instability of the order situation. That involves from time to time requirements for working overtime and on weekends. Two statements by management indicates both the increasing need for flexible employment and the arising conflicts with the works council about that.

My goal always is: Better to work full-time than part-time. To the works council I always say, better to work overtime than to lay off staff. That they do not understand. Instead they want to employ more staff. But if I employed more staff, it could be that I have less work next month and I have to lay them off again (Interview, 1b/1).

In that time, at the beginning of the year, where the orders declined, we said to our workers, you can stay at home and catch up on work later. But the works council would not agree. For our industry flexibility is necessary (Interview, 1b/1).

Both statements document different problems in the relationship between local management and the central works council which disintegrated after privatisation and was replaced by local works councils. Management tried to get the approval of the works council for their flexible employment policy and modifications of regular work but the works council did not want flexible employment but instead wanted to hire more people. One possibility would have been to negotiate and find a compromise, but both parties stuck to their position. So local management decided to handle this problem more or less illegally through a confrontation with the works council. And the works council which was not in a position to pay an equal amount of attention to all profit centres in monitoring the economic and social conditions dealt with this situation by overreacting and overstating demands.

At this point the problem of inconsistency of participation at the local level became evident. In addition to the increasing and broadening skills of workers and managers, the promotion of social competencies of employees was not developed with the same intensity. That became clear after privatisation when the cost strategy of the new owners led to increasing management claims for control of work flow which openly conflicted with the established cooperative interrelations between workers and workers as well as managers and workers. At first the foundation of a local works council was not seen as a chance to negotiate resolved solutions of conflicts between management and workers about ways of flexible employment. However, the local management was not against the foundation of the works council, but reserved. The head of the works council explained the situation as follows:

> The management had shown no initiative for the election of the works council. They neither supported it nor restricted it. Moreover, I do not think that the leading manager is pleased about having a local works council (Interview, 5b/1).

The first conflict arose out of the fact that the new head of the works council has to legally be exempted from work on some occasions, when training in codetermination and other participation issues is necessary. And the leading manager did not want to exempt him because he did not want to lose his 'key turner'.

Here the lack of experience in dealing with the new situation became evident. Nevertheless, it has to be assumed that both parties will be able to deal with this issue in the future. Some indicators show that management has taken the first steps in this direction. The leading manager bought the code of the codetermination law to inform himself about his own rights and duties as well as the rights of the works council to participate in the normal decision making process. And one has to observe that besides the head manager, the other managers could see that the relationship between management and the works council might offer a chance to deal more openly with internal conflicts:

> The relation to the works council is ambivalent. The works council has to be more established. And they must counterbalance the interest of the workers with the interest of the firm. However, a works council is necessary. There are particular things that have to be negotiated internally. We are not being frightened of dealing with such conflicts, but the process of negotiation must be more collegial. Only grumbling is not enough (Interview, 4b/1).

At this point one could conclude that if the established path of flexibility can be combined with the development of participative and social competencies on the sides of both managers and workers, the process of organisational learning could become more complex and intense. The chances for that are not bad, because most of the local managers do not see irreconcilable conflicts between their own interests in organisational development and the interests of other employees. However, the employees' questions about the firm's future possibilities for growth seem to be much more dependent on the redefinition of firm B's social embeddedness between local management and new owners.

4.2.3 Organisational Learning: Starting Conditions, Enacted Conditions and Possible Perspectives

What can we learn about the process of organisational learning, summarising the process of organising within firm B? We can see that both the strength and style of interrelating between actors and groups of actors change over time.

At the beginning of our research it became obvious that the search for new customers and the need to redefine interorganisational relations was seen as the main task. Here the actors could use what they had learned from past experience to deal with complex problems. The actors' strength of loosely coupled artisanal manufacturing allowed for unconventional ways to cooperate and attract customers. Nevertheless, one has to notice that this phase of organisational development was affected by (externally prescribed) extensive reductions of employment that limited the development of adequate human resource strategies by local management.

However, in turn, management was able to develop scripts that made their actions appear to be efficient. They could give the privatisation agency the feeling that they really were investing in the future, because firm B could demonstrate success, and again this demonstrated economic success, gave management a chance to design their organisation themselves. The local management could show by comparison to the other profit centres of the holding company that the firm was able to self-organise their functions for future viability.

However, the plan of the THA to sell the holding company as a package to one investor did not take into consideration the specific needs of firm B. After privatisation the possibilities to self-design their organisation were restricted through the exchange of soft budgeting of the THA for stringent cost management of the new owners. That affected the opportunity had by local management to experiment and create independent solutions to new problems.

At this point, the consequences of the previous human resource management and the underdeveloped regular participation became problematic. Local management saw that task primarily in the broadening of the formal skills of employees and underestimated the task of developing social competencies which would enable the actors to find more participative solutions for emerging conflicts which resulted from increasing attempts by managers to make employment conditions more flexible. On the one hand there seemed to exist self-organising capabilities within the firm which where undermined by the desire of management to rationalise the organisation through internal profit centre organisation and their lack of acceptance of the workers legal rights of codetermination. Nevertheless, the firm had rationalised some of its processes through automation and the implementation of an effective accounting system. However, the future development of the firm and not at least its flexible adaptability depended on the creativity of their human resources and at this point stringent control strategies of local managers became counterproductive.

We can summarise that firm B on the one hand increased its organisational learning capabilities through the creation of heedful and cooperative interrelations to their customers and through the improvement of the skills of employees. On the other hand we have to conclude that the neglect of the ownership constellation and their inadequate attempts to further develop employees' social competencies created problems for the process of organisational learning. At the beginning these shortcomings had to do with the need to reduce employment, but later the local managers underestimated the link between organising creativity and responsible development of human resources.

There is still the need to establish a style of organising whereby the actors learn to deal with the ambivalence of being flexible and productive at the same time. Learning could help the actors find a solution to their unsettled ownership situation as well.

4.3   Case Study C: The Creation of 'New' Markets

The Origins of the Organisation

- **Short introduction to the structure and history of the firm's organisational development**

The background to the foundation of the firm – a job creation centre – was the massive lay-off of workers by a large hydraulics manufacturer. In 1989 there were more than 2,500 employees, but by 1994 this number had shrunk to a meagre 175. This enterprise was the biggest employer in a small mono-structural town in the north of the former GDR. Besides the hydraulics firm, there were some small craftshops and a lot of agricultural activities. The near total decline of the region's industry and agriculture was accompanied by rocketing regional unemployment.

In 1991 there was already a job creation centre which initiated projects for unemployed people in the traditional sectors of job creation. It was responsible for local authority tasks, for social projects and for tourist development of the attractive countryside. Therefore the foundation of firm C at the end of 1992 took place relatively late, when the possibilities for the creation of new jobs appeared limited.

If the THA, the owner of the hydraulics company, again laid off nearly 400 employees, not only would there be the problem of enormous social decline in the whole region but the political climate would become volatile. Besides its narrow 'privatisation dogma' *Treuhand*-managers were therefore more or less forced to take into consideration the broader context of any lay-off decision. They began to give support to job creation projects and to start partial redevelopment projects of industrial sites (Geppert and Kachel, 1995). Using the existing institutional framework the THA primarily negotiated with the trade unions for the establishment of another job creation centre. The former head of the works council was put forward by the trade union for the position of executive manager. Jointly with the trade union he was able to select a 'crew of initiators', comprising 12 people. From the THA and other public institutions they were given material resources, like money, technology and real estate within the hydraulics company.

However, unlike other job creation centres in East Germany whose only aim was the short-term preservation of the workforce, the management group wanted to develop longer perspectives for their labour.[15] With a lot of enthusiasm, the 'crew of initiators' began to search for partners and know-how to create projects that would open up new vistas.

As a result, the firm was involved in various entrepreneurial activities in both the non-profit as well as the private sector. To encourage and also legalise its emerging business activities, the legal status of the firm was changed on several occasions. The firm was initially founded within the legal framework of its parent company, another job creation centre whose activities were primarily focused on developing projects in the non-profit sector. The reason for this legal construction was the need to react quickly. Conflicts then emerged between management of the two firms, ultimately leading to firm C taking over the property and projects of its parent company. At the same time, in order to legitimately secure profits of their spun-off business activities, in addition, firm C founded a private company. This made it possible for involvement in both the non-profit as well as the private sector.

4.3.1 Organisational Learning Problems

1) Challenges of enacting an external relations environment After the foundation of the job creation centre the 'crew of initiators' began to develop various project ideas. However, the difficulty was to find out whether and how these plans could be realised. For that, the actors had to develop social networks to attract potential sponsors and cooperation partners. Here one needs to ask: How were such cooperative relations created? and: Did these approaches guide collective learning processes within the firm and if so, how?

The most important potential sponsor in the initial phase was the local job centre which had to permit and finance all planned activities of firm C. Then there was the THA which was interested in having firm C develop some projects to combat the increasing unemployment and social upsets in an always declining and mono-structural region. Both institutions were the first partners which provided the basic resources. To illustrate, the THA supplied the real estate, the plant, machines and other equipment. Moreover, there was a special *Treuhand*-fund for supporting the shipbuilding industry in the North of the former GDR. As an employer of job creation schemes for former shipbuilding labour the parent company was able to apply for financial assistance from this fund. As a related company firm C therefore had the same access.

From the beginning, the crew of initiators did not see their business as only a limited undertaking with a focus on the job creation sector. In its early stage the actors were less interested in classic job creation schemes such as social or tourist projects. Instead, they wanted to develop medium and long-term employment prospects. They therefore looked for project ideas which would offer prospects for sustainable entrepreneurial activities.

For the establishment of the two basic projects which were used later as a platform to create various new projects, the cooperation with a specialised management consultancy, with the former employer (the Hydraulics Company) was important. Therefore the 'crew of the initiators' received the necessary knowledge about which projects would have a chance of getting public sponsorship and where the proposals should be focused. The chief executive explained what he expected from the new established interrelations:

> We expected that we would get the support for the development of workable project ideas and to formulate viable project proposals. We wanted to learn the art of applying for public projects. And to understand how to develop the necessary skills for the accounting processes (Interview, 1c/3).

The created cooperative relations with the local job centre, the Hydraulics firm and the management consultancy were essential to deal with the conflicts which emerged through the foundation of a second local job creation centre in this small northern German town. There always existed a local job creation centre that also was founded to support past lay-offs in the region. The strategy of the other local job creation centre was tightly coupled to the tasks of the communal authority. At the beginning there was less interest in supporting the building of a new local job creation centre which seemed to be a competitor for public sponsorship. Instead, they pleaded for the integration of the planned job creation schemes into the existing communal job creation framework. Moreover, hostilities between the leading management group within firm C and some influential municipality representatives created problems. The roots of that rested in the radical critique by the former works councils, now managers in the newly founded firm C, of the local authority. In their past position as works councils they had blamed the local representatives because of their failed initiatives in avoiding further economic decline and rising regional unemployment. However, beyond these problems of the past, firm C was now dependent upon support from the local authority. In particular, in planning entrepreneurial activities the actors had to rely on the assistance from all local institutions which were closely related to the community.[16]

Moreover, there was another problem of external interrelating, the ambivalent dependence on the parent company. On the one hand firm C had profited from its quick integration into the already established settings of the parent company, especially because they received access to the extra resources from the special *Treuhand*-fund. On the other hand, there emerged direct limitations. The parent company developed different organisational goals and strategies for further organisational development. Unlike our firm C, there were less entrepreneurial activities. Instead, the interests of the parent company were concentrated on the standard tasks of job creation in the non-profit making sector and on the further qualification of its staff for a limited duration.

2) Challenges of enacting an internal relations environment The two early job creation projects that got support from the local job centre were founded on the plan to overhaul old machines and then to sell or hire out the renovated equipment to local firms and customers in Eastern Europe. The obligatory machines and tools, both of which were used to do the renovation work and which had to be renovated, were taken over from the hydraulics company or from other local enterprises for a low or a symbolic price. The industrial decline in the region offered various possibilities for such bargains.

However, in the interviews, the chief executive always stressed that the success of such bargaining in receiving the essential resources was contingent upon the enactment of trust relations. One example is the development of the firm's relationship with the hydraulics company where change in senior managers opened up opportunities for future cooperation:

> At the beginning the communal authority and the hydraulics company were not interested in our problems. Then the new senior manager, Mr. L., was appointed [from the THA]. He strongly supported our establishment ... He sold us the old machines. He signed the cooperation contract with our firm and supported the inclusion of our manufacturing building on the terrain of his company for which a long-term lease was negotiated (Interview, 1c/1).

The two early (basic) projects for which the firm got public sponsorship from the local job centre and the European Social Fund were called *techno-trans* and *techno-pool*. The first would serve as the base for the planned selling activities and the latter was intended as a rent station for lending the reconstructed machines. Both projects would combine manufacturing and marketing operations.

In preparation for the planned task, the 'crew of initiators' began to select the first cohort of future employees. About 30 were employed right away to prepare the future plant and craft shops for the planned projects. All in all, the number employed on both projects has increased to almost 70. After their appointment, most of the new workers were sent on vocational training courses.

Management processes were structured into three main divisions: executive, project realisation and personnel management. Although all groups had a special task, the firm's strategic orientation was developed through mutual communication and agreements. The aim of the internal work organisation was to lead basic and more advanced projects from conception to realisation. It was therefore necessary for the actors to develop a wide range of skills. However, the main task was not only to create realistic project ideas for which they could get public grants. The actors also had to learn to defend and explain their projects to all interested actors and groups of actors because they were dependent on public subsidies. They had to prove that they were able to manage the project subsidies properly.

Unlike other job creation centres, or the already established local job creation centre or its parent company, firm C's management focused their interests on an industrial business. As we discussed above, one reason for the specific orientation towards technology and manufacturing came from the specific economic situation. Moreover, most of the members of the newly founded job creation centre had been previously employed in the maintenance sector of the Hydraulics Company. That is why the actors were much more familiar with manufacturing tasks than other potential job creation domains such as social services. Later, after the firm was established, the actors became more open to such ideas.

Management's first goal was not to make a profit. They wanted instead to develop medium and long-term job-saving organisational structures and routines. For this task, the actors had neither well-established markets nor well-established work routines which they could fall back upon. Of interest to us is how the actors learned to combine their non-profit-making activities with their interests in creating small profitable businesses, and how they learned to develop sufficiently flexible work routines to deal with this uncertain entrepreneurial task.

3) Challenges for human resource management and participation Beyond the search for realistic project ideas which might lead to future employment opportunities, the primary problem in the early development of the firm was finding qualified and motivated staff. There was of course a pool of about 400 former hydraulics workers, but they had not learned to deal with the new uncertainties of unemployment and an insecure future. They nevertheless hoped to get short-term contracts in the newly founded job creation centre.

However, the management goal to create more sustainable job opportunities demanded that an increasing amount of effort be placed on developing human resources. For that task the actors took advantage of the offers of the local job centre for worker qualification and further education. Most of the initially hired staff took part in such training courses, especially for the artisanal jobs.

Staff selection was carried out in conjunction with the job centre. The latter was responsible for drafting the employment contracts which were limited (by law) to two years, with the possibility of a one-year extension. Having sufficient space for a relatively autonomous personnel policy, the management of firm C was always interested in keeping up its favourable relationships with the local job centre. Local management thus became involved in the processes of staff recruitment, something not originally intended by law.

Aside from the recruitment and further education of new staff for the planned projects, there emerged the need to build a competent core of permanent staff to enable the firm to maintain and further develop work routines and social practices which were being established. Both were essential for the long-term success of organisational development. However, just at this point, firm C came into conflict with the law that did not allow employment in the job creation sector for a period longer than three years.[17] Another uncertainty arose from existing problems to attract and keep higher qualified employees within the firm. The contended legal position of the job creation, less manoeuvring room for guaranteeing wage hikes, and a limited long term employment perspectives were the main reasons. Moreover, the economic and social decline of the whole region had always caused younger and more flexible workers to migrate.

The following section will discuss how the actors learned to develop their human resources to produce a flexible platform organisation with a fixed core of permanent staff. It will also focus on emerging constraints to setting up a valuable human resource management.

4.3.2   The Process of Organisational Learning

1) Enactment of the external relations environment In the early stages of development of the firm, learning to create sustainable external relations predominated. Later on, a focus on the enactment of the internal relations environment became equally as important. In the beginning, the search for external partners or potential customers with whom the firm could collaborate was the challenge for leadership. The actors therefore had to learn to present themselves as interested partners to communal and regional representatives as well as to other potential sponsors. The latter task became important as the firm became more established and had developed a reputation for being a reliable local institution.

The initial steps of getting the firm established and known in the community could be characterised as having been a concerted action. Especially the access to the advisory capacities of the management consultancy, the socially tight relations with the job creation centre and the development of a cooperative relationship to the hydraulics company assisted in making the firm viable.

Establishing contact with the management consultancy occurred in the early stages of the firm's foundation. Through his relationship to the trade unions, the former leader of the works council and later chief executive of firm C got the go-ahead to contact the management consultancy. The consultancy had manifold experiences in dealing with the problems of the East German labour market. Its knowledge and assistance was focused on the development of sustainable project ideas and developing them into viable projects.

However, ideas for future projects were developed by the local management group themselves. In various interactions, the managers tested their original project ideas and got tips about which ideas could get public sponsorship. Especially the strong interrelation with the job centre helped to improve the project concept. They began to modify their original project ideas and discussed the advice given on where they could apply for public sponsorship. From the consultancy the actors learned how to put the project proposal together and present it to potential sponsors.

Firm C also retained good links to the hydraulics company. As mentioned above, the shift in the senior management enabled firm C to develop an essentially cooperative relationship with the hydraulics company. From this base, the establishment of their two main projects and the further development of the firm in the direction of the private business sector became much easier:

> It was right to have strong contacts with the hydraulics company. Compared to other job creation centres which are primarily involved in the social and tourist sectors, we are different. Our close contact to the hydraulics company protected us against external attacks. We could cooperate without disturbances, because nobody knew exactly what we do. Moreover, nobody dared to criticise the hydraulics company about their close cooperation with us, because they are still the largest employer in our region (Interview, 1c/1).

After the establishment of the firm's two basic projects, the redevelopment of the hydraulics company was organised and financed by the THA. The aim of the privatisation agency was to attract private investors for the not yet privatised enterprise. Through its agreement with the hydraulics company about future cooperation, firm C got exclusive offers. The actors therefore got the job of renovating and building up the entire industrial site for which more than 30 workers were employed. This was sponsored in part and the rest by the local job centre.

Later on, the excessive dismissal of employees in the maintenance sector of the hydraulics company led to the search for an external service. Here firm C could again could profit from its proactive human resources development strategy. In the early stages of organisational development, the firm had retrained their staff. Now these supplementary resources enabled our firm to supply maintenance service to the old employer, the hydraulics company.[18]

However, these business activities provoked the suspicion of some private firms in the area. It was repeatedly claimed that firm C was using public sponsorship 'to disturb the benefits of free competition within the region'. Especially small and medium sized regional firms filed complaints with the local Chamber of Commerce.

In the beginning, firm C tried to deal with the external attacks through appeasement. On the one hand they tried to influence the regional authorities to support firm C in its initiatives against regional unemployment. For this political task they hoped to get support from representatives of the communal authority. On the other hand they applied for certification from the regional Chamber of Commerce to document that firm C, despite its business activities, remains a non-profit organisation. Later on, this appeasement strategy lost its importance, because the actors became aware which of their established ventures would be profitable. Then they wanted to gain legal permission to make a profit. That is why they founded a private firm which, next to its ever-increasing non-profit transactions, is also allowed to make a profit. Moreover, they went one step further: in order to be able to influence the neo-liberal attacks from the Chamber of Commerce directly, they became a member.

Another problem of external relations emerged from the different business profiles and strategies between firm C and its parent company.[19] The parent company orientated their organisational development primarily on non-profit operations, along with training and short-term saving of its employment. Instead, firm C decided to use their basic projects as a platform for both non-profit and profit-making operations. The chief executive of firm C described the situation:

> The use of the legal framework of our parent company was helpful in encouraging the foundation of our firm. Moreover, we got access to the specific Treuhand-fund, to which we would not have had access without them. However, we now have to conclude that both organisations went in different directions. And that caused a lot of problems (Interview, 1c/1).

In terms of where the main problems with the parent company came from, the chief executive mentioned two limitations: the liability for one another and the restricted autonomy to make one's own decisions. Against this backdrop local management began to negotiate with the partners who held the assets of both companies. A presentation by management about the organisation's performance and future development was successful. In the end, the associate directors voted in favour of the liquidation of the parent company and that firm C take over its assets. The local management used the impetus gained from this successful outcome to question the existing articles of association. They recognised that it might be possible to become directly involved in the necessary negotiations about the firm's future partners. 'The question for us was, who will lead the association in future. And we wanted to take this task on ourselves' (Interview, 1c/1).

According to the chief executive the result of having shifted the association structure was that he and the project manager took over the leadership.

All in all, the management of firm C did not interpret their external environment as predominant. They instead they saw various situations and events to enact. They developed management competencies to create realistic project ideas, find partners and co-ordinate all initiatives for a successful realisation of the projects. However, for the development of long term employment perspectives, the firm needed political support. There were spin-offs that made their own profit, but a large part of the firm's business was still dependent on public subsidies. In response to how the firm dealt with the problem of shrinking public support for job creation schemes in East Germany, the chief executive argued strategically and politically. Both positions he had learned to play in the past, the latter as a former works council chair and the former in his new managerial position:

> For all our projects and especially for the new ones we have to give presentations to all relevant regional representatives. If the chances to receive public resources become doubtful, we use such meetings to ask the audience: Do you need us? And we add, as long as the social situation is precarious the question has to be answered with a yes. What is important is that we are able show that the public money is and will be well invested (Interview, 1c/2).

2) Enactment of the internal relations environment For the organisational development of the firm both the external and internal enactment of the environment were essential. The acquisition of necessary resources and the search for potential partners had to be managed with the same care as the organisation of already established projects. In the further development of the firm it became clear that the actors had learned to utilise their two basic projects as a platform for further business activities. The actors used the early public investments as a basis for the development of new projects in the non-profit as well as in the private business sector.

The firm was divided into a non-profit and profit-making sector to legalise the flourishing profit-making activities. Before the foundation of a private business sector, the actors could not openly represent their profit interests.[20] With the foundation of an independent private sector the firm was able to expand their profit-making activities without any legal restrictions. The formal separation of the profitable from the non-profitable business was an essential precondition to enlarge the already started profit-making activities.

In the non-profit projects there was more space for the employment of specific labour[21] and for experiments with new ideas than in the newly established private businesses which now had to break even. However, as before, employees were moved from one work task or project to another. Labour was partly lent to the hydraulics company. The flexible organisation of work emerged through the different demands for performance and efficiency within the specific projects. The coexistence and mixture of a different logic of organising enabled the firm to deal with new challenges more flexibly. The firm could therefore easily combine different organisational tasks. New projects were implemented, profitable projects were outsourced or spun-off and new partnerships emerged.

The project organisation was sufficiently open to change. It became clear that the original ideas of the two main projects to sell and to lend overhauled machines to regional customers were not viable. The regional industrial decline led to depressed demands for such products. Moreover, it turned out that the production cost much more than was first assumed. However, for the organisational development of firm C a precise realisation of the originally planned project ideas seemed to be less sustainable. One of the side effects of this emergent strategy (Mintzberg, 1991, pp. 39–55) was that the actors developed new project ideas and business activities not originally intended.

The original 'techno-pool' project which first was developed as a hire station for the overhauled machines was developed into an external service station that worked for regional firms and also for the hydraulics company. They offered services such as maintenance, construction work, redevelopment and logistics. After privatisation, the hydraulics company took over a part of these services and re-engaged some of their former staff. The 'techno-trans' project that was originally responsible for the overhauling and selling of the renovated machines had developed into a small tool producer. First it was a part of the private business sector of the firm; later the managers planned a spin-off.

There are a lot of examples of how the firm developed its initial project ideas further. The established project organisation was used as a platform to combine contradictory organisational tasks: saving jobs and experimenting, and working in the interest of the public welfare and making a profit. In such complex processes of organising the actors learned to deal with ambivalent situations and make strategic choices for the creation of long-term job prospects. They could therefore deal more flexibly with emerging challenges and new situations. That a project was going to be profitable in the end was often not clear in the early stage of the project's development. Later on it might be modified, given up or transformed. Some of the projects only saved the jobs of specific target groups whilst others appeared to be more profitable and offered longer-term job prospects. In the latter case, management had to decide whether the business should remain within the firm, sponsor other non-profit activities, or be outsourced.

The development of the redevelopment project is another example which shows both, how the actors had learned to elaborate an original project design and their openness for realising new innovative ideas. As discussed above, the firm got the job to redevelop the industrial estate of the hydraulics company. As the chief executive explained, the actors were able to use this project to develop further business and create more skilled job opportunities:

> At the beginning we did relatively easy redevelopment tasks, painting, tidying up etc. From there we began successively to take over more elaborate business tasks, the redevelopment of floors and walls. Later we did more and more construction work (Interview, 1c/3).

This description shows how the actors developed their initially simple jobs further allowing for more complex businesses to develop. Unlike private firms, they had the necessary time available to enhance their skills. There was no direct pressure to break even. Rather, the actors had time to learn on the job and to experiment with new work methods. The firm was open to implementing unconventional ideas which were neglected or seen as risky by conventional construction firms. The chief executive gave the following example where an inventor developed an environmentally friendly method of wall coating for a construction firm.

> We met the inventor in Rostock, who was not able to find a firm which wanted to realise his new method of working. We had a look at his method, made calculations and made a decision ... After our decision to realise the new work method we sent members of our firm to him for free training. For the hydraulic company we renovated one plant with this new method. Now we hope to get a job for renovating the whole industrial estate. However, our long-term aim is to spin-off this part of the project into a profit-making venture (Interview, 1c/3).

The firm developed other projects which at first were not profitable for private firms. Another one was a project for former unemployed engineers that would analyse the potential to re-establish regional water power stations in Mecklenburg-Vorpommern. They would research where water power stations were situated in the past and what possibilities there were to rebuild them. After that exploration phase which ended with a research report, the firm searched for potential investors for a green business project. Moreover, they hoped that new job opportunities might emerge later on.

All in all, management developed a platform organisation that was able to deal flexibly with the complex uncertainties of the labour market. The actors had learned to recombine their strategies and processes to become viable in the long-term. They were capable of presenting themselves as a solid regional company with a future. For this difficult task, the actors had developed social capabilities in linking non-profit and profit-making activities in such a way that they were able to apply for financial assistance from both public and private sponsors. Management had developed a specific leadership talent to organise and secure the contribution of resources, money, equipment, personnel etc. Leadership in our case study often meant being able to apply unconventional methods in response to external political decisions which might not take the firm's basic interests into consideration. The following report of the chief executive referring to a problematic situation emerging from the privatisation of the hydraulics company gives a good impression about the challenges that the actors had to deal with:

> With the privatisation of the hydraulics company the THA cancelled all contracts with us, including the cooperation and rental agreements. They told us that we now had to negotiate with the new owners again ... In the Ministry of Trade and Commerce (of the state Mecklenburg-Vorpommern) a party had been planned where the 'gentlemen' wanted to celebrate the privatisation without the participation of the employees who had fought for the existence of this enterprise. People who had willingly wanted to close the hydraulics company wanted to celebrate themselves. We heard about that. Accordingly I phoned the new senior manager and told him that I planned to come to the party too. And that I thought about disrupting the party, if he did not offer a new contract. After that I went directly to the Ministry [to the party] and spoke with the responsible under-secretary of state and the minister of trade and commerce. As a result we negotiated a new rental agreement. The rental agreement was later supplemented with a new cooperation contract with the new owners (Interview, 1c/3).

This statement documents how leadership and micro-political strategies were combined to secure the firm's future development prospects. The decision by the privatisation agency was an open affront to the legitimacy of firm C. With its proactive policy the legitimacy of the firm could be re-established. Moreover, the lack of participation within the privatisation process was criticised. This was the reason for using radical methods to rearrange the firm's position. How the issue of participation was incorporated into the processes of organising within the firm will be discussed in the next section.

3) Human resource management and participation After a period of time, once the firm had become regionally established, partners from the trade unions asked the local managers whether they wanted to introduce a works council, especially as the shift of ownership to the two senior managers and the question of how to reinvest the profits were now interpreted as consequences which needed more participation. Within the management group no one had thought seriously about this question. On the one hand, the instituted processes of organising involved a lot of possibilities for direct participation.[22] On the other, the employees saw the benefits of the recent leadership. They trusted that the management would do their best to increase their employment prospects.

Although the works council was implemented through external request, management had had no reservations about the implementation of the new institution. With their own experiences as works counsellors within the hydraulics company, the leading managers had an adequate understanding about the future role and function of the works council. They knew the rules of the game and how to adequately deal with this new situation.

In competition with purely profit-oriented organisations, firm C employed a broad spectrum of staff with different qualification and skills. After the establishment of the basic projects with jobs for more skilled workers, the firm developed projects for specific employee groups such as the long-term unemployed, women, and the elderly and disabled. Most of them were integrated into the non-profit sector of the firm. There were also profit-making tasks as the redevelopment project for the hydraulics company offered low skilled jobs to specific employee groups. However, nearly all employees had the chance to improve their skills over time, through learning by doing and through participation in public training schemes prior to or over the course of their employment.

A good example which reflects the whole process of organising and its impact on human resource management is the development of the *riverboat project*. The original idea for this project was adopted from a West German job creation centre. In the beginning, the project got no support from the local job centre because it argued that the building of new boats would lead to open competition with private local firms. Furthermore, the local management received the advice that the restoration of historical riverboats would be a more viable project. Now the problem was to find such historical boats. The managers began their search and found two boats which they immediately bought upon their own initiative. However, they had only created the basis for the project. Now the actual problems to realise the project idea arose. They had to check into how to finance the project. The job centre was only allowed to pay a share of the whole investment. Therefore, the firm had to find other interested partners or use their own resources. The management was able to opt for the latter, because available capital existed from their private businesses. In addition, an expansion of public sponsorship became possible, because the firm agreed to employ specific groups of employees such as long-term unemployed youth, and the elderly and disabled.[23] The project manager explained:

> Because we had no shipbuilding experience, for the realisation of the project it was important that there was not so much pressure as in a private shipyard. We had no trained shipbuilder. It was important to have the boats and not have to get more public subsidies (Interview, 2c/1).

The employees did not become professional shipbuilders, but they learned to build riverboats. In the process of organising the actors learned to work flexibly under various conditions. The management group was able to develop their projects from an original idea to its resourceful realisation. In the discussion it became clear that the original idea – to restore historical riverboats – lost its meaning in the process of organising. Instead, it was the managers' capabilities to make viable project applications that became valuable. The project manager explained the situation of management as follows:

> Less consequential was the project goal. Rather significant was that we stress why the projects were necessary. You have to go beyond the subject riverboat. It could have been an old railway coach. The basic conditions for sponsorship are always the same … The question within the negotiations was always what is possible and what not. For this task we were ready to take risks and to work hard (Interview, 2c/1).

The initiative and talent of local managers to take risks helped make profits and integrate employee groups that would be usually less attractive for private business such as long-term unemployed or elder people. At its largest, the firm employed about 200 employees,[24] approximately 30 per cent of whom were outsourced in the organisation's private business activities.

However, despite the increasing success of project management, the structural effects of industrial and agricultural decline of the regional economy influenced the organisational development of the firm and limited the scope for human resource management. Even in the riverboat project, management had difficulties finding skilled workers for some specific manufacturing tasks. Artisans such as joiners or electricians in particular, were not available in the local labour market. Moreover the moving away of higher educated staff limited management's chances to realise more complex and sophisticated project ideas. In interviews the local managers claimed that over the course of time the qualifications of their accessible human resources had shrunk. More and more they had to integrate the mentally ill, alcoholics and the long-term unemployed providing less opportunity to realise risky and highly qualified project ideas.

Other problems emerged from the fact that the firm needed a core of skilled employees to stabilise and improve the management of the base projects. Most of the employees could only receive two or a maximum of three years of public employment sponsorship. If there were no possibilities to integrate them within the firm's private businesses, they had to be discharged. In an interview the project manager stressed this problem:

> I suggested which employees should work in the private businesses. I also assembled the teams for spinning-off. However, we discussed this all beforehand with the employees. It was clear that everybody had a chance to apply for such a job. But only those employees who had the best performance had a good chance of getting the job. Still there are some as elder and disabled persons who have less chances to find long-term jobs (Interview, 2c/1).

The organisational learning of the firm either led to a spin-off into a private business with long-term job perspectives or to temporary jobs where the employees received a chance to improve their knowledge. However, in this case study temporary employment led to a loss of valuable human resources which could not easily be compensated by the hiring of new staff. In this sense the processes of organisational learning were not only blocked through the worsening labour market situation, but through the obligatory labour turnover as well.

4.3.3 *Organisational Learning: Starting Conditions, Enacted Conditions and Possible Perspectives*

Originally the organisation was created as a political response to compensate for the massive redundancies of the largest regional employer. The primary management strategy was to save as many jobs as possible. First, managers took advantage of public job creation schemes to build up the firm's basic job creation projects. For that task the local management developed cooperative relations with different regional organisations, and groups and actors to complement and enlarge the organisational knowledge base. Elementary here was to learn how to apply for public money. Later on, the basic projects were developed further and corresponding businesses with public and private interests were established. Besides the essential non-profit activities, a part of the firm was set up to make its own profit.

The core business was to create supportable projects ideas and to acquire the necessary resources through enacting sustainable interrelations with public and private partners. However, the operational tasks were open enough to experiment with the original project ideas. Some of their first plans became more elaborate in the process of organising, others were given up and promising ideas were developed further to make a profit. The profit gained was used to co-sponsor their own public projects or to attract investors for spin-offs. So, especially the hydraulics company profits from the business activities. The whole of the outsourced maintenance department before the privatisation could be reintegrated after the retraining and successful development of such jobs under firm C's leadership.

Human resource management was seen as a meaningful task for the development of the firm. From the beginning, the firm used the offers from the local job centre to transfer a large number of their employees to public training courses. Most of the public projects combined the operational task with the external retraining of staff. Moreover, there were a lot of possibilities to experiment and learn new capabilities, because most of the projects included unfamiliar challenges (like the building of riverboats).

However, the chances for a sustainable development of human resources were limited. Some of the projects, like the redevelopment project, offered but only a few chances for the creation of qualified jobs. Nevertheless, the spin-off of a small part of this business is planned for the innovative and ecological procedure of wall coating.

Besides internal problems affecting its ability to offer skilled jobs, management also had the problem of trying to implement innovative and sustainable projects. Given the social decline in the region as a whole, high unemployment rates, the drifting away of skilled labour, it became difficult for management to realise resourceful project ideas and it became increasingly difficult to find staff who were motivated and qualified for such complex tasks. Another difficulty for the further development of the established organisational learning capabilities emerged from the problem of maintaining a core of human resources. The obligatory personnel drift of employees who could not be integrated into private business activities after the completion of job creation schemes always led to the loss of practical knowledge that could not easily be replaced.

All in all one can conclude that within firm C quite comprehensive and intensive collective learning processes took place. The actors enacted a corporate identity so to speak which enabled them to experiment and implement new ideas. However, the firm's prospects to maintain and improve its established flexibility will depend on the firm's ability to win future public sponsorships.

Notes

1   The creation of the combines at the end of the 1960s and the beginning of the 1970s was embedded in a process of economic concentration that came together with an intensification of hierarchical control. This means that the combines 'were directly assigned to responsible ministries, and the main suppliers and R&D capacities were integrated into the Kombinate according to the principle "of reproductive self-containment" (*reproduktive Geschlossenheit*)' (Grabher, 1994b, p. 3).

2   The competitor who originally wanted to buy firm A as well decided to invest in the Czech Republic after the failed attempts to invest in our firm.

3   In the comprehensive literature about the organisation of work in former state-owned firms it is emphasised that in comparison to the West, the firms had a higher degree of integration of supplier functions and that there existed an oversized maintenance sector (Fritze, 1993; Grabher, 1992; Wittke et al., 1993).

4   One purchasing manager claimed that despite the desire to maintain their traditional supplier relations they had problems because a lot of them did not survive.

5   So for instance, in the beginning, the logistical function was interpreted as being part of the 'core business'. Later this activity was outsourced too.

6   However, the high amount of skilled labour did not automatically mean that the employee had the appropriate formal qualification. On the other hand, the monotonous work at the assembly lines does not necessarily demand skilled labour.

7   Other new management methods were implemented too, like Total Quality Management (TQM), but the local managers placed the emphasis more on the introduction of TOP and CIP.

8   The dismissals took place in different intervals from 1991 to 1993. The bulk of employment reductions occurred in 1991/92.

9   Here I mean the particular demands of other divisions, groups of actors and actors within the former combine.

10   The emergence and handling of this problem will be discussed in the following section.

11   Against the other profit centres of the former *Kombinat* which have traditional, but declining markets in Eastern Europe, firm B produced from the beginning primarily for Western

markets. The leading manager told us: 'The money has to be earned in the West. But there is the pressure of markets to work much harder too. We are the first-hand supplier for West German firms, but we have customers in France and in the Netherlands' (Interview, 1b/2).

12 Only the accountancy and contracting departments were organised centrally for all three profit centres.

13 Nevertheless, this form of direct personal control was given up in exchange for regular meetings and tighter budget controls.

14 'Ossi' is a common idiom for people who used to live in the former GDR. The opposite is 'Wessi' for the West Germans. Both idioms are often used as stereotypes.

15 A study by Knuth (1994) indicates that job creation centres were on average 24 months in business.

16 The German labour law prescribes that activities in the job creation sector must have primarily non-profit-making aims. This often conflicted with the interests of firm C to develop small business prospects, next to their activities in the non-profit sector.

17 At the beginning of the third year, employees are entitled to a permanent contract.

18 Later, parts of the service sector were sold to the hydraulics company.

19 As mentioned before, at the beginning firm C was integrated in an already established job creation centre.

20 There were not only legal limitations to the job creation schemes. The firm also had to be careful to avoid conflicts with representatives of regional enterprises which had started complaining about unfair competition.

21 Integrated into the non-profit sector were unskilled youth, women, and the elderly and disabled workers.

22 There was less standardisation and bureaucratic control. Thus, the interaction between managers and employees was quite close.

23 In the planning was a spin-off of a part of the project as a rent-a-boat station for regional tourism.

24 Temporarily firm C had even more employees than the hydraulics company that shrank from 2500 in 1989 to 180 in 1993 (Geppert and Kachel, 1995, pp. 97–8).

5 A Systematic Comparison of the Cases

5.1 Introduction

In the conceptual part of this study we introduced seven key arguments which are quite common in the debate about organisational learning and learning organisations. It was stressed that these seven concepts are sort of seen as universal properties for the establishment of new organisational modes, such as double loop and deutero-learning. It was illustrated that students in the tradition of intervention researchers such as Argyris and Schön (1996), Garrat (1987) or Senge (1990) emphasise adaptability over adaptation, thought over action, and, last but not least, reflexive learning over institutionalisation. Moreover, it was argued that the model of the learning organisation in particular has a one-sided affinity for radical change, planning and reflexive learning modes. Looking upon organisational learning as a socially embedded process, we furthermore criticised the deterministic perspective of neo-institutionalism which reduces organisational learning to processes of adoption and imitation. Contrary to the 'radical' assumptions of common organisational learning approaches and the mainstream discussion of the neo-institutionalist debate, we suggested analysing organisational learning processes from an enactment perspective. In this sense organisational learning is seen as being neither context-free, universal concept so to speak which can easily be planned and transferred from one organisation to another, nor it is understood as being determined by certain institutional environments. From an enactment perspective, the question of emerging opportunities and constraints within the process of organisational learning is an empirical one.

On the basis of the case study reports, in the previous chapter we concluded that it makes a difference whether we analyse organisational learning processes in a company which has a long tradition of producing mass products as in case study A, whether the firm produces more customised products as in case study B, or whether the enterprise has just begun to develop job creation projects. We have seen that highly structured institutional arrangements as found in firm A tend to remain in place despite the introduction of new management programmes by actors. New meanings and new ways of thinking were rarely observed. Instead, old meaning and justification seemed to be sustained. Compared to this case study, it would appear that the actors in the other two companies developed more open organisational learning approaches. However, unlike the case study reports where we placed an emphasis on describing how the actors in each case study enacted their internal and external environments over time and what this meant for human resource management and participation, this chapter aims, through a comparative research perspective, to analyse differences within the organisational learning processes of the three case studies.

In the next sections we will use the seven key ideas introduced in the conceptual part as a guideline to interpret and compare how the actors in each case study socially construct the interrelated constraints and opportunities for organisational learning. We will illustrate that each concept, no matter if we take identity construction, recipes on how to learn, the role of participation, etc. does not have much of a universal meaning and provides quite different evidence for the actual processes of organisational learning. The introduction of a comparative research design fits within the context of our thesis that organisational learning processes cannot be separated from their social context. We therefore emphasise the differences in how the actors in each case study generate meaning through their particular commitments and justifications. We assume that the differences between each case study in institutionalisation, in terms of how things are done, consequentially influence the ways in which actors learn (Weick, 1993, pp. 33–4).

In the following chapter we will compare and critically review some of the key arguments of common organisational learning approaches:

1) how the actors socially construct the identity of their company;

2) how they enact the recipes on how to learn;

3) how they learn from the experience of others;

4) which role participation plays within the process of organisational learning;

5) to what extent organisational learning can actually be understood as a continuous process of improvement;

6) which role organisational slack resources play within the process of organisational learning;

7) to what extent organisational learning can really be understood as a designable process (chapter 2, pp. 31–6).

The function of this chapter is to focus our analysis on the microdynamics of organisational learning processes. From the meso-perspective taken here, we neither search for universal recipes on how to create the learning organisation typical for common organisational learning approaches, nor do we overestimate the consequences of the macrostructure on internal organising processes as neo-institutionalism does. Unlike the micro-perspective of students of organisational learning and the macro-perspective of neo-institutionalist approaches, the enactment perspective shows that macro structures are not distinct from what emerges within the microdynamics of organisational learning. From the comparative perspective taken here, we will thus come to grasp more clearly and in greater detail that 'the macro is constructed and pursued within micro interaction' (Weick, 1993, p. 24).

5.2.1 Identity Construction

The aim of this section is to prove one of the basic assumptions in the discussion that the focal organisation ought to be the prominent learning unit. This section focuses on two interrelated questions. It will first be explained which commitments and justifications characterise the companies' organisational development and social construction of identity. Secondly, we want to ask whether the focal organisation and its underlying design strategies played a significant role in this process and if so, to what extent (chapter 2, p. 32 and chapter 3, p. 64).

In contrast to the other two case studies, the identity construction in firm A was closely related to the transformation of ownership and authority. To some extent this can also be said about case study B, because the local management faced a problematic ownership situation after privatisation. However, even before its privatisation the firm had developed its own reorganisation strategies; it was only after the take-over by the real estate company that a series of interest conflicts emerged between local management and the new owners.

In case study A organisational development was seen before and after privatisation as if it were dependent upon some central decisions about the future of the whole industrial group. Local management remained loyal to the politics of the old headquarters and welcomed the take-over. No consideration was given to the emerging internal demands of some of the employees and the works council to develop their own organisational concept. Reminiscent of times past, local management believed that the firm's future market strategy, its product profile and reorganisation and job security was not their job, but largely the responsibility of a central authority. Local management saw it as their task to administer and realise the centrally developed production plans and organisation programmes.

As in the past, the business of the firm was primarily understood as an administrative and technological task. In this sense the expectations of local management about how to improve the organisation's performance was similar to the new owner's strategy. Both the old local management, as well as the two newly appointed CEOs who took over the firm after its privatisation, emphasised that the modernisation of the firm was the main task of the reorganisation process. The local managers stressed the 'underdeveloped state of the firm's technology' and were convinced that only investment in new technologies would make it possible for the firm to survive in a competitive international automobile market (Interview, 1a/2). Similarly, both senior managers from the West saw technological design as a central issue for the reorganisation process. In the interviews they stressed the importance of having the firm adapt to Western technological, operational and organisational standards.

The modernisation of the firm was realised under the motto 'concentration on the core business'. This meant mainly the production of metal reflectors[1] for car headlights and the assembly of car headlights. All businesses or services that had nothing to do with this primary job were outsourced or shut down. One of the leading managers explained the reason for this strategy as follows: 'The main problem is the increase in our production costs. In order to become more competitive, we have to change our rigid work organisation' (Interview, 2a/1). The interesting point for identity construction was that 'concentration on the core business' focused mainly on the shop floor level. At the centre of interest was the optimisation of the production process. Most arguments about the importance of reducing costs in order to be competitive within the global automobile market referred to costs that emerged in the production process. Other transactions and the resulting costs were neglected or externalised.

The organisational development of firm A was focused on technological and administrative restructuring. Internal and external relations were examined under the premise of reducing production costs. The firm's identity as a producer of car headlights would be maintained through the technological modernisation of the firm and the optimisation of the established organisational design strategies. Actors in firm A learned to project their identities onto the changed environmental context according to the new owner's interests and experiences. The firm's identity had to fit in with the structure of the multinational industrial group.

In contrast to case study A, the organisational development in firm B was more self-defined. With the founding of the industrial holding, the local management of the newly founded profit centre organisation was confronted with the problem of defining their future business strategy. In case study A, this meant that regardless of any attempts to reorganise the firm, it maintained its identity as a mass producer of car headlights. Despite the implementation of new management concepts such as TOP or CIP, consideration was not given to alternative, and less structured and formalised forms of identity construction. All designing activities were developed to optimise the manufacturing and assembling processes. In case study B we can also find a multitude of management activities developed to control the organising processes, but contrary to case study A, all reorganisation attempts were focused on the organisation as a whole.

In case study B the reorganisation was not only less selective, but noticeable as well was that the process was less intentional and more decentralised. The former department was thrown into a relatively unknown market environment. There was no central authority that defined a general strategy for the future organisational development. The former tightly coupled relationships to other departments within the industrial group – most of which were being transformed into profit centres – lost their significance after the decline in the East European markets. In retrospect, the leading manager described this unusual and complicated starting situation of the firm:

> In the past we worked primarily for the industrial group. We had no customers … There was the industrial group and their dependent firms and departments. We worked for them. There was no marketing, no acquisition. We were not able to offer a proper customer service. We had to learn all that (Interview, 1b/1).

No investor was interested in directing the reorganisation process in case study B. The actors had to find out by themselves how to develop sensible and long-lasting customer relations. In contrast to case study A, they had never produced for mass markets. Based on their experience, they saw themselves as a firm that could offer specific technological solutions – tools, special machines, services etc.- in order to solve the problems of small and medium-sized industrial firms.

Local management saw the broadening of the employees' skills as a central task of organisational development. Because the firm had lost more than 80% of its former workforce, human resource development was seen as essential. Unlike in the past, the firm not only had to be more flexible in serving their customers, but do so with fewer staff. To deal with these challenges the management was interested in developing multiple skills at the shop floor level. One worker was to be able to work in different positions and with different technologies. The traditional division of work where the workers had to perform the same job during most of their production time was now seen as inflexible and less productive.

Contrary to case study A, firm B had various problems legitimising its commercial activities. Firm B had to show potential customers, partners and other institutions, including the governmental privatisation agency, that it was reliable, and that it would be a stable supplier. Before privatisation this had been one of the main problems of the local management. After privatisation, the question of how to legitimise the business activities of the firm resurfaced, but now primarily as a fiscal problem. The new owner – a real estate group – was not really interested in the industrial activities of firm B, but rather in its location and its market share. Even though the law required that the new owners maintain the level of employment in the firm, local management made it clear that in the future the continued existence of the firm would depend much more upon its profitability. As a real estate group, the new owners did not develop a sense for the specific needs of an industrial firm. The question of material and human resources that was central to any strategy aimed at ensuring a firm's progress became a point of contention between local management and the new owners.

Reorganisation in case study B was not focused on the improvement or restructuring of the established organisational design, but on the development of close interorganisational relations to attract customers, partners and sponsors. The firm was not limited to a specific core business. Instead, the firm's business activities were continuously redefined and reinterpreted. The 'core' activities were not limited to one particular market segment, as in case study A. The internal processes of organising were directed to different market segments. The organisation was decentralised into three divisions – also called profit centres – with divergent product and service designs. Each of these three profit centres developed their own ideas to attract customers. The main management problem of this decentralised configuration was to prevent the self-interests of one profit centre from paralysing the internal communication and cooperation processes of the firm as a whole. The newly developed modes of organising could not be managed through administrative or technological control, but only through moderating, negotiating and developing overlapping forms of cooperation between the three profit centre organisations. The reduced number of employees and interdependence of the three profit centres demanded more intensive modes of communication and cooperation than originally intended by local management.

Unlike the other two case studies, the organisational development in case study C was not as planned. Firm C could not fall back upon established work routines and relatively unchanging market relations as in case study A, nor could it focus existing social competencies on the development of viable market potentials as in case study B. A new investor who persuaded or had been forced to protect jobs did not exist. Similar to case study B, the people in the newly established job creation centre had to develop a new strategic orientation on their own.

Unlike case study C, the local management in firm B did not actively deal with the emerging conflicts. As in the past, the new ownership situation was understood as an extrinsic problem that was difficult to handle. Local management developed a strategy for denying conflicts. What this means is that negotiations over such issues as budgeting and resource allocation were avoided. In case study C, such situations were instead seen as a challenge requiring active leadership and ongoing negotiation between relevant actors. In the organisational development of firm C one can repeatedly find situations where local management learned to defend and increase their autonomy against the interference of externally controlled interests.[2]

In contrast to the other two case studies, firm C was not forced from the start to adopt a primarily commercial strategy. The firm was founded as a non-profit organisation with the mission to save and create as many jobs as possible. Although in the other two case studies all business activities were charged with protecting jobs as well, for firm C job creation meant economic success. In case study C, the economic success of the firm was not at the centre of the management process right from the start. Instead of a narrow strategic business orientation, the actors in case study C developed a well-defined mission to create jobs. This was a 'constant reminder to look outside the organisation' (Drucker, 1996, pp. 162–3) not only for customers as in case study B, but for measures of success. Contrary to the case studies A and B, the criteria of success in firm C were much more open and shifted over time.

The firm had to develop project ideas and to find sponsors. From the beginning, the process of project development was dependent on various interrelations with other organisations, institutions and actors in the region.

The leading manager of the job creation centre emphasised that for the development of projects, defining clear goals for effective project management was not as important as demonstrating that the project would be helpful in realising the firm's mission to create jobs:

> The aim of the project, the reconstruction of historical boats, was less important. The problem was to make clear why the project is important for the region and for the creation of jobs (Interview, 2c/1).

Furthermore, the firm used its close contacts with the previous employer of most of its employees (the hydraulics company) in order to develop various supplier functions. The firm's openness to the offers, demands and interests of others outside the organisation could only be developed because the project organisation of the firm did not follow fixed organisational schemes. The original goals of the projects were continuously redefined and adapted to the perceived environmental circumstances. The actors had less structured plans, job schemes or design principles defining how the organisation should look in the future. It was more important to present the projects to potential partners and sponsors and to develop new projects on the basis of the experiences of the established project management. Management continuously reinterpreted the firm's mission in order to legitimise their projects.

In contrast to the other two case studies, the collective identity of the firm was ever changing. In the beginning it cultivated the image of a non-profit organisation and from there moved on to more commercial activities. While involved in its non-profit projects, the firm used its time wisely to find out which of them could be developed further into commercial activities. In this sense, new jobs were created through a process of trial and error. In the end, the commercial and the non-profit activities of the firm became interdependent. Local management learned to argue that the commercial activities were necessary not in order to maximise individual profits or improve the share-holder value, but to develop new job prospects in the region. Thus, the local management that was first limited to narrow non-profit tasks was able to learn to deal with the contradiction of maintaining a job creation centre on the one hand, and extending its identity through commercial activities on the other.

Unlike case study A, but similar to case study B, the legitimacy of firm C was permanently challenged. However, contrary to case study B, here the new identity was endangered on an ongoing basis. Beginning with its commercial activities, the firm was confronted with attacks from various local organisations that complained about the distortion of free market competition because the firm was being subsidised through public programmes. However, local management learned to deal with these problems and developed two strategies: 1) besides their publicly sponsored job creation activities, they founded a private enterprise; 2) the firm sent its own representatives into important regional institutions, such as chambers of commerce. Moreover, management used its various contacts with regional politicians, the trade unions, the media etc., to make these attacks against the firm public.

The comparison of the three case studies indicates the fading impact of the focal organisation for identity construction. In case study A the optimisation of the focal organisation was at the centre of the organisational development. In the other two case studies, the organisational development was much more sensitive to the perceptions of other actors, agencies, organisations and institutions. Through such interdependent learning approaches, the actors were able to understand the meaning of their actions. In both case studies, the people had to learn by themselves how to locate the firm in a specific social context to be viable. In case study A, the actors were less sensitive to the meaning of their actions, because the intention was to optimise the production-dominated management processes which in turn limited opportunities for new learning experiences.

In case study A, the optimisation of the organisational design of the focal organisation was interpreted as more important than establishing links between local management, teams and work groups. In spite of the fact that management introduced organisational concepts that would enable various forms of cooperation, the established 'functionally crystallised' organisational design (Sorge, 1985) hindered cooperative processes. The whole manufacturing process remained centrally controlled and the demands for reorganisation were mainly limited to the shop floor. The main tasks of the firm were considered to be a reduction of production costs and an increase in output.

In case study B the significance of the focal organisation was not as great, and management put less emphasis on the modernisation or optimisation of a given organisational design structure. The development of knowledge-intensive products geared towards the specific interests of customers became the main task of the organisation. For this, the whole firm had be to organised in such a way that internal production units were configured to react immediately to the specific needs of the customer. The organisational configuration was not focused on output, but on marketing and product development in favour of the customers. The customers were not seen as representative of an impersonal environment that can be served by a separate department of the industrial group as in case study A. Instead, the market was understood as an area that needed ongoing and thorough consideration. At the centre of the organisational development was the interrelationship with customers and the cooperation with potential partners who were to support the future development of the firm. Acquiring external resources became much more important after the privatisation of firm B. Although the new owners expected increasing profits from the firm, the distribution of the necessary material and immaterial resources to secure the firm's future business was not clear. The interest of local management to make profits from their industrial business conflicted with the main interest of the new owner to make profits by marketing of industrial estates.

In case study C, the creation of jobs was the focus, not the optimisation of organisational design principles nor the search for profitable interrelations to customers, but the management of various projects favoured by the firm and the community. Compared to the other two case studies, it seemed at first as though economic success was secondary. Moreover, the definition of clear criteria to interpret economically successful outcomes was difficult. Every project that the firm developed was reinterpreted in terms of the question of the meaning of success. The logic of profit making often meant that employment became less of a priority which is why the firm tried to define and establish new publicly sponsored projects into which remaining employees could be integrated and new jobs created. The economic success of the firm was coupled to its ability to create jobs. This ability in turn was subsequently linked to the firm's capacity to make its own profit, especially after the dismantling of government job creation schemes.

Table 5.1   Identity construction

	Case study A	Case study B	Case study C
Commitments and justifications in identity construction	optimisation of production and output	customer orientated (flexible) specialisation	job creation orientated project management
Significance of the focal organisation for identity construction	high	medium	low

5.2.2   The Role of Recipes on How to Learn

Students of organisational learning stress the importance of making the actors' implicit recipe knowledge explicit for the purpose of making higher-level learning loops and learning organisations. However, from our perspective the exaggeration of the intentional nature of organisational learning is misleading. Instead, we stress the social context which led to the emergence of more or less intentional learning approaches. Thus, we have to prove: 1) where, meaning at what level; and 2) how the recipes on how to learn were developed in each case study (chapter 2, p. 32–3 and chapter 3, p. 64).

In case study A the firm was reorganised according to the blueprint of another car headlight production firm at the West German base of the multinational. After the takeover, local management began to adjust the organisational and technological processes to the practices prevailing in its West German counterpart. Assembly lines were brought from the West and set up in the East. Local managers and labourers worked for several days in the West to learn how work was organised there. The two newly appointed CEOs, responsible for production and commerce, had worked for years in different countries. Before they took over the leadership in the East both worked in the USA. They had learned several times and under various conditions how to set up newly bought or founded industrial bases all over the world.

The criteria of the firm's success were clearly defined from the beginning. The primary aim of management was the efficient manufacturing of car headlights with lower costs than in the West. All organisational functions were checked to see if they belonged to the core business or not. Functions which had been integrated before were outsourced, such as the maintenance unit or the production of synthetic supplier parts for car headlights. The manufacturing of other products, such as car horns, was given up all together.

The introduction of new management ideas such as TOP or CIP was an ambivalent issue. On the one hand, local management stressed the importance of these concepts to improve possibilities to self-design their work. On the other hand, all interviewees, from the top to the bottom, replied to the question about the reasons for the introduction of these organisation methods by stressing efficiency and output. The purpose of implementing TOP was to streamline the assembly of car headlights, and the introduction of CIP was intended to limit the waste of time and resources, especially at the shop floor. All this, it was expected, would reduce production costs and improve the firm's competitiveness.

According to the previously learned behaviour, the people in firm A expected and accepted the knowledge transfer from the West to the East. They were familiar with the fact that someone else outside the firm at the headquarters, or before, in the central agency of state-owned firm, developed recipes and programmes that defined the ways of organising. Management and the workers did not agree upon the necessity of integrating strategic and operational tasks at the shop-floor level. Rather, both sides considered it to be sufficient that each fulfilled its function, and that this would automatically lead to the improvement of the efficiency of the firm. Thus, the implementation of new management methods was organised by experts that were responsible for selecting the people to become team leaders, the teams or the team members that had to be taught.

Within the firm a new position was created, the position of a CIP-coordinator, who was responsible for directing and controlling the implementation process. In the past this manager belonged to the leading management group of the firm. This seems to be the strategy of the new owners to integrate the former leading management from the East. Some of them were selected for new management tasks, were trained in the West and became responsible for controlling the manufacturing process.

The CIP-coordinator explained on the example of TOP how the introduction of this management concept was developed and controlled:

> The stimulus to implement TOP came from S [the headquarters]. There is a central work group that is responsible for the development of the team concepts in the whole industrial group. I was invited by the multinational department in H to take part in a training course ... Then I developed our own training programmes for our staff. First the management and the white-collar workers were trained. After that we created and trained the first teams in O ... One important aspect of the training process is that I determine when each work group should work as a team (Interview, 8a/1).

This argumentation shows a tightly planned introductory process in which the aggregation of the teams was centrally planned, the team leaders were centrally selected and the moment when the team should work under the new label TOP was centrally set. As we have seen in the case study report, the introduction of CIP was organised in a similar way and mainly concentrated on managing interests to rationalise the manufacturing process and reduce production costs. For this task, other management functions such as purchasing were instructed to check the supplier and reduce their number for specific parts. On the other hand, the relationship to the customers continued to be centrally organised by a specific sales department, a kind of wholesale shop responsible for selling all products that are made by the multinational. This function did not belong to the firm's core business activities.

In contrast to firm A that had developed various and detailed recipes to direct the reorganisation process, firm B reconsidered its established organising recipes after the loss of its supplier function within the state-owned industrial group. The formal transformation of the former department into a semi-autonomous profit centre brought the firm into the unanticipated situation of how to self-define a future business strategy. However, there were no certain recipes on how to succeed and get the necessary resources to guarantee the future development of the firm. There were no new owners with a clear strategy on how to modernise or reorganise the firm as in case study A. Here the people had to develop or rediscover their own recipes to prepare the firms for the future.

However, in the past they had learned to react flexibly to the demands of other departments within the industrial group. One manager explained the main difference between the new situation and the past experiences with which the firm had had to deal as follows:

> A big challenge for us was the shift of our production from internal to external customers. Before, only 10 per cent of our customers had been external ... After autumn 1989 it was increasingly necessary to compensate for the decline in internal orders through the acquisition of external customers (Interview, 4b/1).

Moreover, local management stressed that contrary to the past learned behaviour where the actors 'always tried to refuse doing any extra work' (ibid.), now they had to be permanently aware of the needs of their customers. They had to learn to serve them which was different to their learned behaviour of the past of delivering rare goods and products and avoiding having to do any extra work. Unlike in the past when orders were continuously in order to secure an ongoing production process, the firm now had to find its own customers and develop a strategy that made the specific quality of the firm known. Contrary to case study A, firm B had a lower reputation and no new owner was interested in allowing the firm into its well-established markets. Also contrary to case study A was that the main problem of the firm was not a question of streamlining the manufacturing processes in order to reduce production costs. The improvement of the firm's organisational design was a secondary question. The main task of management was to redefine the firm's position, to identify the strengths of the firm and ways in which to present these capabilities. The employees had to do both, namely redefine their established recipes about how to organise the firm's business, and find new recipes for previously unknown tasks such as marketing, customer acquisition and service.

The established organisational recipes, based on clearly defined work rules and a greater degree of planning functions, had become inflexible. In addition came the massive reduction in employment in firm B. For dealing with the challenges of the new market environment, all members of the firm, managers, engineers and workers, had to develop more flexible patterns of behaviour. Unlike in the past, job security no longer existed. The actors were now responsible for creating their own employment prospects. It was no longer possible to avoid working more. Instead the constant pressure to have enough jobs to secure continuous employment became evident. Instead, the actors had to deal more flexibly with permanently emerging discontinuities. Sometimes they had to deal with increasing customer demands, sometimes a drop in orders led to working fewer hours. The workers had to learn to work with various technologies and in multiple work situations. The engineers had to work more closely with the shop floor. The organising process became more complex. Management redefined its past functions of planning and administration. The main function of management shifted from controlling to coordination and moderation.[3]

The whole organisation of the former department had to be modified. The informal recipes which had been relied upon before to deal with the challenges of the planned economy were now used to deal with the insecurities of the market economy. In the past the tacit knowledge of the employees was seen as valuable in finding solutions for recurring problems such as broken machines and missing parts. It now became one of the main functions of the former department within the state-owned industrial group. The management has tried to use this 'strength of weak ties' (Granovetter, 1983) to deal with the new circumstances of the new market environment.

Contrary to the other two case studies, the management of firm C had no experience establishing an efficient or effective organisation. In case study C there were no traditional recipes which could easily be applied. Unlike case study A, the redesign of the firm was not at the centre of the management process. Rather, the main purpose of the organisational development consisted of creating various links to regional agencies, organisations and institutions. Neither increasing efficiency as in case study A, nor the need to find external customers as in case study B was a problem. The development of recipes that enabled the firm to create job prospects was much more experimental than in the other two case studies. Skills other than the fulfilment of clear rules or the orientation of long-established organisational routines were needed.

In case study A, as in the past, the application of centrally planned organisational recipes was maintained. Although Eastern European markets declined, headquarters decided to transfer jobs from the West to the East. Local management had to learn to show that the production costs in the East were actually lower than in the West. In case study B the firm had its organisational traditions to offer specific products and services, and management had to learn to check and modify its existing recipes and enlarge them with formerly externalised functions such as marketing and specific customer services.

In case study C the employees who lost their job learned from the grassroots what it meant to develop valuable jobs and business activities. Starting with less planned and vague project ideas, they learned by doing which of the various project ideas had to be rejected, which would be advantageous and how one could develop them further. These learning activities were much more interactive than in case study A and in case study B. The actors had to decide which of their projects would have a chance to develop and which would not. However, this could not be decided in advance, but through various interactions and negotiations with potential partners, sponsors and suppliers. So, the actors developed experience and action-based recipes, upon which they made their decisions. However, this seemed insufficient to deal with the ambivalent and risky character of a lot of their projects. Often the freshly learned recipes about how to develop a viable project had to be corrected. In an interview with one of the top managers, he explained how a specific project which at first was not accepted by the main sponsor were redefined and developed further several times. However, in the end the firm was able to get support for a modified version of the original version of the project application:

> The original idea of our project to build new boats was rejected. However, a part of the project could be realised. In the discussion with our potential sponsor [the Ministry for Social Policy] we got the information that they probably will promote the reconstruction of used boats. So, we decided to change the original idea and we started to search for old boats ... (Interview, 3c/1).

This argument shows how the development of tight and sensible local relations supported internal knowledge creation. The success of the firm was not dependent on the realisation of fixed rules or planned strategies, but on the flexibility to modify its project ideas as long as they attracted private or public sponsors.

The comparison of the development of recipes between the three case studies shows that the degree of experimentation and the extent to which new recipes were learned decreased from case study A to case study B to case study C. In the case studies B and C the actors had to find out by themselves a way to develop their organisation within a specific social context. In case study B, the firm used its experience in applying products and services that improve the technological design of industrial firms. The main problem was to enlarge the specific skills of employees and to integrate centrally controlled management functions such as customer acquisition and marketing. Both management and workers had to take more responsibility. For this complicated task the actors had no redefined recipes, but social competencies. In the past they had learned to deal with such unknown situations. However, contrary to their former experience, the actors learned to apply and develop their social competencies in order to improve the firm's profit.

Contrary to the other two case studies, economic success was not the focal point of the organisational development in case study C; job creation was the primary task of management. The actors thus had the chance to experiment with various ideas and to find out which of these projects ideas would be viable in order to obtain public and private sponsorship. The managers often could not define clear recipes on how to develop viable or profitable projects. Only towards the end of the period, when the projects were established, was management able to express its recipes on how to develop successful projects. In contrast to the other two case studies, the actors in case study C discovered ways to learn in retrospect. There was no investor who transferred explicit recipes which define the ways of learning as in case study A, and the actors could not fall back on specific, previously learned social competencies which would help to deal with the new situation.

Table 5.2   The role of recipes on how to learn

	Case study A	Case study B	Case study C
Development of learning recipes	routinised transformation of the established recipes	recourse to social competencies to modify the established recipes	retrospective discovering of recipes through learning by doing

5.2.3 Learning From the Experience of Others

Both students of organisational learning as well neo-institutionalist scholars seem to agree that the recipes on how to learn can be directly copied and easily transferred from one organisation to another. The idea is that managers can be trained to apply or just imitate obviously successful management concepts. However, in this section we will see that the transferring and borrowing of knowledge cannot be understood as merely a universal process. Instead, the ways in which actors learn from the experiences of others has to be linked to social practice. Thus we want to observe how actors and groups of actors actually learn from and with each other. We will therefore focus our analysis on the following three questions: 1) who are the relevant actors inside and outside the organisation whose experience matters; 2) how were these experiences interpreted and valued?; and 3) in which way were they integrated within the processes of organising (chapter 2, p. 30 and chapter 3, p. 64)?

As in the past, knowledge creation in firm A was limited to a specific group of actors, the operative management. Their main task was to translate the policy of the headquarters into separate operative tasks. In the reorganisation process, the actors and their knowledge were seen as goods that can easily be transferred. In the interviews, former top managers from the East stressed that they saw fewer chances to secure the survival of the firm without the experience of a Western investor who had the necessary know-how and financial resources to improve the firm's performance. The new owner was seen as a kind of teacher who would help to secure the firm's survival. Both sides, the newly appointed managers from the West and the East German managers, saw the transfer of technologies, procedures and routines as essential for the first phase of the organisation's development.

On the one hand, the attempts to transfer routines and technologies were interpreted as a favour because firm A had little difficulty in meeting the efficiency and quality standards of other locations of the multinational. On the other hand in some interviews it was also mentioned that the explicit nature of the firm's knowledge base could be a threat to the long-term survival of the firm:

> We have to search for possibilities to integrate knowledge intensive production functions too, such as the production of dispersion plates ... This is a key part of a car headlight and we always experienced quality problems with our suppliers ... When we limit our production capacity to assembly functions, there is always the danger that the production capacity of our firm can be easily shifted to cheaper locations in Eastern Europe (Interview, 2a/2).

The reorganisation process was tightly planned and guided by experts, such as technological and commercial professionals. This was also true for the implementation of TOP and CIP in the next step of reorganisation after the firm met the technological and organisational standards of the multinational. These management ideas were seen as an explicit knowledge that can easily be transferred and controlled by operative managers. In this sense, the creation of work teams and the formation of temporary project groups were mainly understood as a management instrument and not as a chance to develop social competence and close links between different subunits and groups of actors. The introduction of new management concepts, such as TOP or CIP, can be understood as 'espoused' management theories that did not shift the established ways of how things are organised. Although management implemented new work teams, the division of work organisation into experts who are concerned with service and control, and shop-floor employees who look after increasing output at the assembly lines. Thus, the reorganisation was dominated by operative management interests to find solutions for mainly technical issues to improve output on the assembly lines.

In case study B it was less important to transfer standard knowledge or to copy from others. At the centre was the development of broader skills to be more responsive to their customers. So, from the beginning the question was not how to improve the efficiency of the established technological and organisational design, but how to develop close connections to potential customers. With the decline of former customer relations within the industrial holding, the firm was increasingly forced to develop new external customer relations. Contrary to case study A, firm B did not produce large-batch standard products such as car headlights. The actors could not hope to make profits through copying well-tried out standard experiences or just optimising their production function.

In case study B, various actors in different positions had to communicate about and negotiate the development and manufacturing of products and services. They had to find a mutual understanding of each other's responsibility and capability in the process of organising. As a consequence, the traditional distinctions between blue and white-collar work became blurred. Not the capability to control the outcome of the other, but cooperation with one another became increasingly important.

However, the introduction of the internal cost centre structure challenged the existing rather informal and less planned modes of knowledge creation. In applying this model, management overlooked the social competence of the employees to handle emerging problems in their daily work. With the creation of cost centres, these traditional informal relations between workers, engineers and managers were seen in a new light. Exchanging information and experience among the three profit centres now became costly.

> The idea of a cost centre has of course some drawbacks. It is not as flexible as we originally expected. The existing reserves cannot be used optimally. Sometimes it becomes increasingly difficult to support other cost centres and to take over some of their orders (Interview, 3b/1).

The focus on specific group interests often hindered the ability to recognise the advantages of internal collaboration through the sharing of key technologies or the mutual exchange of resources. Moreover, the development of selfish interests between the profit centres conflicted with the intentions of local management to create overlapping skills and share experiences throughout the firm as a whole.

The firm had to adapt its skills according to the demands of their customers that went beyond the usual establishment of marketing and sales functions. Both parties, the customer as well as the firm, had to develop close relations during the whole process of organising. The exchange of information and experiences in firm B regularly covered the product development, the manufacturing and after sales service. In case study A the transfer and development of explicit knowledge to increase the output of standard products was of central importance. Compared with case study B, the integration of others' experience was extremely formalised, because the optimisation of the manufacturing process was the focus of organisational development.

Compared to the other two case studies, in case study C the exchange of experience was less formalised and not primarily commercial. To a large degree, the creation of knowledge was embedded in the regional context. Contrary to case study A and to a great extent also to case study B, the firm was a part of the local community. The business of the firm was not only focused on commercial interests, but also on particular local problems, such as those concerning the environment, unemployment or poverty.

One of the main problems of the first phase of organisational development was to ensure that the representatives of the local authority would accept the firm as a local player. Once firm C was established, traditional projects in the area of social work or tourism were limited. Another local job creation centre had specialised in these areas. Firm C had to develop new ideas to apply for public sponsorship. The process of developing and realising the projects was closely linked to the local context in which firm C operated. Developing projects, modifying them and developing them further was intensively coupled with tight interactions to various local actors and groups of actors. In contrast to the two other case studies, the organisational knowledge creation in case study C reasonably followed the interests of the local actors and was based on the employees' own experiences about how to organise an efficient outcome.

Even in difficult situations, local management did not give up or search for external reasons which were determining the firm's development, such as the new owners (case study B), or such restraints as the pressure of market competition (case study A). Instead, they tried to be proactive and develop alternative strategies. One example of such a proactive leadership was the takeover of the business of the former parent company by firm C:

> Very quickly after the foundation of our firm it became clear that there were very different interests between our firm and our parent company. We wanted to expand our non-profit functions and develop commercial projects. They wanted to limit their activities to traditional job creation schemes ... It was a long way to make clear to our partners that this constellation is not sufficient for our firm (Interview, 1c/5).

In the end firm C succeeded in convincing its partners that the firm was indeed capable of developing viable job creation projects. The parent company subsequently lost its reputation and power and firm C took over its business.[4]

The actors in firm C started their business activities through a process of learning by trial and error. In the process of organising, when the actors started to realise their projects, the ideas were modified and continuously adapted to the new situation. Because they only received limited public resources they had to find partners to share risks. Risk-taking on one project always meant sharing risk with others or to using the surplus from one project to create or develop additional ones. For the development of project ideas it was often not clear who had the idea, someone within the firm or somebody outside. The main task of local management was to develop a feeling for which of the ideas were to be realised and to find the people and resources to do it, the process which Sabel (1991, pp. 26–30) calls localisation. On the one hand, localisation seems to have had a favourable influence on firm C's organisational development because the risks of trial and error learning could be shared. The development of mutual trust relations between different actors, groups of actors and organisations supported the exchange of explicit as well as tacit knowledge. However, localisation in a declining region also had negative effects. In firm C the realisation of sophisticated project ideas became more and more problematic, because it was difficult to find skilled employees as the firm had few material resources to attract and hold key workers.

In case study A the experience of others was understood more as a kind of transferable product than as a particular social competence of the employees. The operative management functions directed and controlled the exchange of experience within the firm. In case study B the transfer of explicit knowledge was secondary. Operative management functions, such as controlling and technological effectiveness, covered only a small part of the knowledge creation process. As important was the formal as well as the informal exchange of experience between the customers and within the firm. The growth of close personal relations within the process of project development and the embeddedness with the local community was the key to the organisational knowledge creation in case study C. The mission of the firm was not self-centred, but embedded in a broader social context. In a declining region, the employees developed both the ability to meet the particular problem of the region as well as the necessary professionalism to attract partners and launch profitable projects.

In case study B and case study C learning from the experiences of others was more oriented towards developing a shared understanding with customers or local actors. Developed social practices were necessary in order to deal with constantly emerging uncertainties. In case study B, the uncertainties emerged through the complexity of their products and services. In case study C it was difficult to develop prospective calculations about the success of a project. The sponsors and partners often could not make meaningful estimates of the economic success of a project. Often they supported a project because the management of firm C could convince them about its local importance. For this it was not sufficient to know that something can be done in a certain way, more important was knowing how to realise it in a politically and economically uncertain and controversial environment.

Table 5.3   Learning from the experience of others

	Case study A	Case study B	Case study C
Learning from the experience of others	through close control of the operative tasks	through steady relations with the customers	through close relations within the local community

5.2.4 The Role of Participation Within the Learning Process

The main aim of this section is to compare the role of participation in each case study. In the literature the combination of participative and reflective skills is seen as key in the creation of learning organisations. However, from our perspective of analysis this argumentation is insufficient because it reduces the role of participation to a kind of general tool for intervention researchers to detect learning disabilities and initiate double-loop learning. Instead of this view, we want to stress the practice of participation and the differences in meaning of participative learning in each case study. Our analysis will be guided by the following three questions: 1) how were participative approaches developed; 2) who is learning with whom; and 3) how is collective learning related to participatory approaches (chapter 2, pp. 33–4 and chapter 3, p. 64)?

In contrast to the other two case studies, in case study A participation turned out to have a highly formalised and highly functional character. The works council was not seen as a partner that ought to be involved in the decision-making process. Instead, management understood the role of the works council as functionally specific, with legally fixed possibilities to influence already established decisions. In this sense participatory approaches were interpreted as consuming too much time and energy, as a cost factor. Effects of participation were understood as more disturbing than enabling for the organisational development. Although management emphasised the potential for a mutual exchange of experience at the shop-floor level after the implementation of new management instruments such as TOP and CIP, the rigid technological regime at the assembly lines left little room for collective learning processes. Participatory approaches as well as reflexive openness did not emerge automatically through the creation of teams. The regular team meetings were planned and controlled by the leaders of the teams. In discussions they explained management decisions to the workers. They had a vested interest in ensuring that teams complied with technical norms and quality standards but would not develop participatory approaches.

In interviews, the head of the works council claimed that a too narrow definition of core business restricted the firm to a simple manufacturing unit within the structure of the multinational. With the reduction in product diversity, he argued further, the survival of the firm was at risk, because the firm would probably lose out in the price competition against the rapidly growing Eastern European suppliers. This danger was seen by the local management too, though they drew a different conclusion from it. They argued that production had to be optimised in order to decrease these costs and that supplier parts had to be bought at lower costs. This, they argued, would increase the firm's competitiveness. In the end the role of the works council was limited to compensating for this narrow organisational strategy. The council did not participate and did not influence the decision-making process. Instead, the main task of the works council consisted of protecting the losers in the reorganisation process.

As seen in the case study report, especially the introduction of TOP led to an increase in group pressure against weak employees within the work teams. In this sense one can summarise that the established modes of participation in case study A did not enable new forms of collective learning processes within the firm. Collective learning was constrained to a limited group of actors. Managers learned together with managers or from experts; workers learned together with workers and were controlled by managers and experts. The learning experience at the shop-floor level was neglected. So, the original intentions of local management to improve communication between different subunits and groups of actors failed. 'Continuous improvement' was mainly seen as a management instrument to realise an optimal production output. Emerging conflicts, such as in the newly introduced teams, or passive opposition such as the increasing number of employees who were calling in sick, were not seen as chances to develop new forms of collective learning, but as problems which endangered the firm's productivity.

In case study B the modes of formal participation shifted. Based on their experience, local management saw the participation in decision making by the holding's works council as a problem. The interests of the firm as a profit centre organisation were different from the interests of the works council which represented the employees of the entire holding. Local management thus had many conflicts with the holding's works council. The main goal was to protect as many jobs as possible within the holding and place less emphasis on the particular requirements of profit-making dominated outcomes.[5] In the beginning, firm B received instructions from the privatisation agency to reduce its staff. Later on they adopted their own staffing policy. Thus, they started to think about the development of broader skills, the flexible reduction or extension of working hours depending upon customer demand, etc. These arrangements always conflicted with the position of the holding's works council of upholding legal standards in working hours. Increasing the workers competence was in the interest of both sides, but the initiative to organise training courses came from the local management. Despite this, local management welcomed the disintegration of the holding's works council and the foundation of a locally embedded one, the role of the works council was not seen with mixed feelings and not as a chance to develop more forms of learning and working, as in case study A. However, both management as well as the councils accepted the formal representation of the employees' rights.

But participation in the decision making process was more difficult to realise than in case study A. The more decentralised decision-making processes and highly specialised jobs prevented employees from developing a shared understanding of each other's jobs. Moreover, it was important that they reflected upon and developed an awareness of the problems of others. Important for the organisational development was not so much developing participatory or reflective approaches, but work processes where actors and groups of actors could decide by themselves about how and when to do the work. This self-organised action had to be coordinated. Cooperation between actors, groups of actors and cost centres became problematic. Neither local management nor the works council understood that the council could no longer take a formal position. That might be necessary in individual cases, when the legal rights of an employee had to be secured against the intentions of local management or the policies of new owners. However, such tasks appeared to be becoming secondary. The new role of the works council might rather be to become a kind of mediator that has to deal with conflicts of interests that emerge in day-to-day work. One major issue is to mediate the conflict between the individual interests of one cost centre to maximise profit with the interests of the firm as whole to improve the cooperative relations between all cost centres. However, in the interviews these problems were always recognised by the local management, but the necessity to moderate these conflicts of interest were primarily interpreted as a task of the top management.

In case study C, the works council was founded upon the initiative of local management. Some of the executives were familiar with how a works council functions. They had been works councillors for several years.[6] That is why in contrast to the other two case studies, local management could imagine that the interests of management and the employees were different. Moreover, they were prepared to institutionalise an internal form of control. However, the installation of formal participation possibilities were not sufficient to transform the established modes of organisational learning. Instead, for the companies B and C it was more important to develop project ideas which would be supported, and to participate in regional decision-making processes. These specific forms of participation were necessary to secure the firm's position within the region and to develop a reputation as a serious firm. Internal participation was not seen as a problem, because the management of the project involved mutual communication and exchange of experiences between employees. Not unlike case study B, the specific environmental conditions and the lack of possibilities to define or reflect upon the outcome of their projects hindered the development of certain modes of participation and a broadly shared understanding of what went on. More important than internal participatory approaches was the development of close relations with sponsors and potential partners.

Similar to case study B, in firm C the decentralised modes of organising and the requirements to professionalise the projects made traditional forms of participation complicated. Moreover, in both case studies diversity of tasks, products, and services was much higher than in case study A. Coherent solutions concerning more participation were more difficult to support. In case study C, collective learning was not coupled with the existence of representative forms of participation, but contingent upon the steady development of established projects and the creation of new projects.

It can be summarised that classical participatory approaches such as the protection of the workers rights and the employees developing a strong identification with the goal of reorganising were mainly relevant in case study A. In firm A participation was chiefly interpreted as a functionally specific issue whose goal was to increase the output. The concern of participatory approaches was to achieve and control externally planned production targets.

In case studies B and C, industrial relations between management and the works councils were not at the centre of the management processes. In both case studies the development of new forms of work and action were tested. However, this was not primarily a task of reflective openness as assumed in learning organisation approaches, but a question of shifting patterns of interacting. The continuously shifting tasks and the need to adapt to new situations required rather more informal and direct modes participation than just the creation of systematic possibilities for participative learning, as in common organisational learning approaches assumed. In case studies B and C, establishing formal conditions for workers' participation was less important than improving and challenging the permanent informal modes of interacting and negotiating which were internally and externally embedded in the social context. In case study A, participation was interpreted as a formal issue in the management process whose task it was to support the goals of management and to avoid conflicts.

Table 5.4   The role of participation within the learning process

	Case study A	Case study B	Case study C
The role of participation within the process of organising	… was mainly understood as a functional and formal method by which to secure employee rights and avoid conflicts	… was formally conflictual, but informally established in the work process	… was formally recognised, but mainly informally established in the management of the projects

5.2.5 Beyond the Ideal of Continuous Organisational Learning

In the debate over organisational learning the importance of continuous learning is stressed. In this sense, the creation of possibilities for continuous learning is interpreted as the most important quality of learning organisations. It is argued that the members of such an organisation must become continuous learners by correcting and avoiding failures. However, from our perspective it is insufficient to concentrate on the continuity of learning and to neglect the question of how the actors deal with the unintended events and discontinuities within the organisational learning process. Instead of searching for explanations as to how actors continuously improve their organisational learning loops, we want to shift the focus to the ways in which actors develop plausible interpretations about their ongoing processes of organising. The reasonably experimental nature of learning processes thus becomes visible. The central questions of this section are: 1) where were discontinuities most likely to occur; 2) how did the actors deal with the emerging discontinuities within the process of organisational learning (chapter 2, pp. 34–5 and chapter 3, pp. 64).

In case study A, discontinuities were most likely to appear in the production process. The production process should be protected against disturbances caused by technological and human factors. Collective learning was focused on preventing the occurrence of failures. All activities of both management and the workers had to be focused on improving the production functions of the firm. The quality and the output of production were at the centre of all learning activities. The definition of core business, technological growth, the introduction of CIP and TOP, all these ideas were used as instruments to attain this goal.

Management initiated CIP which were used to streamline the internal organisation of the teamwork. The main goals included increasing the speed of the assembly lines and reducing the number of team members. However, technically attempts to improve the output led to an increase in stress at the assembly lines. One of the leaders of the work groups explained the differences as follows:

> Before we could go on working when something broke down on the assembly line or when one team member was not working at full capacity. Now this is hardly possible (Interview, 2a/3).

The problem of management was to bring the right person at the right time to the right place to improve the organisation's output. In this sense management forced the teams to perform well by initiating 'continuous improvement processes'. The possibilities for collective learning were limited to events when the technologically tightly coupled manufacturing processes were interrupted. The actors had to become capable of taking on the increasing demands of a technologically efficient organisational design. Unskilled or inexperienced workers within the teams who were not able to deal with this increasing pressure to perform were selected for less demanding tasks in the packing department or the small-batch production unit.[7]

One could argue that the traditional ways of thinking and acting were reinforced by the collective learning process. This turned out to be different in the other two case studies where traditional ways of thinking and acting were challenged and collective learning processes had a more irregular, comprehensive and shifting character.

Contrary to case study A, the actors in firm B could not fall back upon their traditional ways of thinking and acting. The previous functional integration of the firm was given up. With the foundation of the industrial holding the actors could not rely on the security of obtaining regular orders from related departments within the former industrial group. Their past experiences had to be used to deal with the challenges of the new situation. The actors had to learn to create an organisation that was more adaptive to the demands of their specific customers. Contrary to case study A, the product specificity hindered standardisation and formalisation of manufacturing tasks. From the development of the product to its sale, actors had to be prepared to modify and shift the original intentions of the very process of designing and producing the product and its related services. They also had to be much more concerned about the process of organising as a whole. Merely concentrating on technological and human capabilities to optimise the manufacturing issues was no longer sufficient to cope with this more comprehensive task. Moreover, the manufacturing functions had to be socially coordinated with other functions, such as procuring, product development and sale. However, the difficulty was to produce continuous social linkages between different functional tasks that contained various discontinuities.

The focus was not the development of an efficient output, but the creation of plausible solutions to satisfy the customers' specific needs. The necessity to develop mutual understanding between the firm and its customers led to many interruptions of the originally planned organising process. Recurring frictions and unplanned moments in the organising process prevented the establishment of routinised learning approaches. Instead, collective learning had to be both more intensive and more comprehensive, because the actors had to become capable of making their own decisions and reacting flexibly to the unconventional demands of their customers. The chief executive contrasted the tasks of his firm with those of a traditional mass producer as follows:

> One has always to distinguish between our enterprise which must steadily develop new products and produce a broad variety of other specific products

and a firm which produces the same product over a period of many years. Approximately every three months we introduce a new product ... We have continuously to rethink and develop our capacities (Interview, 1b/2).

In case study B, the actors became aware that these events were not exceptions that could easily be avoided, instead they recognised those non-intended events as an inherent product of their business activities. Discontinuities in the organising process occurred mainly because of the nature of products and services which the firm offered to its customers. Whereas firm A received mass orders of highly standardised products, firm B mainly produced a small quantity of very specific products. The actors often had to develop the appropriate design of the product during the manufacturing process. They had to be able to find and offer solutions for an individual problem of the customer. As such they had to develop a specific tool for a specific task. It turned out to be difficult both to plan and control the process of developing and producing the product. It was difficult to anticipate the quality of a job from the moment the firm took the order from its customer.

However, contrary to case study B, the intensity and comprehensiveness of collective learning processes were larger in case study C. Firm C also distinguished itself from the other two case studies in that previously learned ways of thinking and acting were seriously challenged. With the foundation of the job creation centre, people were confronted with a totally new situation: they had to define a new social identity and develop new ideas about how to secure employment. Collective processes of making sense of it all relied less on past work routines. Instead, new experiences emerged within the process of project development. However, contrary to the other two case studies, the expectations about the outcome of the projects were very vague. The design of the projects and the participating actors within the projects were shifting over time. In this sense discontinuities within the process of organising are seen as a normal outcome of experimentation within the projects. As in case study B, disruptions were not mainly concentrated on manufacturing tasks, rather, discontinuities could emerge in all phases of the organising process and at all levels of the organisation.

Firm C was less specialised than the firms in our other two case studies. The process of specialisation often just began when the project seemed to be profitable or attractive for an outside prospective buyer. Just before the spin-off of a project the actors worked out how they could improve the efficiency and which of their employees would be capable of working in the new institutional context.

However, the success of one project often only became visible after one understood the shortcomings and neglected potential of an individual project. The actors constructed their projects in such a way that made them capable of learning from their failures. As we will discuss in the next section, for such an experimental development of the projects, an unspecified amount of time and resources were necessary. Through a loosely coupled management of projects, learning by doing was possible. One of the leading project managers saw the success of the 'boat building project' as due to less economic pressure:[8]

> Because we had fewer experiences in boat building, it was important for the success of this project that there was not just a pressure to perform as in a private dockyard (Interview, 4c/1).

Because they were less experienced and enjoyed the freedom to act without having to focus first and foremost on economic success criteria, the actors had enough room to manoeuvre. They could learn the skills needed for constructing a boat and, if necessary, they could take some training courses. They had the opportunity to find their level of efficiency which of course also involved the possibility to make failures, correct them and search for alternative solutions without running the risk that these activities would jeopardise the survival of the project or the firm as a whole.

Discontinuities in the organising process were not the exception as in case study A or particularly related to specifying the product as in case study B, but everyday experience. Local management had to learn to deal with these discontinuities and if necessary accept the failure of one project to secure the future of another project idea that was more likely to be supported by potential sponsors.

It can be summarised that the creation of conditions for continuous organisational learning was most important in case study A. These settings favoured mainly adaptive learning approaches that stabilise the traditional ways of thinking and acting.

However, for organisational learning processes in more turbulent environments the effects of routinisation are vague. As we have seen in case study B, the specificity of products and services did not allow for strict routinisation. It was more substantial for the organisational development that the actors became capable of dealing with permanent modifications of the original design of products and services.

Costly disruptions occurred in case study A because the firm had specialised in the large-batch manufacturing of a standard product. Failures had to be avoided. Small-batch production of specific headlights such as for motor bikes was interpreted as a necessary exception that was not part of the firm's core business.

In case study C the discontinuity was not the exception, but the rule. To secure the firm's development the actors had to learn to reinterpret and modify their original project ideas. Important for this was to use the first-hand experiences of day-to-day work. Such experiences were allowed to determine which projects were to be considered as viable or profitable from a long-term perspective.

From case study A through case study B to case study C the importance of developing accurate, foolproof and uninterrupted modes of organising declined. The accurate organisation of work had the most significant impact in a stable social and economic context. In a learning environment where non-intended events were more common, the development of plausible organisational design strategies became more important. Here the actors had first of all to search for plausible solutions, commitments and justifications that made sense of the outcome of their previous actions, both for themselves as well as others.

Table 5.5   Beyond the ideal of continuous organisational learning

	Case study A	Case study B	Case study C
Modes of dealing with discontinuities within the process of organisational learning	learning from avoiding discontinuities and failures	learning from dealing with discontinuities and failures	learning from discontinuities and failures

5.2.6   *The Role of Organisational Slack Resources Within the Process of Organisational Learning*

In the literature it is stressed that a surplus of resources can provide the firm with the capability to deal with the uncertainties which emerge in daily work processes. Moreover, organisational slack is interpreted as an important resource for increasing the organisation's adaptability. It is expected that the existence of a surplus of unspecified resources will give the actors more possibilities for learning to learn and the organisation more room to manoeuvre. However, from our point of view the quality of the process of organisational learning turned out not to simply depend upon securing or developing unspecified material or social resources. Quality was also affected by: 1) how organisational slack resources had been socially constructed; and 2) how this process is directly related to the openness of the particular organisational learning approaches in each case study (chapter 2, p. 35 and chapter 3, p. 64).

Contrary to the other two case studies, the technical, financial and personal resources in firm A were centrally planned, assigned and controlled. After the take-over this kind of hierarchical coordination of the manufacturing process and its separation from other tasks such as marketing or R&D were similar to what the actors had previously experienced. Even under the conditions of the state-socialist centrally planned economy the continuity of the manufacturing processes in firm A was at the centre of the management process. Uncertainties such as experiments and conflicts had to be avoided in order to enable an accurate and efficient organisation of work.

After the take-over, the production process was streamlined. For that purpose, the implementation of new management ideas such as TOP and CIP were used to detect and diminish 'unnecessary work activities'. The main idea of CIP was to streamline the production process. Unnecessary functions and actions were to be 'continuously' avoided and reduced. One of the essential tasks of CIP was characterised in an internal document as follows: '... the exclusion of waste as surplus, waiting, breakdowns, transport, handling and buffers in all parts of the firm' (CIP-Instruction and Internal Company document).

All employees and especially the operative management at the shop-floor were seen as being responsible for reducing the 'waste of resources', as well as for decreasing the costs of production. In this sense organisational slack lost its character as a resource, and came to be understood as a kind of ballast which had to be overcome. However, to avoid conflicts and resistance by employees, management assured that all CIP activities, irrespective of whether they were initiated from management or from the workers, would not lead to dismissal. As an alternative, management offered redundant employees other jobs within the firm or in another subsidiary of the multinational near the location of firm A.

In the production process the employees on the assembly lines were seen as technical parts that could easily be traded for technological systems or for other employees. As in the past, the employees with planning and coordination tasks received a leadership function. Thus, after the introduction of the TOP team-leaders were significantly empowered. However, not all the planning and coordination tasks were taken over by them. The foremen continued to have the main responsibility for these functions, especially for the coordinating and monitoring on the shop floor. Moreover, the work on the assembly lines did not shift. The work tasks were not integrated. Job rotation or job enlargement played no role. As the smallest unit within the firm, the team maintained a structure similar to the organisation as a whole. Every employee played his or her part within a well-defined work environment, controlled and planned by the supervisor.

The organisational development in firm B was devoid of such a planned process as in case study A. With its shifting demands, especially the low standardisation of products and the high amount of one-off production given the necessity of close customer contacts during the whole production process, the firm's market environment required a different kind of access to the organisational slack resources than in case study A. Employees were not treated as parts which could easily be directed or replaced. The creation of capabilities to self-organise the work from the product development to its marketing became an important 'slack' resource. Contrary to case study A, the emergence of overlapping functions and the exchange of information was essential for the firm's development.

The local management initially understood the new market challenges as being a matter of restructuring the organisational design. Their main interest was to decentralise the decision-making processes and to develop product and cost-centred subunits. Every cost centre became responsibility for a specific group of products. However, management neglected to address the emerging conflicts between the three cost centres. The tendency of each cost centre to work in its own interest made spontaneous cooperation difficult. It became difficult to coordinate joint use of scarce resources such as technology and decision-making conflicts emerged. These problems could often not be solved locally, but required the authority of the senior manager. One of the leaders of a cost centre described the emerging difficulties and conflicts to find an optimal load rate of technology, especially when all three cost centres required a specific machine at the same time, as follows:

> Sometimes we all need the same machine simultaneously. And we all face enormous pressure to meet a deadline. Then there emerges the question which of the three cost centres will receive priority. However, all have solid arguments as to why they should be given priority. Here cooperation is necessary, but for this reason often not possible ... At this point we often must consult our senior manager who has the final in such matters (Interview, 2b/1).

In other interviews lower-level managers and employees spoke of problems relative to a decline in voluntary and mutual support between the cost centres.

In the past, spontaneous cooperation within the production process used to be quite common, but now it was often seen as problematic even for meeting their own narrow efficiency goals within each cost centre. The decline of established support networks and the appearance of an egoistical cost centre mentality made the established slack resources appear costly. As in case study A, any cooperation that went beyond the operational requirements came to be viewed as a 'waste' of time and resources.

However, even if local management recognised these obvious shortcomings of a too tight interpretation of the function of the three different cost centres, they also stressed the advantages of this organisational principle when the firm was confronted with other emerging market uncertainties. The cost centre structure of the firm was seen as problematic even when all cost centres could not keep up with the demands of its services, but was considered beneficial when each cost centre had different order demands. In the interviews the managers emphasised the flexibility of the firm as a whole to support one another when one cost centre had a backlog of orders and another had a decline in orders. Because of the establishment of multiple skills, in such situations each cost centre was able to take over jobs from one another. Unspecified resources in the form of broad skills became an organisational slack resource that enabled a flexible adaptation to the uncertainties of the market.

In comparison to the other two case studies, the development of organisational goals in firm C was more open. The management and work processes were less specialised and a greater chance existed to integrate new project ideas. The project goals were less fixed and shifted over time. In this case study the relationship between complex learning and the creation of organisational slack resources becomes evident. The actors did not know which of their project ideas would be successful in the end. They developed a surplus of diverse social relations to potential sponsors and other actors within the local community. They presented their project ideas in meetings and discussions with the members of local firms, the job centre and other regional actors, and thereby tested and redefined the original project goals.

Thus, the existence and creation of organisational slack was essential, but not sufficient for more complex learning processes. Complex learning processes developed because of the ambiguity of goals and the ongoing necessity to redefine them. In the other two case studies organisational slack appeared to be a problem of organisational design. All social relations which were not seen as necessary to meet the tight production goals were questioned. The introduction of new management concepts were used to streamline the production process and to find out which tasks and activities were unnecessary in order to fulfil these narrow goals. Similar problems emerged as the local management in firm B introduced the cost centres. Established modes of spontaneous and more informal cooperation between actors from different levels and subunits of the organisation became invalidated. Thus, the tightening of organisational goals led to the reduction of organisational slack resources and a lower complexity of the learning process.

In the case study C, the emerging relationship between complex learning and organisational slack becomes evident. Because the actors had open project goals, they could not define beforehand which of their social relations were unnecessary. This became evident at the end when a project was successfully realised or spun-off, at which time the actors were able to explain what the slack resources looked like which enabled complex and further learning.

The lower level of goal and resource specificity allows for more experimental and open learning approaches than in the other two case studies. The local manager responsible for the project organisation explained that after the start of a project, modifications of the original project ideas were possible. In his view, the development of viable projects was not cost-centred or directed to a specific outcome in the first place. In an interview he stressed the importance of trial and error learning which also involves giving up particular projects: 'It is not tragic when one particular project failed. If we find out that there is no market or possibility for permanent sponsorship for a new project, we have to make a decision' (Interview, 2c/1).

Contrary to the other two case studies, the creation of organisational slack is not a problem of organisational design, but of lower goal specificity. The comparison of the three case studies shows that the definition of clear goals for organisational development and the establishment of mechanisms to control its outcome made a surplus of time, functions and skills appear costly. The loose specification of the projects in firm C did not allow for the development of clear cost-benefit analysis. However, such an analysis was indeed crucial for finding out in which markets the firm and its projects were more likely to survive. In contrast to the other two case studies, public financing led to the integration of specific employees who had a lower productive capacity. However, the problem of firm C was to maintain its more experimental organisational learning modes, because of the increasing impact of public interest to integrate a problematic workforce into the firm's projects. The firm experienced problems in finding a skilled workforce to develop creative projects because it had to operate in a region suffering from social and economic decline, a problem that was only aggravated by the reduced public sponsorship.

It can be summarised that the complexity of organisational learning and the access to established or created organisational slack resources depends upon the openness of the organisational goals. The focus on competition in mass markets, as we observed in case study A, led to tightly controlled management strategies that sought to decrease production costs. The orientation to customer specific markets we could see in case study B required less defined goals that were more open for modification within the whole organising process and less controllable. On the other hand, the introduction of internal market relations hindered internal coordination processes between the semi-autonomous cost centres. In case study C the creation of sustainable projects and the choice to spin-off profitable projects required wide-open organisational goals. This left room for an ongoing redefinition of the methods to acquire resources, modify the project organisation and increase the organisation's adaptability to the shifting and ambiguous environmental demands.

Table 5.6   The role of organisational slack resources within the process of organisational learning

	Case study A	**Case study B**	**Case study C**
The role of organisational slack within the organisational learning process	close production goals and tight modes of control mean that unspecified resources appear as 'waste'	the introduction of internal cost centres means that spontaneous and voluntary cooperation appear costly	the openness of project goals means that organisational slack appears a valuable resource

5.2.7 Organisational Learning as a Planned and Pragmatic Process

Students of organisational learning seem to overestimate the voluntary quality of learning and acting. However, from the perspective adopted here organisational learning is more an emergent process than a reflexive one as is often assumed. We will therefore not focus our discussion as much on how actors realise well-established management strategies, but rather more on how these strategies were formed in the first place. We assume that the concentration on planning, designing and analysing prevents an understanding of the particular quality of organisational learning as a process. From our perspective, the emergence of innovation and adaptation is not purely the outcome of explicit programmes and plans, but rather the result of pragmatic or less reflexive learning approaches. There are two leading questions in this section:

1) what was the meaning of planning in the development of each organisation; and 2) how were these planning approaches linked to more pragmatic modes of organising (chapter 2, pp. 35–6 and chapter 3, pp. 64)?

Operational planning played a major role in case study A. In contrast to the other two case studies, the attempts to realise and improve the planned organisational outcome was at the centre of the whole management process. Even when critical events such as the decline of established markets and change of ownership occurred, local management saw no reason to more actively attempt to understand their task environment. As in the past, local managers preferred conventional interpretations of the environment. In spite of all the changes, local management interpreted the environment largely as stable and predictable. So, quantitative data and formal knowledge appeared to be more essential for the firm's performance then the personal experience and tacit knowledge of the employees.

In the discussion with one of the leading CEOs about the newly implemented organisational concepts, it became evident that the creation of teams was seen as an instrument to improve the firm's productivity. To the question whether the narrow and technologically controlled work tasks within the work teams had not been given up or modified, the respondent answered in the negative. He stressed that the growth of the firm's performance was not so much a question of the reorganisation of teamwork, but more a question of effective calculation. This opinion was elaborated further as follows:

> The question here is not whether or not to alter the design of our assembly lines. When I look at the attempts by other firms to take alternative paths, I am disillusioned. They all failed, because they did not meet the requirements of an increased outcome. All organisational or technological modifications must be measurable. I require serious facts and figures (Interview, 2a/1).

This is a clear example of decision-making and planning as process of rational calculation based on quantitative data. This tight focus on formal knowledge led to the underestimation of informal modes of organising and related social practices which cannot be measured as scientific data. It can be said that management attempts to increase intended outcomes hindered strategic learning. This means that we can assume that learning in case study A occurred whenever technical control, fixed work schemes and tight work routines broke down or lost their meaning. This is well reflected in interviews on the shop floor in particular in the employees' description of how they were capable of beating the system. Moreover, the increase of absenteeism on the shop floor can be interpreted as a kind of subversive behaviour and reaction to the attempts of local management to tighten the technological control in the manufacturing process. It can be summarised that in firm A new forms of organisational learning did occur in spite of the attempts to secure some degree of self-regulation of work within and between the teams.[9]

In case study B planning had a different meaning than in firm A. In contrast to firm A, the actors in both firms B and firm C had to be much more active in order to penetrate the environment. They failed to establish certain departments and standardised mechanisms to discover the environment or to plan internal operations. After the former internal department was transformed into a profit centre, the actors could not behave in the same passive way they were used to and simply wait for instructions. As newcomers in the market environment they had less experience in marketing themselves. Instead, they sought to test out what could be feasible in the new market environment.

In both firms, processes to discover the task environment were much more informal and non-systematic. Actors saw the environment not as something given to which they only had to respond, but one that they could influence; something which required tacit knowledge and which was based on informal processes of organising. In firm B the leading manager described this certain situation as follows:

> We were newcomers and could not wait for the customers to come to us and ask for our services and products. We always understood that we must go to them, find out what they want, offer our service and show competence (Interview, 1b/3).

According to these open and strong customer-oriented strategic arrangements, the operational activities were less formally planned and centralised. However, the steady pressure to act and work closely with their customers made planning difficult and left more space for learning. Moreover, possibilities to routinise and formalise discovering procedures were small because all three subunits produced unique and less standardised products. Each of the three cost centres tried to discover its own task environment and make its own tests on how to introduce themselves to their potential customers.

The quality of the products and the variety of customers made it less possible to calculate the outcome. That is why learning occurred not so much in spite of planning as had been in the case study A, but more as a requirement that was to compensate for the lack of possibilities in the operational planning process.

The problematic relationship between learning and consciously calculating outcomes became evident as the development of strained cost centre arrangements blocked the established rather than the emergent forms of mutual support and cooperation between and within the three subunits. The calculation of internal outcomes within each cost centre devaluated former informal relations, and boundaries between the cost centres appeared to be obligatory.

In comparison to the other two case studies, operational planning in case study C played the most subordinated role in organisational development. Moreover, opportunities for long-term strategic planning seldom arose and mostly in such situations where the actors were responding to external pressures to present accurate explanations about the quality and the future of their projects. Operational planning became important when the firm decided to spin-off one of its projects. Then local management had to define a basic strategy, to develop work schemes and to decide which employee would be the member of this new organisation.

Compared to the other two case studies, the enacting of the environment was the most comprehensive. This means that the actors' assumptions about the environment were less pronounced and more open to experimentation. In contrast to firm A which tried to improve the effectiveness of the firm in its traditional task environment and contrary to firm B which searched for ways to establish the former internal department as a semi-autonomous profit centre within a market niche, the actors in firm C learned in a more pragmatic way. They had lower expectations about their future tasks or possibilities in the market and gathering quantitative data made less sense. Instead of developing more or less elaborated modes of strategic and operational planning, the actors tried out new behaviour and tried to make sense of what was happening. For them experimentation often meant ignoring customary and fixed rules and expectations about the outcome of their actions.

> To realise new ideas you often have to give up common expectations. Developing projects where you cannot really be sure whether they will succeed, often means you have to try things in you are very inexperienced. And for this we cannot always check the legal situation. Had we always acted politically and legally correct, we would not have been able to develop new projects. We would simply not exist anymore (Interview, 2c/2).

Even when one of their projects appeared in retrospect to be successful or when actors were asked to define certain outcomes they began to reflect and develop strategic explanations. The discussed pragmatic learning approaches that are at the centre of our argument were mainly developed through the evolution of personal networks to local actors and organisations. This led to a relatively open search for feasible project ideas, possible partners and likely sponsors.

The management approaches in firm C to create viable projects and small business firms can instead be understood not so much as systematic trial and error processes but rather as reflexive learning modes. With such a pragmatic orientation the actors tested which of their projects could be extended in a more systematic way in the future. However, pragmatic and systematic learning approaches were not separated from each other as in the other two case studies, they were instead dialectically linked. In order to secure the pragmatic development of their projects, the firm had to show that they were able to develop into small business firms capable of surviving on their profits alone. The actors had to demonstrate on the basis of hard data and work schemes that they had learned to produce efficient outcomes.

The comparison of the three case studies indicates that the pragmatic learning approaches extended from case study A through case study B to case study C. The affinity to planning blocked pragmatic learning approaches. Those approaches appeared in a rather hidden and subversive manner. The discussion of all case studies shows that overestimation of formal data made tests and experimentation appear to be costly. But in case studies B and C the actors' need to introduce themselves in a relatively unknown task environment provided a reason for more pragmatic learning approaches. In both case studies informal and tacit knowledge was the key to organisational learning. However, in case study B trial and error principles in the learning process were both more directed and more systematic. Not operational planning, but the development of cost-conscious subunits made modes of learning appear problematic that had previously tended to be of a more pragmatic nature.

Table 5.7 Organisational learning as a planned and pragmatic process

	Case study A	Case study B	Case study C
The relation between planning and pragmatism within the process of learning	preference for planning made pragmatism appear subordinated	undefined relationship between planning and pragmatism	preference for pragmatism makes planning secondary

5.3   Summary

The systematic comparison of the three studies has shown that the quality and nature of organisational learning processes is quite different in each case study. Contrary to common assumptions of organisational learning approaches, the process cannot be understood simply from the micro-perspective of individuals 'learning to learn' within an organisational context. Moreover, our comparison shows that it is not sufficient to deduce the properties of organisational learning from the macro-structures of society as neo-institutionalists indicate. From the enactment perspective introduced here we have seen that the structure and development of internal and external relations between actors and groups of actors were quite different in each case study.

The development of organisational capabilities of learning how to learn can be understood in part as 'relational learning'. The relational 'style' becomes visible to the extent to which the activities are connected and in how different experiences become involved in the learning process. The relational 'strength' is dependent upon the social tightness of the internal and external relations (Weick and Roberts, 1996; Weick and Westley, 1996). An appropriate synopsis of the discussion in the last seven sections would be that the openness of relational learning processes becomes ever more narrows from case study C through case study B to case study A. According to the argumentation above it can be seen that in case studies B and C the style as well as the strength of relational learning shifted. In these case studies the openness of organisational learning was much broader than in case study A.

The argument of this chapter shows that organisational learning cannot be discussed without consideration of the institutional arrangements which were stabilised and/or modified within this process. The sensitivity of organisational learning processes increase when the actors develop more socially coupled internal and external relations. When the process of organisational learning was more open, actors had increasing possibilities to make sense of new emerging problems. Relational learning that transformed the traditional forms of organisational learning was not limited to an individual organisation, but embedded in various externally oriented action networks.

In other words, the style and the strength of the relational learning approaches were driven by the institutional micro-dynamic corresponding in particular to how traditional forms of organisational learning had been stabilised and had shifted. According to the changes in the institutional order, traditional beliefs, narrow expectations and long-established modes of organising can lose some of their influence as in firm B and mainly in firm C, or they can be strengthened as in firm A.

Notes

1   For the assembly of car headlights, the firm uses various types of steel reflectors (depending on the product design) they made themselves, or synthetic reflectors made at the multinational's West German base.
2   In section 4.3 it was documented that the legitimacy of the firm was continuously endangered by various interest groups outside the organisation (chapter 4, pp. 110–13).
3   The traditional distribution of work was also no longer suitable because of the massive reduction in employment. See section 4.2 (chapter 4, pp. 96–100).
4   As we discussed in section 4.3, the parent subsequently lost public sponsorship and most of its projects came to an end. With the agreement of the main sponsors, local management took over the leadership of both companies and the remaining projects of the parent company (chapter 4, pp. 110–13).
5   The tough position of the holding's works council is only understandable, when one takes into consideration the massive reduction in personnel in this case.
6   See section 4.3 (chapter 4, pp. 104–21).
7   See section 4.1 (chapter 4, pp. 79–83).
8   See section 4.3 (chapter 4, pp. 117–19).
9   See section 4.1 (chapter 4, pp. 79–85).

6 Intertwining Organisational Learning and Institutional Settings

6.1 Introduction

In this concluding chapter we will discuss the advantages of the enactment perspective and in doing so also review our empirical findings within the context of our introductory critique of organisational learning and neo-institutionalist approaches. We will thereby focus on our initial thesis concerning the social embeddedness of organisational learning processes.

Despite having highlighted the idea of bringing society back into the analysis of organisational learning, we have criticised neo-institutionalist concepts for their static view about the relationship between macro-structures and micro-processes. The examination of the role of institutions in the process of organisational learning from an enactment perspective as undertaken in this study, goes beyond mere generalisations about the dominant role of macro-institutions and how they impact upon the outcome of organisational learning. To continue the argumentation of the previous chapter that institutional environments are less homogeneous and compelling than neo-institutionalism assumes, in the next sections we want to reconsider how micro-level learning activities in organisations are intertwined with institutional settings on the macro-level of society (Orton 1996; Weick 1993). Despite having agreed with neo-institutionalist scholars that institutions always have an extra-organisational nature (Meyer and Rowan, 1992, pp. 21–44; DiMaggio and Powell, 1991b, pp. 63–82), from our point of view the degree to which environmental conditions become more objective in nature in the ongoing processes of organising can be determined neither in advance nor in the abstract. Institutionalisation at the macro-level of society cannot be divorced from micro events emerging through interactive learning processes and is therefore an important focus of analysis for empirical research of organisational behaviour.

We started this study with a detailed critique of the voluntary definition of organisational learning. Here it is argued that managers can simply choose to transform their firm by switching from single-loop learning to double-loop learning (Argyris and Schön, 1978; Senge et al., 1990). The crucial point is that individual choice has been overestimated and less consideration paid to the role of institutions. In organisational learning approaches, institutions either block the transformation of traditional organisational forms into learning organisations, or they are not seen as relevant for higher-level learning loops. Accordingly, the discussion in the conceptual chapter can be summarised as follows: when students of organisational learning overvalue choice, neo-institutionalists simply argue that managers have nothing from which to choose.

The primary arguments in the discussion about organisational learning as illustrated in the conceptual chapter are considered universally applicable. However, in the last chapter we have seen that their meanings can be interpreted quite differently depending upon the social context. Thus, through the application of our enactment concept, we have seen that different institutional frameworks led to an increase or decrease in strategic choices (Child, 1972). We have summarised these arguments employing the concept of relational learning and illustrated that modes of relational learning in each company were different in style and strength.

The purpose of the concluding chapter is to review the dialectical relationship between organisational learning and institutions more generally. For this we will move our emphasis from the more elementary question of whether there is choice or no choice to the more tangible question of this study of how the actors in each case study actually developed opportunities and constraints to learn more openly. From this position we distinguish in section 6.2 three institutional tensions. On the basis of our empirical material, and so to speak as a completion to the discussion of the previous chapter, we recognised: 1) the tension between traditional and novel tasks (old and new); 2) the tension between homogeneous and heterogeneous knowledge creation (open and closed systems); and 3) the tension between intended and non-intended forms of organisational learning (theory and practice). Instead of seeing organisational learning as improvement over individual learning in a singular organisation, as a continuous improvement process or as planning process, we will turn our attention to the institutional nature of organisational learning processes. Thus, we will come back to our critique that beyond the undersocialised view of common organisational learning approaches there seems to be dialectical tensions between organisational learning and institutionalisation. As we will see, the actors dealt with each of these three institutional tensions in an empirically different manner and in doing so applied modes of learning not recognised in the common debate over organisational learning, such as creative forgetting, learning through networking or learning from side-effects.

The variance between our three companies in dealing with these institutional tensions in their learning processes shows the significance of the local cultural system. This is the topic of section 6.3. Here we again highlight the advantages of the applied enactment perspective by contrasting our approach with some key arguments of neo-institutionalism. In this section we will pay closer attention to the micro-dynamics between the observed forms of organisational learning and their degree of institutionalisation. Therefore, we will illustrate that what people know and how well they know it has to do with the dissimilarities of the actors' awareness of the significance of their cultural system, with the dissimilarities in how they socially construct it and with the dissimilarities of how temporary it sometimes can be. As we will see, all these aspects have consequences for how actors and groups of actors learn with and about each other.

We will conclude this chapter with some general reflections in the final section (6.4) about the benefits of an institutional framework for the analysis of organisational learning processes and suggest to compare the paths of organisational learning. We hope that the research results of this study have shown the necessity to replace mainstream research practices which are mainly interested in specifying the relationship among abstracted concepts such as the learning organisation to improve organisational effectiveness.

6.2   Institutional Tensions in Processes of Organisational Learning and their Impact on the Micro-macro Problem

6.2.1   The Tension Between Traditional and Novel Tasks

In the conceptual part we have shown that the idea of the learning organisation assumes that actors who dispose over more and more detailed knowledge are able to act more successful. We also demonstrated that those organisational systems that are capable of developing systematic learning cycles are in a better position compared with other organisations that are less capable of learning in a regular or systematic way. Our initial expectation was that the more a certain organisation knows and the quicker it learns, the more successful it will be. However, the systematic comparison of our three companies did not support this view about the new 'one best way' to develop a prosperous enterprise. In contrast to conventional organisational learning approaches, we found that the openness of learning emerged not through a better understanding of the learning context, but through the dialectic between traditional organisational behaviour and the capacity of a firm to be open to new tasks. This process depends upon institutional dynamics; the stability as well as the breakdown of the established institutional arrangements.

Similarly to Bechtle (1998) who observed the problematic relationship between organisation and innovation in the West German region of Baden-Württemberg we came to the conclusion in all our case studies, albeit decreasing from case study A through case study B and case study C, the 'strong presence of the past' hindered more open organisational learning processes. As we saw the orientation on past experiences and on instituted *learning recipes* was quite strong in case study A but much weaker in the other two case study. Traditionally enterprise A favoured technology, specialisation and the production of high quality products for the mass market. At the centre of its organisational development were accuracy, stability and high technological standards. As in the past the highly standardised production tasks were seen as central for the *identity construction* of the firm. Reorganisation was not focused on development of new skills and *learning recipes*, but on securing a stable production process. As in the past organisational learning was mainly concentrated on securing a continuous output and not on making sense about new emerging challenges. The learning processes of local managers and employees were locked into traditional user-producer relationships.

Contrary to the other two case studies the shifting of ownership did not lead to decline or convulsion of established institutional arrangements. The reorganisation of the firm included the closure and outsourcing of some departments and product lines after the firm was taken over by the new owners. This did not lead to more open learning approaches but to the optimisation of the traditional manufacturing tasks. Rather than developing or starting new jobs as in the other two case studies, the focus of management activities consisted of improving traditional tasks of enterprise A.

In case study B the disintegration of the established institutional settings did not support the implementation of systematic *learning recipes*. After the decline of the large combines, the actors where confronted with the unfamiliar situation of having to attract customers in an unknown market environment. They could not develop the same closeness to the traditional ways of organising as in case study A. The customers were not seen as anonymous partners that expect a well-calculated number of products with a certain quality.

In firm B the actors recombined the established modes of internal coordination and cooperation to deal with the new market environment. The reconstruction of the firm's *identity* was not directed towards the systematic refinement of the established modes of organising as in case study A, but towards the reassembling of the established *learning recipes*. The past learnt organisational behaviour such as informal strategies to circumvent absurd administrative orders or to avoid extra jobs lost weight and were modified. In this sense the opening of the firm to new tasks did not improve the established processes of knowledge creation as conventional organisational learning approaches assumes. Rather, the process of organisational learning went hand in hand with the recombination of past *learning recipes* and work routines. It became clear that the new knowledge was not institutionally supported, did not fit into the established cultural context and tended to be forgotten or ignored (Douglas, 1991, pp. 113–2; Johnson, 1992, pp. 23–44). Just as had been the case in firm A, the implementation of continuous improvement process ideas in firm B did not encourage workers to participate more directly and the internal cost centre came to be questioned. The novel tasks of customisation required not only more external cooperation with the customers, but also the development of more discursive internal coordination. However, right here the cost centre logic led to the dilemma that the internal development of cost awareness gave birth to the decline of the established modes of spontaneous internal collaboration.

In case study C we could observe the largest tension between tradition and an openness for new tasks in the organisational learning process. The breakdown of traditional institutional settings led to loss of traditional institutional securities. The long-established skills and competencies of the employees lost their value with the decline of their traditional jobs. The question here was not the implementation of well-established *learning recipes* as in case study A, nor could one observe an attempt to transform existing recipes into established socially tight user-producer-relations. The learning processes which emerged in case study C did not so much aim to accomplish a certain market goal such as high quality production for mass consumption or for specific customers. Contrary to case study A where management tried to refine the past routines to secure the firm's presence in the traditional market and contrary to case study B where the management tried to recombine the profitable competencies to attract customers in a certain market niche, the actors in firm C began to develop new activities. For this relatively unfamiliar task the actors had less institutionalised *learning recipes*. The *identity construction* of the firm was not directly linked to economic success, but to the relatively open learning goal of creating jobs. In this sense the economic success of a certain project was ambiguous in the beginning and not immediately calculable. The insecurity about the economic success and the relatively inexperienced realisation led to rather experimental learning approaches. This rather *pragmatic learning* approach emerged neither through the refining of the established *learning recipes* as in case study A nor through their customisation as in case study B, but through learning by doing.

The preceding discussion has shown that the tension between the retaining of traditional tasks and the opening for new tasks is linked with the evolution and the dynamics of the institutions. The decline and breakdown of institutional settings forced the actors to engage in more open learning approaches. In the case studies B and C the actors learned to deal with the *discontinuity* of the new situation (section 5.2.5). Contrary to case study A where adaptive learning modes were seen as sufficient, in the other two case studies interactive search and learning processes appeared. In case study B the actors had to develop viable customer relations by themselves after the former combine was transformed into an industrial holding. The social competencies, developed in the past, were transformed and recombined to meet specific requirements of the customers. In case study A in contrast to the other two case studies, the emerging modes of organisational learning appeared to be very close to the firm's traditional tasks. Although that the ownership relations shifted and that a part of the traditional markets in Eastern Europe declined, the established institutional arrangements remained relatively unchanged. More open search and learning approaches were not considered or seen as a function of particular specialised departments within the industrial group such as R&D or the centralised sales organisation.

In case study C on the other hand the tension with the past was far more pronounced than in case study A and B. The process of learning was more closely coupled to practical experimentation. The planning of actions and their routinisation appeared to be difficult. In this case it was not that important to refine original plans or adjust them to the requirements of a certain group of customers. Instead the actors learned retrospectively how to modify and reinvent their original project ideas to empower the firm's further development.

On the basis of this evidence, one could conclude that the tension between traditional and new tasks in institution building does not only influence how organisations learn, but also how they forget. Moreover it seems to be the case that the openness for new tasks is more related to ignoring the established organisational knowledge base rather than improving it. In the conventional literature these aspects are often discussed as a problem of unlearning. It is assumed that the learning of novel tasks requires unlearning. In this context it is argued that learning and unlearning are problem triggered, for example after standard operating procedures break down (Hedberg et al., 1981) The question of organisational learning tends to be discussed as a mere problem of design. Organisational design is seen as the key to systematic learning aimed at generating new knowledge and 'to adjust and update existing knowledge'. 'Unlearning abilities are needed in order to make room for more adequate interpretative frameworks and responses in organisational memory' (ibid., pp. 19–20). However, from the perspective adopted in this study, the term 'unlearning' can be better understood as forgetting and ignoring. Not only do we ask how actors purposefully unlearn a certain organisational behaviour, but also how institutionalised forms of organising led them to forget habits and traditions and ignore emerging risks in the process of developing new tasks.

In the comparison of our three case studies we have seen that the openness for novel tasks cannot be compared with an intentional discovery process. Instead the emergence of more open learning approaches and the forgetting of established ways of thinking and acting are driven by the dialectic between the decline of established institutional arrangements and the building of new ones. In this sense organisational learning cannot be understood as a cumulative process which delivers more detailed information about a certain problem and increases the organisation's knowledge base. And 'unlearning' cannot be understood as deleting a certain amount of past learned behaviour in order to increase the firm's flexibility. We have seen that only knowledge which is institutionally supported is developed further and refined as in case study A, and that the decline of institutional stability influenced the processes of forgetting as in the case studies B and C (Douglas, 1991; Johnson, 1992). In case study A the reorganisation process was seen traditionally as the improvement of the firm's technical core and its functions. In this sense the implementation of teamwork was not understood as a process that gives more space for direct participation and self-organisation, but as an attempt to optimise production processes. Team orientated production was not directed to the humanising of the work organisation, but to improve its output. The perfection of the established modes of organising involved forgetting and ignoring implicit learning potentials.

We have seen that the retaining of a certain organisational domain with its well-established modes of competition and customer relations led to rather customary forms of learning and forgetting. In case study A forgetting played a functional role in the management's attempts to optimise the production process in order to increase competition within the established organisational domain. Functions and departments which did not fit this task were closed. The remaining activities within the firm were focused on the continuous improvement of the production task. In the other two firms the decline of established institutional settings, the ambiguity about the future ownership of the firm and the market situation did not support the development of more systematic forms of forgetting, but led to the development of forgetting patterns which Johnson (1992, pp. 29–30) has called 'creative forgetting'. With 'creative forgetting' the author meant that institutional forgetting can be reasonably proactive. Learning and forgetting can as in case study A be directed along the established technological trajectories or it can be more orientated to develop and do different things as in case study C. In this enterprise the decline of traditional institutional arrangements did lead to more radical learning attempts which not only led to the forgetting of past learned habits and routines, but also involved more than in the other two case studies a certain ignorance about the risks at stake and the ambivalence of the output. In case study B the ties between traditional and novel tasks are closer than in case study C, but contrary to case study A the search for new market segments involved forgetting and more radically learning approaches. The loss of traditional user-producer-relations led to the recombination of established work routines and to the creation of new customer relations.

Contrary to common arguments about learning organisations and their improved capabilities to develop systems thinking (Senge, 1990) or their well-directed interventions that seek to uncover and defeat internal learning blockages (Argyris and Schön, 1996), ignorance somehow seems to deal with institutional dynamics and its ambiguities. In case study A we have seen that the actors tried to avoid interruptions and failures. At the centre was the improvement of the established routines and procedures. But in the other two case studies the actors learned to deal with the *discontinuities* of the institutional environment. Especially in case study C organisational learning was not guided by elaborated *learning recipes* that were to regulate avoiding the failures and interruptions as was the case in firm A. The opening for such novel tasks as the realisation of uncertain project ideas required to ignore to a certain degree the risks and failures that could be faced during the realisation of a project. These processes are reminiscent of Albert Hirschman's observation regarding the initiation of developmental projects in the developing countries. Like Weick (1995b) he has pointed to the retrospective nature of 'making sense' and the impossibility to calculate and plan creative learning modes:

Creativity always comes as a surprise to us; therefore we can never count on it and we dare not believe in it until it has happened. In other words, we would not consciously engage upon task whose success clearly requires that creativity be forthcoming. Hence, the only way we can bring our creative resources fully into play is by misjudging the nature of the task, by presenting it ourselves as more routine, simple, undemanding of genuine creativity than it will turn out to be (Hirschman, 1967, p. 13).

This argument is supported by our empirical findings in case study C and allows us to argue that actors did not simply ignore or play down the risks of a certain project to themselves. They also learned to present themselves as more routinised and competent to their relevant partners in order to gain the necessary support and resources. Overlooking some important problems and the redefining of their original project ideas were both the result of past and precondition for future learning.

It can be concluded that organisational learning processes that are developed in tension to the traditional task environment have less to do with continuous perfection of the organisation's knowledge base or the development of accurate *learning recipes*, than with the 'art of ignoring' (Kühl, 2000; Luhmann, 1999). Moreover, the comparison of the case studies showed that the 'creative forgetting' of traditional modes of organising and openness for novel tasks is not a question of improving reflexive learning modes (Senge, 1990) or of improving the speed of organisational learning (Wildemann, 1996), but of practising. Following Weick (1995a and 1995b) we can even argue that when organisations act without detailed plans or when they act in a confused or discontinuous way they learn to make sense retrospectively of the outcomes of their actions. The association of organisational learning with acting also refers to Marx's understanding of practice. A reinterpretation of his eleventh Feuerbach-thesis (1985)[1] could be that understanding a social reality is less important than changing it as organisations are produced by actors who learn and forget through acting.

6.2.2   The Tension Between Homogenous and Heterogeneous Knowledge Creation

In the conceptual part we mentioned that debates about organisational learning emphasise the intentional modification of the particular organisational design. The creation of learning organisations is mainly seen as a problem of internal design and of optimal fit. However, from an institutional perspective it is problematic to distinguish between the formal organisation as a learning system and its particular environment. If one considers the role of institutions and institutionalisation in the organisational learning process, one can question to what extent organisations can be adequately explained as systems with predictable actors (Sorge, 1996, pp. 3793–810). We saw that the notion that learning goals, organisational design, boundaries and other patterns are fixed only seem to be convincing in the case of firm A. In the case studies B and C the learning goals and recipes were continuously modified and developed further. Even in case study A organisational learning could not be interpreted as a completely functional process. However, contrary to the other two case studies the nonfunctional learning modes were not seen as opportunities to develop more creative modes of organising, but as interruptions of the well-established internal designing processes.[2]

The thesis of this section is that organisational learning involves more homogeneous or heterogeneous knowledge creation processes. In this sense we would like to ask why and how in firm A knowledge creation appeared to be rather homogenous, whereas in the other two case studies this processes appeared to be rather heterogeneous. We also would like to address the implication of this for the processes of organisational learning in each case study. The discussion of our three case studies shows that organisational learning involving an openness for novel tasks requires more intensive external collaboration and partnering than learning process whereby organisations try to exploit the tasks in which they are traditionally successful.

We have seen that the knowledge creation process of firm A can be characterised as a more or less homogenous *identity construction*. The development of internal and external modes of organising was limited to a clear mission. Other activities which were less institutionalised, such as the small-scale production of headlights for motorbikes were interpreted as secondary for the firm's further development. As we saw, the focus on optimising established modes of organising led to a certain neglect of *organisational slack resources*. All these activities that were not directed to the improvement of production output were seen as too costly or were considered unnecessary. Direct participation in decision-making processes was less developed. Instead the guarantee of formal *participation* rights was to assure the avoidance of interruptions of the foremost production tasks. In this sense it was shown that learning from the *experience of others* was closely related to the improvement of internal processes.

The closeness of organisational development to production tasks was embedded in more or less narrow producer-user relations. On the one hand, the firm was seen as a competent supplier of car headlights and no more. On the other hand, the firm presented itself as a competent supplier of one particular product. Other activities were seen as supplementary, not as an opportunity for the future development of the firm.

With the support of the new owners, the firm was able to hold on to and extend its position in the highly competitive car supplier market, this in spite of the decline of the traditional markets in Eastern Europe. Internal and external forms of collaboration even if modified, were not changed in any substantial way. After the change of ownership the stated aim of the firm's reorganisation consisted of a reduction of the production process to its core activities. Contrary to the other two case studies, one can describe the learning process in case study A as rather exploitative, internally centred and homogenous. Exploitative because the learning process focused upon the refinement and extension of existing competencies, technologies and paradigms (March, 1996, pp. 102–4). The learning process was *internally* centred because there existed a clear dichotomy between the importance of internal knowledge, closely related to the production process, and the relevance of external knowledge, less related to these traditional tasks. External impulses for learning came foremost from a familiar community of actors including customers of the firm as well as its competitors in the same market segment (Bechtle, 1998). In this sense one can say that organisational learning led mainly to a relatively homogenous improvement of the established knowledge base. At the centre of organisational learning was the stable production of a relatively homogenous product for a well-known group of customers. Like in the past the interrelations to suppliers and customers remained limited to technological improvement of the product quality.

In this specific institutional context organisational learning was primarily seen as a design problem. Only in this case one could observe the consistent learning system predicted by conventional learning approaches. However, contrary to the mainstream debate, the learning process observed was limited to a certain institutional context which was more exploitative, internally centred and relatively homogenous. In the other two case studies the attempt to distinguish between a single learning unit as the organisational learning system and its outer environment appeared to be misleading. Here the process of organisational learning appeared not so much as a design problem, but as a problem of a heterogeneous largely externalised knowledge creation process. This study like earlier investigations (Powell et al., 1996; Bechtle, 1998; Hustad, 1998) indicates that the potential of an enterprise to be open towards new modes of knowledge creation does not seem to reside exclusively inside one single organisation. The locus of innovation should not be looked for in the formal organisation of the firm, but in the interorganisational networks of learning (Powell et al., 1996, pp. 116–45).

In the other two firms collective learning activities were contrary to case study A not directed to refine a certain organisational design, but more intended to put into practice which meant becoming a practitioner (ibid., p. 118). The process of learning was not directed to the improvement of a particular practice, but towards the learning of new practices through their active development. The learning unit was not the learning organisation. The development of novel tasks took place in the context of a more heterogeneous process of knowledge creation. Networking and external collaboration played an important role which enabled the actors in both firms to deal with the new situation after established institutional settings started to decline.

However, the way in which the actors dealt with the problem of more heterogeneous knowledge creation was different. The focus of the institution building in case study B was directed to the development of decentral modes of decision-making and the customisation the former centrally guided internal department. In firm C on the other hand the institutional decline was much more comprehensive. The chances to follow a certain structure of tradition as in the other two case studies was lower. However, the process of organisational learning did not start from scratch: the firm used the established institutional framework of another well-established job creation centre as a basis for its own organisational development. Moreover, the firm never gave up the close relationship with the former employer, the hydraulics company. Similarly to case study B the learning process was driven mainly by the intensive development of interorganisational relations (section 5.2.1).

On the basis of these findings one can conclude that the ways of learning to learn or deutero-learning in these cases appears not as self-centred designing, but as a process of *learning through networking*. The development of internal learning capabilities for building and utilising new knowledge seems to be socially closely linked to the development of external collaboration.

We saw that in case study B the process of organisational learning was mainly orientated towards the search and creation of socially close customers' relationships. Learning *from the experience of others* meant mainly the creation of cooperative partner relations with its customers. However, the intensive collaboration between firm B and its customers not only meant a compensation for the lack of internal *organisational slack* resources, but learning the practice of networking. Internal and external coordination was not, like it used to be, centrally *planned* nor was it guided by well-established *learning recipes* as was the case in firm A. Instead, it was more discursive and relied on less formal rules or routines. In firm C the process of organisational learning was contrary to the other two case studies neither driven by the calculated development of the organisational design nor by customisation. Instead the firm's development was more intertwined with the problems of the region. In this sense *learning from the experience* of others was largely related to the creation of regional partnerships. The acquisition of project ideas, their realisation and the spinning-off of small businesses were managed through the development of broad interrelations with heterogeneous communal actors, such as the former employer, the hydraulics company, the local job centre, other job creation centres, etc. For the development of the firm it was not so much important to develop more or less formal modes of internal *participation*, but to create participatory relationships with external partners which originated in different spheres of the community. Whereas in firm A the learning community was composed quite homogeneously close to the car industry, in the case studies B and C the *networks of learning* turned out to be more open to actors with distinct experiences from different social spheres. However, at the same time there appeared the problem of developing a common perception towards an inventive solution for combining the diverse interests of the various actors so that they could do something together. It can be concluded that heterogeneous knowledge creation that emerged in the process of organisational learning was derived from a greater institutional diversity. That diversity emerged because of the decline of established interrelations. In case study B the former internal department of a large industrial group was transformed into a semi-autonomous profit centre. This led to the emergence of explorative learning activities. These can be contrasted with the exploitative learning activities that we observed in case study A. The established flexible work routines and specific skills appeared to be a solid bedrock for the development customer-oriented products such as a particular tool, a machine or a robot. However, specialisation of the internal cost centres led to problems of internal coordination that resulted in conflicts. Heterogeneous knowledge creation in this case implied that each cost centre was specialised in addressing the needs of particular customers. This in turn led to problems of developing an overlapping vision for the organisation as a whole. This empirical finding indicates that organisational learning may be orientated by goals, but these goals do not necessarily need to be systemic. For case study C we observed similar results. However, the heterogeneity of learning goals and their ambivalence were much greater. In spite of the fact that the projects were often promoted by the very same partner such as the local job centre, the realisation of the project did not allow for the development of relatively homogenous *learning recipes*. Each project required a different configuration of external collaboration. If in case study B each cost centre had to develop a certain degree of specialisation, in case study C specialisation even occurred after the development project had come to an end. Actors had to develop a more systematic organisational design and more homogenous interorganisational relations. As in case study B, firm C developed a closer customer orientation and a more settled mode of internal coordination.

However, the main problem in both firms continued to be the development of a balance between exploitative learning processes directed to the specialisation and utilisation of former learning results, and an openness for novel tasks requiring more explorative learning approaches. The problem did not as the conventional organisational learning debate indicates simply consist of designing a learning organisation that was to free actors from blockages and allow them to learn. From our point of view the problem rather seemed to be how to sustain the institutional diversity within the learning community enabling actors to continue to learn further and be open for the learning of novel tasks. As we saw in the discussion of case study A, the overestimation of calculated exploitation of well-established organisational design complicates further learning. In that case exploitative learning strategies clearly dominated. However, in the other two case studies, the maintenance of a balance between these two learning modes appeared to be a fragile and a complicated issue. This question always emerged when the actors in firm B oriented the firm's strategy towards a certain type of customer or when the actors in case study C started to specialise in a former project in order to prepare its spinning-off.

Similarly to Powell et al.'s study[3] of *networks of learning* in sector of biotechnological firms it can be argued that:

> ... exploitation and exploration, and calculation and community are intertwined. Organizational learning is both a function of access to knowledge and the capabilities for utilizing and building such knowledge (1996, p. 118).

The question of *exploitation* which refers to reduction of institutional diversity and *exploration* which refers to its creation and sustainability can also be discussed from an evolutionary perspective taken by Galar (1996). He distinguishes between hard and soft selection in organisational and regional development. The first produces incremental improvements and provides a better adaptation in an already attained domain as we observed in case study A and to some extent also in case study B. The second led to critical innovations and carries adaptation into new domains which we observed foremost in case study C. However, the new ideas and innovations which emerge are often interpreted as a disorder that has to be reduced, because actors look for the 'perfect solution'. Soft selections change into hard selections. Exploration loses its consequence in order to exploit the common organisational domain.

Furthermore, it can be concluded that the higher the institutional diversity and the more heterogeneous the process organisational knowledge creation, the more important will be the role of actors and leadership for the process of organisational learning. If in case study A local managers acted reasonably as designers or dispatchers which direct and control the highly routinised work process, in the other two cases we could observe local managers acting more like networkers or mediators.[4] Here the learning goals were open and *learning recipes* were developed more *pragmatically* and it was not possible to plan, design and control the organising processes. The competencies of the various members of the learning network were combined in such a way that the fragile balance between explanatory and exploitative learning approaches continues. They started to learn to mediate conflicts, because the absence of clear *learning recipes* and goals required a constructivist and productive settlement of interests between different actors and groups of actors inside as well as outside the organisation.

6.2.3   The Tension Between Intended and Non-intended Forms of Organisational Learning

In the last two sections we have seen that the transformation of traditional forms of organisational behaviour and the openness for novel tasks did not emerge through cumulative learning processes. New organisational solutions and innovation occurred not through a better understanding of internal decision-making nor through the perfection of organisational designing. The exchange between different forms of knowledge and resources allowed for the sort of blurring of the organisational boundaries that we observed in the case studies B and C. Innovation and creativity emerged not so much through planned and calculated attempts to reorganise the firm, but through forgetting and ignoring traditions and eventual risks, as well as through decentralised learning within the interorganisational networks.

Hence social institutions support the emergence of more decentralised and heterogeneous network learning approaches not directly, but in a dialectical way. This implies not only that more creative and innovative organisational learning approaches cannot be directly targeted, but also that it is hard to know beforehand if certain steps of organisational designing will lead to a better performance and new organisational solutions.

In this section we will discuss the tension between intended and non-intended forms of organisational learning as a complement to the forms of institutional learning we have been discussing in the past two sections. At the centre of this section are the ways in which actors make use of the unforeseen learning possibilities emerging in the ongoing processes of organising. The central thesis of this section is that in all of our case studies the emergence of creative learning modes was not planned, nor was it the result of better designing or decision-making. Instead, the openness for novel tasks appeared to be rather a secondary effect of the intended reorganisation goals.

We saw that there existed considerable differences between our three case studies as to whether emerging secondary effects are seen as a chance, and as such as irrelevant or even counterproductive to further learning processes. In case study A the focus of management activities was on highly analysed, routinised assembly operations. This led to side-effects which again were interpreted as counterproductive to the attainment of the narrow production goals. Following Sorge (1982/83, p. 126) one can argue that the intentions of the management to analyse the workers' attempts of beating the system in fact led to the persistence of such practices. We saw how middle managers, such as production engineers, were most prone to see the idea of CIP as an instrument for improving the control of the assembling operations. Technological solutions were to replace human work and avoid side effects of organisational designing such as the opportunity for workers to beat the system. The concentration on reorganisation and on technological design led together with the introduction of formal rules to the neglect of internal and external interrelations. The tradition of planning and designing in this case led to the systematic underestimation of non-intended learning modes. The focus on technology and production output made human work and the non-intended consequences of work practice appear as a less important side-effect of the *planned learning process*. The way in which actors tried to work around the established set of rules was neglected or was seen as an interruption of the well-established work flow. In contrast to the other two case studies experimentation and search processes were systematically delegated to certain specialists and departments.

In firm B and C the development of *learning recipes* were less structured and linked to efficiency. In this context Walter-Busch has argued that problem solving is not linked with efficiency, but effectiveness (Walter-Busch, 1996, pp. 196–7). For the latter it is less important to 'do things right' (ibid.) such as to optimise a specific task environment. This is precisely what we observed in case study A. Instead, it is argued that for development of more effective forms of organising one has to find out how to 'do the right things' (ibid.). That was exactly the case in firm C and to some extent also in firm B. In other words, in these two case studies learning processes were not so much driven by the attempts of management to develop an accurate organisational design for a particular problem, but by the goal of developing plausible solutions for problems which from the start which were less clear (Weick 1995b, pp. 55–61). Learning was solution driven, not driven by a particular problem and the requirement to develop a perfect output. Planning was more difficult and experiences of past learning appeared to be less sufficient for new emerging tasks. Hence the ambiguity of institutions brought about the search for and development of new solutions. Not only the first intentions of actors were relevant for understanding the organisational learning processes, but also their secondary effects. Original intentions can change over time and lead to the emergence of new or recombined intentions.

At the centre of firm B's reorganisation was not the development of an efficient calculation of means to meet certain production goals, but the creation of effective ways to meet the rather ambiguous goal of customisation. The rather decentral modes of organising allowed each cost centre to develop its own strategy on how to deal with the new market environment. If in case study A non-intended outcomes of organising were neglected, in case study B non-rational problem-solving was put at the centre of its organisational development. The main difference between these two firms was the quality of products. Product development and manufacturing had much more to do with craft work than with the mass production of highly standardised products of the sort we could observe in firm A. So in case study B, we identified a process of organisational learning that appeared to be more *pragmatic*, than planned. As in case study C, it was not the search for the 'one best way' of learning and organising, but the development of more holistic work processes involving skilful experimenting. The lower adjustment of the firm to a particular group of customers required a more open search processes, less formalised work rules and more intensive social coordination of internal and external relations.

In firm C it was impossible to develop the sort of efficient solutions for a certain problem or to develop new products for particular clients that we could observe in our other case studies. Actors were more aware of the non-intended opportunities arising in the process of realising particular projects. Organisational learning was more closely integrated with practising learning than with the learning of a single practice. Whereas in case study A strategic planning remained at the centre of the firm's *identity construction*, in case study C managers had more problems with making sense of the outcome of their actions, because original project ideas became problematical and had to be redefined (section 5.2.1). Organisational learning involved more than in the other two case studies the need to make sense of the non-intended side-effects of the original project ideas. First predictions were given up and new emerging solutions that appeared to be more plausible were developed further. However, the transformation of the firm's identity by redefining the original project ideas can be contrasted with the *identity construction* in case study B. Here the firm's identity resulted from the strategies used to attract customers. This strategy was different in each cost centre making internal cooperation within the firm as a whole more difficult. As in case study A, the cost centre logic required that more time was spent on the calculation of certain outcomes and of the possible profits than on the non-intended consequences of these actions. In case study C actions were affected by preferences and intentions, because the involved actors developed more chances to learn from emerging *discontinuities* and failures (section 5.2.5).

The dialectical relationship between intentional and non-intentional organisational learning can also be conceived of in terms of the metaphor of a game. Gehlen distinguishes two kinds of such learning games (1986, pp. 205ff.). A first type, so-called 'polyphone games', lack both an obvious goal as well as a clear intention. People play such 'amusing' games just for the purpose of having fun and entertainment. More serious purposes of such games at best develop at a later stage of the organisational development. This second type of games become more structured and serious over time. They are successively played with quite specific goals in mind. Such games take place in the context of stricter rules of the sort that characterise chess games or soccer matches. However, compared with 'polyphone games' the new quality of these more institutionalised games is not just their seriousness, but the increasing regularity and homogeneity of the learning process between the players of the game.

Comparing the organisational development in our three case studies, we found that games were most institutionalised in firm A. Games in firm C, on the other hand, exhibited the lowest degree of institutionalisation, with firm B occupying a position somewhere in between these two extremes. The more institutionalised a game was, the more specified its goals became and the more detailed its rules were. In firm C it was not necessary to develop a perfect solution for a certain problem, what counted more was the realisation of a broad variety of distinct projects (section 5.2.7.). Finding out how 'to do the right thing' required the development of experimental learning modes, rather than the perfection of established ways of increased organisation. It was not possible to realise the sort of reduction of *organisational slack* we observed in case study A, nor was it possible to realise any specific goal. Instead we found that slack in case study C manifested itself under the form of 'redundancy of relations' (Grabher 1993, pp. 25–48). It therefore became imperative to specify and realise a project idea. Networking and redundancy of relations effected that projects were both socially acceptable and creditable.

The discussion showed that all attempts to increase efficiency such as technological perfection in case study A or cost awareness in case study B led to the disappearance of creative learning modes and to the decline of spontaneous cooperation. It also became evident that the lower degree of intended learning approaches in case study C (to a lesser extent also in case study B) appeared to be useful for creative learning and for the openness towards novel tasks. In contrast to the conventional debate about organisational learning which is concerned about the limitations of institutions on deutero-learning or neglects it altogether, one can argue that those institutional arrangements that are not created for economic reasons are beneficial to the emergence of creative learning modes. However, according to Streeck (1997) it is difficult to institutionalise creative learning modes. Even in case study C the spinning off of one specific project involved goal specification and the development of more routinised learning modes. Nevertheless the organisational development of firm C showed that it was possible and even necessary for the outgrowth of its projects to protect them from the pressure of economic success. In reference to Streeck (1997) one can argue that emerging side effects which differ from intended learning modes are the prerequisites for creativity and further learning:

> ... even in economic life, it is often the nonfunctional that is the most functional, and indeed that where everything is functional, functions may be less than optimally performed. Protecting the nonfunctional from rationalist pressures for functionalist streamlining, even though its benefits can, at best, only be guessed, may well be the most difficult challenge today for societies and decision-makers, economic and non-economic, private and public (Streeck, 1997, p. 212).

In this sense we can conclude that 'polyphone games' as described by Gehlen (1986) are always in danger of losing their openness and creative character. Even in case study C the more playful character of projects changed when goals got more closed and became focused more upon more specific outcomes. Organisational arrangements became more functional with and came to be characterised by settled rules and work routines. However, what makes case study C different from the more structured learning processes in firm A is that *learning recipes* were less perfectly defined beforehand and that they were often retrospectively acknowledged by the actors. Learning processes in case study C were more pragmatically driven by sub-optimal solutions than by the search for accurate designing principles for a single problem. We have seen that reorganisation processes that are intended to increase the perfection of established organisational designing principles give less space for creative organisational learning modes. Here actors might know what they can do, they may be aware of who shapes the environment and of what capabilities are precisely required to meet the intended learning goals. An explorative search for new solutions is lacking. Organisational learning is perfectly calculated, but less enjoyable.

In brief, the perfection of internal designing principles are in contrast to the postulates of the conventional organisational learning debate not important for the development of more open organisational learning processes. The systematic comparison of our three firms has shown that organisational arrangements that are less reflexive and that have rather biased and shifting goals, provide better conditions for experimentation and creative learning than the ideal of the self-reflexive learning organisation. This appears to be a dilemma for how non-organisable learning forms can be organised. Weick and Westley (1996, pp. 440–58) call this problem oxymoron. For them organising and learning are essentially antithetical processes, because they see learning as disorganising and increasing variety, and organising as heedless and reducing variety.

6.3 Dissimilarities in the Social Construction of Cultural Systems and their Impact on the Micro-macro Problem

6.3.1 Dissimilarities in the Awareness of Cultural Systems

The purpose of this section refers is to examine the leading question of this study of trying to understand the relationship between organisational learning and institutions, or, to put it another way, to assess the effects of micro-level learning processes on macro-level institutions and vice versa. In the methodological part we argued that East Germany seemed to be a sufficient empirical field in which to study organisational learning processes given the challenges faced by the formerly state-owned industrial companies because of the transformation of a planned economy into a market economy. Moreover, in spite of the firms' similar social and economic background, we assumed that the social context and the actual learning situation of each of the case studies would vary significantly.

As we illustrated in the conceptual chapter, neo-institutionalist scholars such as DiMaggio and Powell (1991a and b) and Meyer, Rowan et al. (1992) describe institutional environments as relatively abstract, monolithic and compelling systems. However, both our case study reports as well as the comparative discussion in the last chapter have shown that the degree to which actors took their internal and external environment as a given reality differed greatly in each of the three case studies. Institutions have not affected all three organisations in the same way after the wall came down. However, the question now is how can we explain all these differences at the micro-level of organisational learning. The conclusion reached by this study is that the micro-macro problem reveals the significance of local cultural systems. The systematic comparison of the empirical findings has provided evidence in favour of Weick's thesis (1985, p. 386) that in the practice of learning people may most likely notice the cultural dimension of their institutions when their daily routines break down. Moreover we have criticised the ideal of continuous learning organisations and demonstrated that occasions for more open organisational learning processes were more likely to appear in crisis situations when established modes of organising became ambiguous. However, even in such situations traditional ways of thinking were not simply abandoned, nor was it the novelty of the new situation alone that caused organisational learning processes to become more open. Instead, our comparison has shown that the actors in case studies B and C became more aware of their organisational culture and thus learned more actively. This does not indicate that the actors in firm A have not learned, but rather that in contrast to the other two case studies, most of the people in firm A mainly learned more repetitively and did what they always had done. In contrast to the other two case studies the concentration on the failure-free and continuous learning circles hindered actors in becoming more aware and thinking about alternatives to their traditional ways of thinking and producing. This shows that the degree of awareness of culture or the extent to which institutions were taken for granted varied greatly in each case study. In this sense we agree with neo-institutionalism that the institutions incorporated in the heads of actors as cognitive frames influence organisational behaviour (DiMaggio and Powell, 1991; Scott, 1995). However, what the authors neglect to discuss is that the degree of institutionalisation between organisational forms can differ greatly even when they belong to the same population or organisational field.

Thus, we have illustrated that organisations which see their internal and external environment as less changeable than it actually is fit better into the context of the arguments made by neo-institutionalists who stress that extra-organisational institutions such as national or branch cultures influence the processes of organising. However, whether and which part of these ideological patterns are interpreted as being given cannot be predeter-mined as in the case of macro-institutional approaches. In highly structured cultural systems, how actors interpret organisational design, technology or potential customers seems to be significantly linked to how an organisation conforms to institutional expectations of relevant interest groups as registered in case study A. However, the increase in cultural diversity stimulated through the coexistence of different organisational forms led to less conformity and more adaptive learning forms. This refers closely to the idea of Weick that perfect adaptation would exclude adaptability and with this more open forms of organisational learning (1995a, p. 265).

6.3.2 Dissimilarities in the Structuration of Cultural Systems

The description of how interactive learning processes at the micro-level stabilised and/or altered could be also understood as distinct modes of structuration (Giddens, 1984). Even when the context of social and economic transformation can be understood as conditions or 'triggers' that initiate organisational change, we have experienced that how organisations transform can be quite different because of the way in which actors structure their local cultural system (Geppert and Merkens, 1999; Merkens et al., 1999). As we have demonstrated based upon our systematic comparison of the empirical findings, when actors are strongly committed to their past experiences and traditional ways of thinking, the openness of organisational learning is underdeveloped.

Despite such structural triggers as the shift of ownership or the decline of established markets in Eastern Europe resulting from institutional change at the macro-level of society, in case study A traditional forms of learning survived. Here it is evident that the commitment to and justification of traditional organisational design had significant consequences for how the firm enacted their internal and external environment. Through concentration on planning, the perfection of organisational design principles etc., for firm A the 'map became the territory' (Weick, 1995a, pp. 355–8). Thus we saw that highly institutionalised or structured cultural systems created a sort of collective senselessness or ignorance to learn from their present actions. At one point, actors began to take their ways of organising and even their enduring economic success on the car supplier market for granted. Because of the focus on their past experiences, new management concepts such as team work were seen merely as instruments to improve the accomplishment of traditional tasks. Highly structured modes of organising with a narrow adherence to hierarchy and traditional technological systems constituted inactive and routinised modes of organisational learning. In other words, the actors' preference for a structured and stable cultural system led to interpretations which defended the status quo. There seemed to be no alternative to the traditional production systems and markets. However, this TINA (there is no alternative) effect was less evident in the other two case studies. Here the structural triggers were interpreted differently, although not voluntarily. In firms B and C the actors discredited their old causal maps (ibid.) and with it the structuration of their cultural systems. However, unlike case study A, the change of formal structures in the other two companies had greater consequences, because learning processes involved the transformation of established ways of interpreting and making sense of things. However, the main difference between case studies B and C became evident in the degree to which each firm started to act as a newcomer. And despite the fact that firm B became a new competitor in the local market, it was no real newcomer. Unlike case study C, the transformation of the cultural system was quite moderate in order to meet the new demands of more customer-oriented production. The discrediting of the established cause map was basically less than in case study C where the actors were actual newcomers with no established route by which to gain access to future markets. While the other two firms had fewer problems in justifying their business activities or the existence of their firms because of their established status as a professional production firm and because powerful interest groups more or less supported their business activities, in the case of firm C actors had just begun their search for potential interest groups and had more difficulties in convincing these groups of their loyalty. These less structured commitments and the ongoing problems in justifying job creation projects and commercial activities led to emergence of a much more weakly structured cultural system.

In the last section we demonstrated that the degree of institutionalisation in terms of the extent to which cultural systems are structured mirrors the micro-macro problem from a perspective which differs from the neo-institutionalist approaches. However, in line with neo-institutionalism, we have explained the central role of legitimacy for organisational behaviour, an aspect which is completely neglected in the mainstream studies about organisational learning. And yet unlike neo-institutionalism, we have shown that not only is legitimacy important, but even more so its meaning and how it is created, and that this as we examined, differs according to the degree to which organisational learning processes have been institutionalised.

We agree with neo-institutionalists that the adoption or imitation of institutionally legitimised formal structures is one way to improve the image of an organisation. Especially for development entrepreneurial ventures and projects in firm C it was important to develop strategies to achieve a wider reputation and to document the organisation's professionalism and accountability. However, what neo-institutionalist approaches fail to address is that the degree to which these commitments and justifications are directed can be quite different. In this sense it can be concluded that less structured cultural systems such as projects seem to be more adequate for dealing with uncommon and novel situations than highly structured and well-established organisational forms.

6.3.3 Dissimilarities in the Temporariness of Cultural Systems

Another problem which is underdeveloped in neo-institutionalist approaches is that organisations differ significantly in their degree of temporariness.[5] Students in this research tradition may be right when they argue that the age and nature of an industry are significant for explaining why organisations have problems in altering their established organisational forms. These organisations are accustomed to specific standard operating systems or technologies and view them as the perfect means by which to solve a well-known problem. In case study A we have seen that even new commitments and justifications such as new management concepts may support the transformation of these traditional modes of organising. However, the neo-institutionalist assumption that the institutional pressure causing organisational isomorphism cannot automatically be interpreted as a given. As we have seen in the last two sections, even more important it would seem than this abstract explanation is to look at how local cultural systems are structured and whether there is room for more active knowledge creation. This directly influences how people learn, what they know and how they make sense of the world/of their environment. As we have seen in firm C, temporary systems where actors have fewer possibilities to refer to and make use of their past experiences in order to understand the present outcome of their actions and where tests were necessary in order for them to learn about themselves and their environment, the resulting learning modes where quite open. Thus, actors seem to develop more sensible interpretations about their current actions and in doing so change traditional patterns of interaction. This was discussed in the second section of this chapter when we demonstrated how temporary systems such as entrepreneurial activities and projects always involve alterations in style and strength of relational learning. To put it another way, temporary cultural systems with less structured organisational forms are more apt to alter the direction of established organisational learning modes. Actors thus learn more about which part of the environment they are actually influencing. This shows again the influence of the micro-dynamics of organisational learning on the macro-level of society. The advantages of temporary systems over enduring and more structured organisational forms can be described in terms of Weick's idea of 'avoided tests' (1995a, pp. 215–19). In our case study reports we can surmise that the tendency to avoid tests decreases with the degree of temporariness of the cultural system. Thus, in firm A a pattern of test avoidance was quite common. One example of this was the passive 'wait and see' strategy prior to a shift in ownership. Nor were any tests undertaken to look for alternatives beyond the car supplier market. Later on the actors saw no alternative to the car supplier markets and started outsourcing departments which were not a part of the core business. Thus the avoidance of tests led to a decrease in the firm's cultural diversity. Test-avoidance in case study B mainly involved avoiding the decision about whether or not to spin-off. This in turn made local management more dependent due to the restrictive control strategies of the new owners. However, in contrast to the other two case studies, test-avoidance was a less central issue in case study C. Instead they had the problem to find out where test-avoidance would be functional to secure the exploitation of successful business ideas developed in temporary systems such as projects.

The discussion has shown that it is not only important to create temporary systems because they seem to enable more sensible organisational learning forms. More significant it would seem for the development of viable organisational learning forms would be finding intelligent ways to balance the cultural weakness of temporary organisational forms with the cultural strength of traditional ones. As we have illustrated, highly structured cultural systems are optimal for dealing with stability and known challenges in established markets, but have problems dealing adequately and sensibly with novelty. Less structured cultural systems on the other hand may provide better conditions for creativity and experimentation, but have problems institutionally organising these learning modes for the long run.

6.4   Concluding Remarks and Outlook

This final chapter could also be read as a suggestion to shift the focus of research from 'single-minded' learning organisations to one which reflects on organisational learning paths. Unlike those intervention researchers who focus mainly on the diagnosis of organisational learning disabilities, we have proven that our comparative approach can provide significant insights into the dialectical relationship between organisational learning and institutions. From an enactment perspective, organisational learning is not a new research paradigm and learning organisations are not the new 'one best way', but a new metaphor for an 'old' problem, the search for practical solutions for how organisations and its members balance the requirements of adaptation with the necessity to improve adaptability. This was described as institutional tensions which can be handled quite differently between organisations even in the same national culture or population.

In reference to our discussion in the methodological part of this study where we justified the application of a comparative case study research, this concluding idea to suggest analysing organisational learning paths might not come as such a big surprise. However, no matter whether we start our analysis with a very distinct organisational form of the same population such as a national culture as in this study, or with more similar organisations, the research problem remains the same. Even organisational learning processes in very similar organisational forms cannot be discussed without reflecting on their social context. As we have shown, learning processes at the micro-level of organisations always have consequences at the macro-level of society and these can be very different or quite similar, a fact which again emphasises the prominent role of institutions for the comprehension of organisational learning paths.

In closing, let us return to the social context of our three case studies. We have to say that for the purpose of this study it was of no substantial that we selected East German firms. However, that we analysed companies within the cultural context of social and economic transformation appeared in fact to be substantial for our particular interest in this study of how institutions affect organisational learning and vice versa. Thus, we agree with Weick's (1985, p. 386) research experience that we have obviously learned more about the significance of the cultural systems of our three firms in this historically unique time of change, and we hope that our research method has been improved through having applied it within the context of these exceptional circumstances.

Notes

1 *Die Philosophen haben die Welt nur verschieden interpretiert, es kömmt drauf an, sie zu verändern* (the original was written in spring 1845).

2 The problem of 'functionality of the non-functional' (Streeck, 1997, pp. 197–219) for the process of organisational learning we will discuss more detailed in the following section.

3 The authors adopted the distinction between exploitative and explorative ways of organisational learning from March (1994).

4 We owe this idea to a paper of Klimecki and Lassleben which they presented 1998 at the 14th EGOS Colloquium in Maastricht. There the authors discussed the problem of leadership in learning organisations.

5 Besides Weick (1993), the idea of temporariness of social systems is also stressed by Luhmann (1982 and 1988) in his explanation of the logic of his autopoiesis concept.

References

Andersen, I., Borum, F., Kristensen, P. H. and Karnoe, P. (1995), *On the Art of Doing Field Studies: An experience-based research methodology*, Copenhagen: Munksgaard.

Argyris, C. (1992a), 'Why Individuals and Organizations have difficulty in Double-loop Learning', in C. Argyris, *On Organizational Learning*, Oxford: Blackwell, pp. 7–38.

Argyris, C. (1992b), 'Teaching Smart People how to Learn', in C. Argyris, *On Organizational Learning*, Oxford: Blackwell, pp. 84–99.

Argyris, C. (1992c), 'Strategy Implementation: An experiment in learning', in C. Argyris, *On Organizational Learning*, Oxford: Blackwell, pp. 131–42.

Argyris, C. (1992d), 'Reasoning, Action Strategies and Defensive Routines: The case of OD practitioners', in C. Argyris, *On Organizational Learning*, Oxford: Blackwell, pp. 213–46.

Argyris, C. (1996), 'Unrecognised Defenses of Scholars: Impact on theory and research', *Organization Science*, 7/2, pp. 79–87.

Argyris, C. and Schön, D.A. (1978), *Organizational Learning: A theory of action perspective*, Reading: Addison-Wesley.

Argyris, C. and Schön, D.A. (1996), *Organizational Learning II: Theory, method, practice*, Reading: Addison-Wesley.

Bateson, G. (1992), *Ökologie des Geistes: Anthropologische, psychologische, biologische und epistemologische Perspektiven*, 4th edn, Frankfurt a.M.: Suhrkamp.

Bechtle, G. (1998), 'Das Verhältnis von Organisation und Innovation: Wie reagiert die baden-württembergische Industrie auf die Krise der neunziger Jahre?', Akademie für Technikfolgenabschätzung in Baden-Württemberg, Discussion Paper Nr. 124. Stuttgart.

Beck, U. (1986), *Risikogesellschaft: Auf dem Weg in eine andere Moderne*, Frankfurt a.M.: Suhrkamp.

Berthoin Antal, A. (1998), 'Die Dynamik der Theoriebildungsprozesse zum Organisationslernen', in H. Albach, M. Dierkes, A. Berthoin Antal and K. Vailant (eds.), *Organisationslernen: Institutionelle und kulturelle Dimensionen*, Berlin: edition sigma, pp. 31–52.

Blumer, H. (1969), *Symbolic Interactionism: Perspective and method*, Berkeley: University of California Press.

Brown, R.K. (1992), *Understanding Industrial Organisations: Theoretical perspectives in industrial sociology*, London: Routledge.

191

Child, J. (1972), 'Organizational Structure, Environment and Performance: The role of strategic choice', *Sociology*, 6, pp. 1–22.

Child, J. (1997), 'Strategic Choice in the Analysis of Action, Structure, Organizations and Environment: Retrospect and prospect', *Organization Studies*, 18/1, pp. 43–76.

Child, J. and Heavens, S.J. (1996), 'The Social Constitution of Organizations and its Implications for Organizational Learning', paper prepared for the meeting of the Kolleg on organizational learning, Ladenburg.

Cyert, R.M. and March, J.G. (1963), *Behavioral Theory of the Firm*, Englewood Cliffs: Prentice Hall.

Czarniawska-Joerges, B. (1994), 'Painful Transformations: Privatization in East and Central Europe – Introduction: The tragicomedy of errors, *Industrial and Environmental Crisis Quarterly*, 8/1, pp. 1–6.

Czarniawska-Joerges, B. (1996), 'The Process of Organizing', in M. Warner (ed.), *International Encyclopedia of Business and Management*, Vol. 4, London: Routledge, pp. 3966–81.

DeGeus, A.P. (1996), 'Planning as Learning', in K. Starkey (ed.), *How organizations learn*, London: Thompson, pp. 92–9.

DiMaggio, P.J. and Powell, W.W. (1991a), 'Introduction', in W.W. Powell and P.J. DiMaggio (eds), *The New Institutionalism in Organizational Analysis*, Chicago: University of Chicago Press, pp. 1–38.

DiMaggio, P.J. and Powell, W.W. (1991b), 'The Iron Cage Revisited: Institutional isomorphism and collective rationality', in W.W. Powell and P.J. DiMaggio (eds), *The New Institutionalism in Organizational Analysis*, Chicago: University of Chicago Press, pp. 63–82.

Dodgson, M. (1993), 'Organizational learning: A review of some literature', *Organization Studies*, 14/3, pp. 375–94.

Douglas, M. (1991), *Wie Institutionen denken*, Frankfurt a.M.: Suhrkamp.

Drucker, P.F. (1996), *Managing for the Future*, Oxford: Butterworth-Heinemann.

Easterby-Smith, M., Snell, R. and Gherardi, S. (1998), 'Organizational Learning: Diverging communities of practice?', *Management Learning*, 29/3, pp. 259–72.

Edmondson, A. and Moingeon, B. (1996), 'When to Learn How and When to Learn Why: Appropriate organizational learning processes as a source of competitive advantage', in B. Moingeon and A. Edmondson (eds), *Organizational Learning and Competitive Advantage*, London: Sage, pp. 17–37.

Eisenhardt, K. (1989), 'Building Theories from Case Study Research', *Academy of Management Research Review*, 14/4, pp. 532–50.

Friedland, R. and Alford, R.R. (1991), 'Bringing Society Back In: Symbols, practices and institutional contradictions, in W.W. Powell and P.J. DiMaggio (eds), *The New Institutionalism in Organizational Analysis*, Chicago: University of Chicago Press, pp. 232–63.

Fritze, L. (1993), *Panoptikum DDR-Wirtschaft: Machtverhältnisse, Organisationsstrukturen und Funktionsmechanismen*, München: Olzog.

Galar, R. (1996), 'Europe as a Continent of Regional Systems of Innovations Regarded from the Evolutionary Viewpoint', paper prepared for the Polish Committee of Scientific Research, Technical University of Wroclaw.

Galbraith, J.R. (1974), 'Organization Design: An information processing view', in J.R. Hackman, E.E. Lawler III and L.W. Porter (eds), *Perspectives on Behavior in Organizations*, New York: McGray-Hill, pp. 432–8.

Garrat, B. (1987), *The Learning Organization: And the need for directors who think*, London: Fontana.

Gehlen, A. (1986), *Der Mensch: Seine Natur und seine Stellung in der Welt*, 13th edn, Wiesbaden: Aula-Verlag.

Geppert, M. (1991), 'Untersuchung interner und externer Anpassungsprobleme von Unternehmen der ehemaligen DDR: Dargestellt am Beispiel eines Betriebes der Kabelindustrie unter besonderer Berücksichtigung organisationskultureller Erklärungsansätze', unpublished manuscript (thesis), Humboldt University, Berlin.

Geppert, M. (1994), 'The Problems of Intraorganisational Change in East-German Firms', *Journal of Business Education*, 3/2, pp. 20–28.

Geppert, M. (1996), 'Paths of Managerial Learning in the East German Context', *Organization Studies*, 17/2, pp. 249–68.

Geppert, M. and Kachel, P. (1995), 'Die Treuhandanstalt am Ende: Ein historischer Abriß und kritische Beurteilung aus volkswirtschaftlicher und organisations-theoretischer Perspektive', in R. Schmidt and B. Lutz (eds), *Chancen und Risiken der industriellen Restrukturierung in Ostdeutschland*, Berlin: Akademie Verlag, pp. 69–106.

Geppert, M. and Merkens, H. (1999), 'Learning from One's Own Experience: Continuation and organizational change in two East German firms', *Human Resource Development International*, 2/1, pp. 25–40.

Geppert, M. and Schmidt, S. (1993), 'Von der "DDR-AG" zur Treuhandanstalt in Liquidation? Anmerkungen zum Umgang mit dem ehemaligen "Volksvermögen"', Social Science Research Centre, Discussion Paper FS II 93-202, Berlin.

Gherardi, S., Nicolini, D. and Odella, F. (1998), 'Towards a Social Understanding of How People Learn in Organizations: The notion of situated curriculum', *Management Learning*, 29/3, pp. 273–97.

Giddens, A. (1984), *The Constitution of Society: Outline of the theory of structuration*, Cambridge: Polity Press.

Grabher, G. (1992), 'Kapitalismus ohne Kapitalisten? Kombinatsentflechtung, West-investitionen und Unternehmensgründungen in Ostdeutschland', *Allemagne d' aujourd'hui, Special Issue Nr. 21* (German version).

Grabher, G. (1994a), *Lob der Verschwendung: Redundanz in der Regionalentwicklung: Ein sozioökonomisches Plädoyer*, Berlin: edition sigma.

Grabher, G. (1994b), 'The Elegance of Incoherence: Institutional legacies, privatization and regional development in East Germany and Hungary', Social Science Research Centre, Discussion Paper FS II 94-103, Berlin.

Granovetter, M. (1983), 'The Strength of Weak Ties: A network theory revisited', *Sociological Theory,* 1, pp. 201–33.

Granovetter, M. (1992), 'Economic Action and Social Structure: The problem of embeddedness', in M. Granovetter and R. Swedberg (eds), *The Sociology of Economic Life*, Boulder: Westview Press.

Güldenberg, S. (1997), *Wissensmanagement und Wissenscontrolling in lernenden Organisationen: Ein systemtheoretischer Ansatz*, 2nd edn, Wiesbaden: DUV.

Hatch, M.J. (1997), *Organization Theory: Modern, symbolic and postmodern perspectives*, Oxford: Oxford University Press.

Hedberg, B. (1981), 'How Organizations Learn and Unlearn', in P.C. Nystrom and W.H. Starbuck (eds), *Handbook of Organizational Design*, Vol. 1, New York: Oxford University Press, pp. 3–27.

Hirschman, A.O. (1967), *Development Projects Observed*, Washington DC: Brookings.

Honey, P. (1999), 'A Declaration on Learning', *Human Resource Development International,* 2/1, pp. 9–16.

Hustad, W. (1998), 'Inside and outside the organization learning process: Borrowing Nonaka's keys', paper presented at the 14th EGOS Colloquium, Maastricht.

Isaacs, W.N. and Senge, P.M. (1992), 'Overcoming Limits to Learning in Computer-based Learning Environments', *European Journal of Operational Research,* 59, pp. 183–96.

Johnson, B. (1992), 'Institutional Learning', in B.-A. Lundvall (ed.), *National Systems of Innovation: Towards a theory of innovation and interactive learning*, London: Pinter, pp. 23–44.

Kim, D.H. (1993), 'The Link between Individual and Organizational Learning', *Sloan Management Review,* Fall, pp. 37–50.

Klimecki, R. and Lassleben, H. (1998), 'Leading the Learning Organization: Challenges between visioning and engineering', paper presented at the 14th EGOS Colloquium, Maastricht.

Knuth, M. (1994), 'Zwei Jahre ABS-Gesellschaften in den neuen Bundesländern: Ergebnisse einer Befragung im November 1993', Institut für Arbeit und Technik. Discussion Paper IAT-AM 09, Gelsenkirchen.

Kühl, S. (2000), *Das Regenmacher Phänomen. Widersprüche und Aberglaube im Konzept der lernenden Organisation*, Frankfurt a.M.: Campus.

Luhmann, N. (1982), 'Autopoiesis, Handlung und kommunikative Verständigung', *Zeitschrift für Soziologie,* 11/4, pp. 366–79.

Luhmann, N. (1984), *Soziale Systeme. Grundriß einer allgemeinen Theorie*, Frankfurt a.M.: Suhrkamp.

Luhmann, N. (1988), 'Organisation', in W. Küpper and G. Ortmann (eds), *Mikropolitik. Rationalität, Macht und Spiele in Organisationen*, Opladen: Westdeutscher Verlag.

Luhmann, N. (1999), *Organisation und Entscheidung*, Wiesbaden: Westdeutscher Verlag.

March, J.G. (1996), 'Exploration and Exploitation in Organizational Learning', in M.D. Cohen and L.S. Sproul (eds), *Organizational Learning*, Thousand Oaks: Sage, pp. 101–23.

March, J.G. and Olsen, J.P. (1976), 'Organizational Learning and the Ambiguity of the Past', in J.G. March and J.P. Olsen (eds), *Ambiguity and Choice in Organizations*, Bergen: Universitetsforlaget, pp. 54–68.

March, J.G. and Simon, H.A. (1958), *Organizations*, New York: John Wiley.

Marx, K. (1985), 'Thesen über Feuerbach' (original work written 1845), in K. Marx and F. Engels, *Ausgewählte Schriften in zwei Bänden*, Vol. 2, Berlin: Dietz, pp. 370–72.

Merkens, H., Geppert, M. and Antal, D. (2000), 'Triggers of Organizational Learning during the Transformation Process in Central European Countries', in M. Dierkes, A. Berthoin Antal, J. Child and I. Nonaka (eds), *The Handbook of Organizational Learning and Knowledge*, Oxford: Oxford University Press (in print).

Meyer, J.W. and Rowan, B. (1992), 'Institutionalized Organizations: Formal structures as myth and ceremony', in J.W. Meyer and W.R. Scott (eds), *Organizational Environments. Ritual and Rationality* (updated edn), Newbury Park: Sage, pp. 21–44.

Meyer, J.W. and Scott, W.R. (1992), *Organizational Environments. Ritual and Rationality* (updated edn), Newbury Park: Sage.

Miller, D. (1996), 'A Preliminary Typology of Organizational Learning: Synthesizing the literature', *Journal of Management*, 22/3, pp. 485–505.

Miller, J. and Glassner, B. (1997), 'The "Inside" and the "Outside": Finding realities in interviews', in D. Silverman (ed.), *Qualitative Research: Theory, method and practice*, London: Sage, pp. 99–112.

Miner, A.S. and Mezias, S.J. (1996), 'Ugly Ducking No More: Pasts and futures of organizational learning research', *Organization Science*, 7/2, pp. 88–99.

Mintzberg, H. (1991), *Mintzberg über Management. Führung und Organisation, Mythos und Realität*, Wiesbaden: Gabler, pp. 39–55.

Moingeon, B. and Edmondson, A. (eds) (1996), *Organizational Learning and Competitive Advantage*, London: Sage.

Morgan, G. (1986), *Images of Organization*, Beverly Hills: Sage.

Neuberger, O. (1994), *Personalmanagement*, 2nd edn, Stuttgart: Enke.

Ortmann, G., Sydow, J. and Türk, K. (1997), *Theorien der Organisation: Die Rückkehr der Gesellschaft*, Opladen: Westdeutscher Verlag.

Orton, D.J. (1996), 'Reorganizational Learning: Some conceptual tools from Weick's model of organizing', in B. Moingeon and A. Edmondson (eds), *Organizational Learning and Competitive Advantage*, London: Sage, pp. 185–201.

Pawlowsky, P. (1992), 'Betriebliche Qualifizierungsstrategien und organisationales Lernen', in W.H. Staehle and P. Conrad (eds), *Managementforschung 2*, Berlin: Walter de Gruyter, pp. 177–237.

Powell, W.W., Koput, K.W. and Smith-Doerr, L. (1996), Interorganizational Collaboration and the Locus of Innovation: Networks of learning in biotechnology, *Administration Science Quarterly*, 41, pp. 116–45.

Sabel, C. (1991), 'Moebius-strip Organizations and Open Labor Markets: Some consequences of the reintegration of conception and execution in a volatile economy', in P. Bourdieu and J.S. Coleman (eds), *Social Theory for a Changing Society*, Boulder: Westview Press.

Schultz, M. (1995), *On Studying Organizational Cultures: Diagnose and understanding*, Berlin: DeGruyter.

Scott, W.R. (1987), *Organizations: Rational, natural and open systems*, 2nd edn, Englewood Cliffs: Prentice Hall.

Scott, W.R. (1995), 'Introduction: Institutional theory and organizations', in W.R. Scott and S. Christensen (eds), *The Institutional Construction of Organizations: International and longitudinal studies*, Thousand Oaks: Sage, pp. xi–xxiii.

Senge, P.M. (1990), *The Fifth Discipline: The art and practice of the learning organization*, New York: Doubleday.

Senge, P.M. (1996), 'The Leader's New Work: Building learning organizations', in K. Starkey (ed.), *How Organizations Learn*, London: Thompson, pp. 288–315.

Simon, H.A. (1955), 'A Behavioral Model of Rational Choice, *Quarterly Journal of Economics*, 69, pp. 99–118.

Simon, H.A. (1996), 'Bounded Rationality and Organizational Learning', in M.D. Cohen and L.S. Sproull (eds), *Organizational Learning*, Thousand Oaks: Sage, pp. 175–87.

Sommerlatte, T. (1992), 'Lernende Organisationen', in J. Fuchs (ed.), *Das bio-kybernetische Modell: Unternehmen als Organismen*, Wiesbaden: Gabler, pp. 113–22.

Sorge, A. (1982/83), 'Cultured Organization', *International Studies of Management and Organization*, 7/4, pp. 106–38.

Sorge, A. (1985), *Informationstechnik und Arbeit: Arbeitsorganisation, Qualifikation und Produktivkraftentwicklung*, Frankfurt a.M.: Campus.

Sorge, A. (1991), 'Strategic Fit and the Societal Effect: Interpreting cross-national comparisons of technology, organization and human resources', *Organization Studies*, 12/2, pp. 161–90.

Sorge, A. (1996), 'Organization Behaviour', in M. Warner (ed.), *International encyclopedia of business and management*, Vol. 4, London: Routledge, pp. 3793–810.

Staehle, W.H. (1973), *Organisation und Führung sozio-technischer Systeme: Grundlagen einer Situationstheorie*, Stuttgart: Enke.

Streeck, W. (1997), 'Beneficial Constraints: On the economic limits of rational voluntarism', in J.R. Hollingsworth and R. Boyer (eds), *Contemporary Capitalis: The embeddedness of institutions*, Cambridge: Cambridge University Press, pp. 197–219.

Swieringa, J. and Wierdsma, A. (1992), *Becoming a Learning Organization*, Reading: Addison-Wesley.

Trist, E. (1981), 'The Evolution of Socio-technical Systems: A conceptual framework and an action research program', Ontario Quality of Working Life Centre. Occasional Paper No. 2, Toronto.

Trist, E.L. and Bamforth, K.W. (1951), 'Some Social and Psychological Consequences of the Longwall Method of Coal-getting, *Human Relations,* 4, pp. 3–38.

Walgenbach, P. (1995), 'Insitutionalistische Ansätze in der Organisationstheorie', in A. Kieser (ed.), *Organisationstheorien*, 2nd edn, Stuttgart: Kohlhammer.

Walter-Busch, E. (1996), *Organisationstheorien von Weber bis Weick*, Amsterdam: Fakultas.

Weick, K.E. (1985), 'The Significance of Corporate Culture', in P. Frost, L.F. Moore, M.R. Louis, C.C. Lundberg and J. Martin (eds), *Organizational Culture*, Beverly Hills: Sage, pp. 381–88.

Weick, K.E. (1993), 'Sensemaking in Organizations: Small structures with large consequences', in J.K. Murnighan (ed.), *Social Psychology in Organizations: Advances in theory and research*, Englewood Cliffs: Prentice Hall, pp. 10–37.

Weick, K.E. (1995a), *Der Prozeß des Organisierens*, Frankfurt a.M.: Suhrkamp.

Weick, K.E. (1995b), *Sensemaking in Organizations*, Thousand Oaks: Sage.

Weick, K.E. and Roberts K.H. (1996), 'Collective Mind in Organizations: Heedful interrelating on flight decks', in M.D. Cohen and L.S. Sproul (eds), *Organizational Learning*, Thousand Oaks: Sage, pp. 330–58.

Weick, K.E. and Westley, F. (1996), 'Organizational Learning: Affirming an oxymoron', in S.R. Clegg, C. Hardy and W.R. Nord (eds), *Handbook of Organization studies*, London: Sage, pp. 440–58.

Wiesenthal, H. (1995), 'Konventionelles und unkonventionelles Organisationslernen: Literaturreport und Ergänzungsvorschlag', *Zeitschrift für Soziologie,* 24/2, pp. 137–55.

Wildemann, H. (1996), 'Erfolgsfaktoren für schnell lernende Organisationen', in H.-J. Bullinger (ed.), *Lernende Organisationen: Konzepte, Methoden und Erfahrungsberichte*, Stuttgart: Schäffer-Poeschel, pp. 75–103.

Wittke, V., Voskamp, U. and Bluhm, K. (1993), 'Den Westen überholen? Zu den Schwierigkeiten bei der Restrukturierung der ostdeutschen Industrie und den Perspektiven erfolgversprechender Reorganisationsstrategien', in R. Schmidt (ed.), *Zwischenbilanz: Analysen zum Transformationsprozeß der ostdeutschen Industrie*, Berlin: Akademie Verlag.

Yin, R.K. (1994), *Case study research: Design and methods*, 2nd edn, Thousand Oaks: Sage.